ILLUSTRATED
WORLD OF
THE BIBLE
LIBRARY

ILLUSTRATED

WORLD OF

LIBRARY

McGRAW-HILL BOOK COMPANY, INC.

THE BIBLE

5. NEW TESTAMENT

NEW YORK · TORONTO · LONDON

First published in Jerusalem — Ramat-Gan, Israel

Library of Congress Catalogue Card number 59— 43080

41171

PRINTED IN GREAT BRITAIN

The New Testament

PICTORIAL COMMENTARY

by MICHAEL AVI-YONAH PH.D.
Associate Professor of Archaeology
Hebrew University, Jerusalem

STYLISTIC ADVISER
Merton Dagut

MANUSCRIPT AND PROOF READER
Inna Pommerantz

GRAPHICS AND LAY-OUT
Jacob Zim, Stephan Bengom

MAPS
Eng. Pinhas Yoeli

RECONSTRUCTIONS
Eva Avi-Yonah

INTRODUCTION

THE New Testament, the subject of this volume, may be approached on several ideological levels. At its loftiest, where it touches upon the most profound mysteries of the universe, it is beyond any visual commentary. However, like the Old Testament, the New may be studied in several other ways as well. Although the values it is intended to convey are eternal, they had to be expressed in a language intelligible to those to whom its message was addressed. The evangelical teaching is therefore conveyed in a text written in the Hellenistic Greek of the first and second centuries A.D., which has been transmitted to us in copies written in the fourth century, with a few earlier textual fragments. Hence classical philology, Greek palaeography and their related sciences can help us to penetrate the meaning of the words occurring in the text, as they were understood by its authors.

Furthermore, the tale unfolded in the Gospels and the Acts is set in a definite historical, geographical and material context. The personages and places mentioned in these books, as well as the entire cultural and economic background of the first century of the Christian era, are an integral part of the New Testament story which cannot be properly understood — at least in its mundane sense — without constant reference to this framework.

The illustrated commentary presented here does not presume to approach, even from afar, the sacred mysteries of religion. Its humbler purpose is to elucidate the canonical text of the New Testament by placing the selected verses side by side with the concrete evidence supplied by archaeology, geography, papyrology and the other sciences related to the study of antiquity.

As in the preceding volumes of the "Illustrated World of the Bible Library", its aim is to use only such material as is both authentic and contemporary, avoiding any fanciful pictorial "reconstructions" of the past.

The traditional canonical structure of the New Testament has placed several obstacles in the path of the commentator. The three "synoptic" Gospels of St. Matthew, St. Mark and St. Luke relate virtually the same story, differing primarily in the stresses laid on the various aspects of Jesus' terrestrial activity and teaching and in the selection of incidents, sayings and traditions available to their authors from various sources. As the word "synoptic" indicates, these three Gospels can be "looked at together." With the Gospel of St. John the situation is otherwise: its view of the ministry of Jesus is markedly different from the common view of the other three, and does not easily lend itself to harmonization with the other three into one consistent account. This consideration helped to rule out the first two alternatives before us: to combine the four into one, or to repeat ourselves. To combine would necessarily have violated the fundamental principle of this work, namely that the text be followed in the established order. The second alternative was obviously equally undesirable. The way finally chosen, after much consideration, was to adopt the Gospel of St. Matthew as the basis for a continuous narrative, and to select from the other Gospels such parts as could, in one way or another, amplify the contents of the first.

This decision was made with a full appreciation of the fact that a considerable body of scholars now views the Gospel of St. Mark as the earliest of the Synoptic Gospels and as having been used as a framework by St. Matthew and St. Luke for their fuller and adapted accounts. St. Matthew's Gospel, however, gained early recognition as the most authoritative and comprehensive record of Jesus' life, and many contemporary scholars still regard it as the earliest. Finally decisive, however, was the unchallengeable fact that this Gospel stands at the beginning of the New Testament and, with its birth and resurrection stories, provides a much fuller account on which to base this work.

In the second part of the New Testament, comprising the Acts of the Apostles, the Epistles and the Revelation, the problems were different in character and scope. The first book of this second part, that of the Acts of the Apostles, forms an almost uniform and continuous narrative which presented no special difficulties for visual commentary.

The Epistles of St. Paul and of the other apostles were, on the other hand, much more difficult to illustrate. These texts are not intended to tell a story, but to convey a message. Their theological contents are, by the very nature of the discussion of metaphysical subjects, beyond the scope of illustration. However, as they were addressed to the first Christian communities, composed of men and women integrated into the Greco-Roman society of the period, the metaphors used to bring home the teaching of the apostles were naturally enough drawn from the material world surrounding both the preacher and his audience. This figurative aspect of the epistles enables the commentator to draw upon all the material remains of the Greco-Roman inhabited world. We have here attempted to do this within the limits of the available space.

The Revelation or Apocalypse of St. John the Divine must again be approached differently. In common with the other canonical or extra-canonical apocalyptic writings (for example the Book of Daniel, for which see Vol. IV), its purpose is to forecast future events connected with the Day of Judgment and the consequent end of this world. Its contents are therefore, by definition, outside any present or past context. Nevertheless, the events of the future, as predicted in such sources, seem to contain — at least in their literal sense — a projection of the present into the future. They describe the downfall of the contemporary social structure. In the case of the evangelical Apocalypse this catastrophe had to be connected first and foremost with the destruction of Roman power, the mainstay of the ancient world which, to the authors of this text, was utterly corrupt. The imperial city, its rulers and its enemies appear, thinly disguised, as either the objects or the agents of the divine wrath. Their images can therefore be legitimately used to illustrate a work which, if understood in its transcendental sense, would extend beyond the limits of conceivable time.

The New Testament as a whole may be regarded as the documentation for the gradually unfolding story of the rise and spread of Christianity, its earliest teachings and its hopes for the future. It begins within the confines of the humble provincial townlets of Judaea and Galilee and ends at the point when the new religion is reaching out, by way of the Jewish Diaspora, into the centre of the civilized world.

Following its subject, the present commentary is thus in its first part largely concerned with the Holy Land in the time of Jesus. The sites mentioned in the Gospels are still there for all to see. The Mount of Olives still rises to the east of the Holy City, the blue waters of the Sea of Galilee are still by turns stormy and tranquil, the fertile plain of Gennesaret still stretches out beside the lake named after it.

The regular climate of Palestine and the fact that agriculture was at that time the basis of Jewish society — and in particular the staff of life of the masses for whom Jesus' message was intended — all this made comparisons drawn from nature serve for most of the evangelical parables. These can therefore be illustrated by reference to the weather, the flora and the fauna still to be observed in this country.

The main part of the Jewish people — in importance if not in numbers — was, at the time of Jesus, still living in its own land. Several of the illustrations shown are based on Jewish remains dating from this period. These include, for example, the "jot" and the "tittle" of the Law (Matt. 5 : 18), the "seat of Moses" (ib. 23 : 2), the "rolling stone" (ib. 27 : 60), the "widow's mite" (Mark 12 : 41), the stones and buildings of the Temple (ib. 13 : 2). All these verses can best be illustrated visually by reproductions selected from the archaeological finds excavated in Palestine, from the beginnings of scientific research, which commenced with the Survey of Palestine of the Palestine Exploration Fund in the seventies of the last century, down to the latest discoveries, in 1960, in the caves of the Judaean desert which served as a refuge for the last warriors of Bar-Kokhba in his war with the Romans (A.D. 132-135).

But while striving to safeguard their national identity against the threats and blandishments of Greco-Roman culture, the Jewish contemporaries of Jesus were part and parcel — political-ly, economically and to some extent even culturally — of the world around them. Even while Jesus was still preaching in Galilee, the influence of the Gentile world was felt in some of the parables. The references to items of common dress or household furniture, the order of the meals, the customs connected with mourning, and above all such details as the story of the Gadarene swine and of the census "penny" or denarius (Mark 12 : 15), can best be visualized from the remains of Greek or Roman antiquity, whether found in this country or outside it. Such sayings as that referring to the dogs that "eat of crumbs which fall from their master's table" (Matt. 15 : 27) are appropriately illustrated from a Greek vase painting, while the reference to those "that are called gods, whether in heaven or in earth" (1 Cor. 8 : 5) is directly related to official Roman imagery, in which the emperor, the lord of the earth, appears in the garb and with the attributes of Jupiter, the lord of heaven.

As the story of the New Testament unfolds itself, the Jewish background gradually gives way to a Gentile one; though for some time the Jewish communities, scattered in the Diaspora throughout the eastern half of the Roman Empire, continued to serve as bases for the activities of the apostles. These usually began their mission in the local synagogue, but very soon had to "turn to the Gentiles" (Acts 13 : 46).

The atmosphere of the Roman present thus everywhere pervades the material life of the period, as mirrored in the New Testament. Of course, this life was seen from the lowly provincial standpoint of the class from which the apostles sprang and to whose members they addressed themselves. At the apex of Roman society stand the emperor and his local representatives, the legates and provincial governors, selected from the ruling senatorial class. Their authority is upheld by the army with its centurions, *speculatores,* spearmen and cavalrymen. The merchant navy is seen organizing the transport of wheat from Egypt to feed the hungry masses at Rome. The majesty of Roman law is supported by the magistrature, its tribunals and lictors. All this kaleidoscope of the contemporary world is colourfully displayed in the pages of the New Testament.

Nor can we disregard Greek culture, which flourished side by side with Roman power and under its protection; for it was the Romans who saved the disintegrating Hellenism of the Orient from complete extinction. Even the Jewish communities in the Diaspora were affected by the dominant Hellenistic culture. St. Paul, born and bred in the Hellenized city of Tarsus in south-eastern Asia Minor, was thoroughly familiar with the various aspects of this culture, although he had also for some time sat at the feet of Rabbi Gamaliel, the Pharisee. The apostle refers in his letters to the pedagogues who introduced their pupils to the world of Hellenistic literature, to the athletic side of Greek life with its competitions and prizes, to the craftsmen who laboured to produce the works of art and manufactured articles which we still admire; but he also points to the moral corruption which was the seamy side of contemporary life. Even the Greco-Oriental belief in gods that walked the earth turns up in the Acts, in the story of the incident at Lystra (Acts 14) in which the eloquent apostle was cast in the role of Hermes-Mercury.

Parallel with the Jewish and the Greco-Roman elements in the New Testament there appears a third strain, distinct from, yet related to both. While the prophets and other writers of the Old Testament had to set forth their teaching without reference to anything which preceded them — and if they were influenced by the earlier literature or mythology of the Orient such influences had to remain underground — the Christians from the beginning regarded the Old Testament as part of their own religion. Several of the prominent personalities of the Bible, such as Moses and Elijah, Jonah and Melchizedek, are referred to frequently in the pages of the New Testament. Nor can we escape the assumption that they were envisaged in one shape or another. Ever since the Hellenistic period the Jews — and in their wake the early Christians — had begun to illustrate the Bible with paintings (especially in the form of illuminated manuscripts in the Greek translation, the Septuagint). These illuminations on the one hand reflected the biblical story (sometimes even its later Midrashic interpretations), and were thus rooted in the Jewish past. At the same time, however, in conformity with the liberal-religious tendency of the circles in which these illustrations originated — and the mere fact of their creation, in spite of Exodus 20 : 4, is a proof of that liberalism — they were adapted from the material found in the then dominant Hellenistic art, thus introducing one more Greek strain into the fabric of contemporary Judaism. The originals of these Bible illustrations have been lost centuries ago; but their type persists in the paintings of the earliest Christian catacombs at Rome, in the frescoes of the Dura-Europus synagogue, and in later Byzantine mosaics and miniatures. If we try to form some conception of how the Old Testament characters were envisaged in the time of Jesus, it is to this later material that we have to turn, as has been done here.

In whatever way we approach our subject, one thing is clear: its importance as a documentary source for one of the world's great religions, and as first hand evidence for contemporary ways of life and thought. It is this latter aspect of the New Testament that we have aimed at illustrating here; our task will have been accomplished if this work helps to further the understanding of its contents.

CREDITS

It is our pleasant duty to thank all those who have helped us in this undertaking, whether persons or institutions: David H. Scott, Religious Book Editor, McGraw-Hill Book Company, and Professor Robert C. Dentan, General Theological Seminary, New York, who made revisions in the introductions and the text; R.P. Robert North, S.J. and R.P. P. Nobler, S.J., both of the Pontifical Biblical Institute; Prof. R. Bianchi-Bandinelli and Dr. E. Nash, both of Rome; Mr. M. Dagut, who checked the style, and Mrs. Inna Pomerantz, who helped to read the proofs.

Among the institutions which supplied material were the following: Ecole française d'archéologie, Athens; Staatliche Museen, Berlin; Pergamon-Museum, Berlin; Museo civico, Bologna; University Library, Cambridge; Museum, Cherchel; Archaeological Museum, Chiusi; Ny Carlsberg Glyptothek, Copenhagen; Archaeological Museum, Firenze; Bibliotheca Medicea-Laurenziana, Firenze; British Museum, London; Egypt Exploration Fund, London; Landesmuseum, Mainz; Malta Museum, La Valetta; John Rylands Library, Manchester; Mariemont Museum; Coin Cabinet, Munich; Glyptothek, Munich; National Museum, Naples; Chester Museum, Northumberland; Bibliothèque Nationale, Paris; Louvre Museum, Paris; Museo Concordiese, Portogruaro, Italy; Antiquarium of the Forum, Rome; National Museum of the Villa Giulia, Rome; Capitoline Museum, Rome; National Museum delle Terme, Rome; Villa Torlonia, Rome; the Pontifical Museums and Libraries of the Vatican and Lateran, Vatican City, Rome; The American Academy, Rome; the German Archaeological Institute, Rome; Landesmuseum, Trier; Museo archaeologico, Venice; Museo civico, Verona; Kunsthistorisches Museum, Vienna; Museum, Wiesbaden. And in Israel: the Archaeological Department of the Hebrew University, the Israel Department of Antiquities, the Shrine of the Book, the 'Avdat Expedition, all in Jerusalem; Haaretz Museum, Tel-Aviv; Municipal Museum, Haifa.

The publishers of the works from which the reproductions were made (see Index of Reproductions at the end of the book) and who kindly allowed us to use their publications, namely: Akademie der Wissenschaften, Vienna; Bialik Institute, Jerusalem; E. J. Brill, Leyden; Cambridge University Press; B. Filser ,Vienna; J. Gabalda, Paris; Hodder and Stoughton, London; Letouzey et Ané, Paris; A. Picard, Paris; Pontifico Istituto di archeologia cristiana, Rome; Yale University Press, New Haven, Conn.

Messrs. Scala, Firenze, photographed most of the objects from Italy; The Orient Press Photo Company those in Israel; Schwitter A.G., Zürich, prepared the colour plates.

The author and the publishers are privileged to include, on the title page of this volume, a reproduction of the latest discovery made in connection with the archaeology of the Gospels. This is a fragmentary Latin inscription, found in mid-June 1961 at Caesarea, in which the governor of Judaea, Pontius Pilate, dedicates a building in honour of the Emperor Tiberius. This remarkable find is the first known occurrence of the name Pontius Pilate in ancient epigraphy. We are therefore most grateful to the Caesarea Expedition of the Istituto Lombardo, Milano, and to its director, Dr. A. Frova, for their kind permission to include it here.

THE AUTHOR

The Hebrew University, Jerusalem
July, 1961

ST. MATTHEW

THE book of the generation of JESUS CHRIST, the son of David, the son of Abraham.   (Matt. 1 : 1)

The Gospel which stands first in the New Testament canon is traditionally ascribed to St. Matthew, usually identified with Matthew the tax gatherer, or publican, who was called by Jesus to apostleship from his counting-house at Capernaum (see p. 39); in Luke 5 : 27 this publican is called Levi, and in Mark 2 : 14 Levi the son of Alphaeus. He is identified by Mark and Luke as a rich man who gave Jesus and the apostles a great feast (Mark 2 : 15; Luke 5 : 29); it may be significant that the host's name is omitted in the Matthean account (Matt. 9 : 10). While the traditional view of its authorship continues to be held by many, others regard this view as untenable and believe the Gospel to have been composed toward the end of the first century by an unknown author who made use of written sources, one of which may have been an Aramaic collection of the sayings of Jesus made by the apostle St. Matthew. The very ancient tradition that Matthew made such a collection may possibly be the origin of the idea that he wrote the Gospel. The Gospel of Matthew is the longest of the four; the pattern it follows is similar to that of Mark and Luke, the three forming together the "Synoptic Gospels", i.e. those which can be compared with each other "at a glance". The general order contains, first of all, an account of Jesus' birth and ancestry (beginning in Matthew with Abraham, the common ancestor of the Hebrews, and continuing by way of David, from whose descendants, it was believed, the Messiah would come); this is followed by Jesus' preparation for his mission, his lengthy ministry in Galilee and neighbouring countries, his journey to Jerusalem, and finally the last week, with his passion, death and resurrection. This order is followed by Mark and Luke also, except that Mark has no account of Jesus' birth and ancestry.
The illustration shows the page containing the beginning of the Gospel of St. Matthew in the Sinaiticus Ms. of the fourth century, A.D., one of the two oldest manuscripts of the Greek Bible, discovered in 1844 on Mount Sinai by C. Tischendorf; since 1933 in the British Museum. It includes a complete version of the New Testament.

Column 1

ΒΙΒΛΟC ΓΕΝΕCΕΩC Ι
Υ ΧΡΙCΤΟΥ ΥΙΟΥ
ΔΑΥΕΙΔ ΥΙΟΥ ΑΒΡΑ
ΑΜ ΑΒΡΑΑΜ ΕΓΕΝ
ΝΗCΕΝ ΤΟΝ ΙCΑΑΚ
ΙCΑΑΚ ΔΕ ΕΓΕΝΝΗCΕ
ΤΟΝ ΙΑΚΩΒ ΙΑΚΩΒ
ΔΕ ΕΓΕΝΝΗCΕΝ ΤΟΝ
ΙΟΥΔΑΝ ΚΑΙ ΤΟΥC
ΑΔΕΛΦΟΥC ΑΥΤΟΥ
ΙΟΥΔΑC ΔΕ ΕΓΕΝΝΗ
CΕΝ ΤΟΝ ΦΑΡΕC ΚΑΙ
ΤΟΝ ΖΑΡΑ ΕΚ ΤΗC ΘΑ
ΜΑΡ ΦΑΡΕC ΔΕ ΕΓΕΝ
ΝΗCΕΝ ΤΟΝ ΕCΡΩΜ
ΕCΡΩΜ ΔΕ ΕΓΕΝΝΗ
CΕΝ ΤΟΝ ΑΡΑΜ ΑΡΑ
Μ ΔΕ ΕΓΕΝΝΗCΕΝ ΤΟ
ΑΜΙΝΑΔΑΒ ΑΜΙΝΑ
ΔΑΒ ΔΕ ΕΓΕΝΝΗCΕ
ΤΟΝ ΝΑΑCCΩΝ ΝΑΑC
CΩΝ ΔΕ ΕΓΕΝΝΗ
CΕΝ ΤΟΝ CΑΛΜΩΝ
CΑΛΜΩΝ ΔΕ ΕΓΕΝ
ΝΗCΕΝ ΤΟΝ ΒΟΕC
ΕΚ ΤΗC ΡΑΧΑΒ ΒΟΕC
ΔΕ ΕΓΕΝΝΗCΕΝ ΤΟ
ΙΩΒΗΔ ΕΚ ΤΗC ΡΟΥΘ
ΙΩΒΗΔ ΔΕ ΕΓΕΝΝΗ
CΕΝ ΤΟΝ ΙΕCCΑΙ
ΙΕCCΑΙ ΔΕ ΕΓΕΝΝΗ
CΕΝ ΤΟΝ ΔΑΥΕΙΔ ΤΟΝ
ΒΑCΙΛΕΑ ΔΑΥΕΙΔ ΔΕ
ΕΓΕΝΝΗCΕΝ ΤΟΝ
CΑΛΟΜΩΝ ΕΚ ΤΗC
ΤΟΥ ΟΥΡΙΟΥ
CΑΛΟΜΩΝ ΔΕ ΕΓΕΝ
ΝΗCΕΝ ΤΟΝ ΡΟΒΟ
ΑΜ ΡΟΒΟΑΜ ΔΕ
ΕΓΕΝΝΗCΕΝ ΤΟΝ
ΑΒΙΑ ΑΒΙΑ ΔΕ ΕΓΕΝ
ΝΗCΕΝ ΤΟΝ ΑCΑΦ
ΑCΑΦ ΔΕ ΕΓΕΝΝΗ
ΤΟΝ ΙΩCΑΦΑΤ
ΙΩCΑΦΑΤ ΔΕ ΕΓΕΝ
ΝΗCΕΝ ΤΟΝ ΙΩΡΑΜ
ΙΩΡΑΜ ΔΕ ΕΓΕΝΝΗ
CΕΝ ΤΟΝ ΟΖΕΙΑΝ
ΟΖΕΙΑC ΔΕ ΕΓΕΝΝΗ

Column 2

CΕΝ ΤΟΝ ΙΩΑΘΑΜ ΙΩ
ΑΘΑΜ ΔΕ ΕΓΕΝΝΗ
CΕΝ ΤΟΝ ΑΧΑC ΑΧΑC
ΑΧΑC ΔΕ ΕΓΕΝΝΗCΕ
ΤΟΝ ΕΖΕΚΙΑΝ ΕΖΕ
ΕΖΕΚΙΑC ΔΕ ΕΓΕΝΝΗ
CΕΝ ΤΟΝ ΜΑΝΑCCΗ
ΜΑΝΑCCΗC ΔΕ ΕΓΕΝ
ΝΗCΕΝ ΤΟΝ ΑΜΩC
ΑΜΩC ΔΕ ΕΓΕΝΝΗ
CΕΝ ΤΟΝ ΙΩCΕΙΑΝ
ΙΩCΕΙΑC ΔΕ ΕΓΕΝΝΗ
CΕΝ ΤΟΝ ΙΕΧΟΝΙΑΝ
ΚΑΙ ΤΟΥC ΑΔΕΛΦΟΥC
ΑΜΦΟΥ ΕΠΙ ΤΗC ΜΕ
ΤΟΙΚΕCΙΑC ΒΑΒΥΛΩ
ΝΟC ΩCΠΑCΟΙ ΠΥC
ΜΕΤΑ ΔΕ ΤΗΝ ΜΕΤΟΙ
ΚΕCΙΑΝ ΒΑΒΥΛΩΝΟC
ΙΕΧΟΝΙΑC ΕΓΕΝΝΗ
CΕΝ ΤΟΝ CΑΛΑΘΙΗΛ
CΑΛΑΘΙΗΛ ΔΕ ΕΓΕΝ
ΝΗCΕΝ ΤΟΝ ΖΟΡΟ
ΒΑΒΕΛ ΖΟΡΟΒΑΒΕΛ
ΔΕ ΕΓΕΝΝΗCΕΝ ΤΟΝ
ΑΒΙΟΥΔ ΑΒΙΟΥΔ
ΔΕ ΕΓΕΝΝΗCΕΝ ΤΟ
ΕΛΙΑΚΕΙΜ
ΕΛΙΑΚΕΙΜ ΔΕ ΕΓΕΝ
ΝΗCΕΝ ΤΟΝ ΑΖΩΡ
ΑΖΩΡ ΔΕ ΕΓΕΝΝΗCΕ
ΤΟΝ CΑΔΩΚ
CΑΔΩΚ ΔΕ ΕΓΕΝΝΗ
CΕΝ ΤΟΝ ΑΧΕΙΜ
ΑΧΕΙΜ ΔΕ ΕΓΕΝΝΗ
CΕΝ ΤΟΝ ΕΛΙΟΥΔ
ΕΛΙΟΥΔ ΔΕ ΕΓΕΝΝΗ
CΕΝ ΤΟΝ ΕΛΕΑΖΑΡ
ΕΛΕΑΖΑΡ ΔΕ ΕΓΕΝΝΗ
CΕΝ ΤΟΝ ΜΑΤΘΑΝ
ΜΑΤΘΑΝ ΔΕ ΕΓΕΝΝΗ
CΕΝ ΤΟΝ ΙΑΚΩΒ
ΙΑΚΩΒ ΔΕ ΕΓΕΝΝΗ
CΕΝ ΤΟΝ ΙΩCΗΦ
ΤΟΝ ΑΝΑ ΜΑΡΙΑC
ΕΞ ΗC ΕΓΕΝΝΗΘΗ ΙC
Ο ΛΕΓΟΜΕΝΟC
ΧΡC ΠΑCΑΙ ΟΥΝ ΑΙ ΓΕ

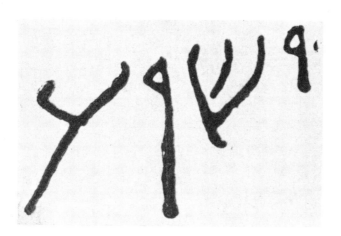

AND she shall bring forth a son, and thou shalt call his
name JESUS: for he shall save his people from their sins.

(Matt. 1 : 21)

The name Jesus, as written in the Gospels, is the Greek form of the Hebrew name Yeshua, a late contraction
of the original Hebrew Yehoshua (Joshua in the English Bible). This is one of the many biblical names in which
the Divine name is combined with a verb conveying a blessing. Yehoshua means originally "The Lord is
salvation"; the Gospel, however, interprets the name as meaning one who shall save the "people from their
sins". The form Yeshua appears frequently in the Bible after the Babylonian Exile, in the names of families
of priests (1 Chron. 24 : 11), Levites (Ezra 2 : 40 and often) and Judaites (Ezra 2 : 6). It continues to be used
among the Jews in the post-biblical period; several high-priests from the last days of the Second Temple and
numerous prominent rabbis were called Yeshua or Yoshua.
The reproductions on the left show the Hebrew and Greek form of the name, as it was written on many ossuaries
(small bone chests) dating from the time of Jesus. Such ossuaries are usually found in rock-cut tomb-caves in
and around Jerusalem. They were destined to receive the bones of the dead one year after the original burial.
For the purpose of identification the name of the deceased was written on the ossuary in one or both of the two
languages (Greek and Aramaic/or Hebrew) current in Jerusalem at that time.

NOW when JESUS was born in Bethlehem of Judaea in the days of Herod the King, behold, there came wise men from the east to Jerusalem.   (Matt. 2 : 1)

Bethlehem in Judaea was the abode of David's ancestors Boaz and Ruth, Obed and Jesse. It was also the scene of the anointing of David by Samuel (1 Sam. 16 : 4), and was referred to in glowing terms by Micah (5 : 2). It is regarded by St. Matthew (see verse above), St. Luke (2 : 4) and St. John (7 : 42), as well as by all later Christian traditions, as the birthplace of Jesus. At that time it was a Judaean city of minor importance, the first convenient halt for caravans travelling from Jerusalem southwards. The view above shows the town and the Church of the Nativity, erected over the grotto where (according to tradition) Jesus was born.

After setting out the locality of Jesus' birth, the Gospel places the event during the reign of Herod, king of Judaea (37-4 B.C.). Herod was born of an Idumaean family. His father, Antipater, was the all-powerful minister of Hyrcanus, one of the latter Hasmoneans. Aided by the Romans, Herod succeeded in destroying the last scions of that dynasty and became king in their stead. His reign was marked by external splendour and material progress, but was marred by tragedies in the royal family and a deep rift between the ruler and the people. The coin of Herod reproduced on the right of p. 20 shows, on the obverse, a sacrificial tripod (a pagan symbol) with the Greek inscription: "Of King Herod"; and, on the reverse, a table on which rests the starred helmet of the Dioscuri (see p. 202). Only the avoidance of any human likeness marks it as the issue of a Jewish ruler.

WHEN he arose, he took the young child and his
mother by night, and departed into Egypt.

(Matt. 2 : 14)

Menaced by Herod, Joseph was guided to seek safety in Egypt. From Bethlehem a comparatively short
journey southwards would bring him, within two days, to Beersheba and thus outside Herod's domain. If it
became necessary to avoid the main highway, the by-ways fringing the Judaean desert could be taken. Egypt
served as a refuge for many biblical personages, beginning with Abraham and including Jeroboam the son of
Nebat, the prophets Uriah (Jer. 26 : 21) and Jeremiah (Vol. III, p. 142), and, in the second century B.C., the High
priest Onias III. In the time of Jesus, Egypt was a Roman province, having been annexed by the emperor Augustus
in 30 B.C., after the defeat of Cleopatra. As such it was but a shadow of its former glory, but the awe-inspiring
monuments of its great past, such as the sphinx and pyramids (see above), stood then, as now, visible to all.
At the time of Jesus' birth, the Jewish community in Egypt numbered one million, a seventh of the total population. Joseph and his family could thus easily find shelter and sustenance with their compatriots, whether
in Alexandria or in one of the Jewish villages on the banks of the Nile.

A ND he came and dwelt in a city called Nazareth . . .   (Matt. 2 : 23)

After Herod's death, and in accordance with his will, his kingdom was divided by the emperor Augustus among his descendants. Archelaus, the eldest surviving son, was made ruler of Judaea and Samaria, with the title of ethnarch. He inherited his father's cruelty, but not his ability, and was deposed by the Romans after a troubled reign of ten years (A.D. 6). Joseph could hardly hope to live in peace under this ruler and he therefore settled in Galilee under Herod Antipas, another of Herod's sons, a shrewder but less dangerous character (Luke 13 : 32). The place selected by Joseph was a small locality called Nazareth, perched on the southern slope of the mountains of Galilee, with a wide view over the Esdraelon Valley. It was situated about seven miles south-east of Sepphoris, the principal city of Western Galilee. Nazareth is not mentioned in any source outside the Gospels till the Byzantine period. Even then it was a purely Jewish village, having been settled after the destruction of the Second Temple by the priestly family of Happizez (1 Chron. 24 : 15) which had fled from Jerusalem. The relative insignificance of the locality made it safe for Jesus to grow up there, in the shop where Joseph worked as a carpenter (see p. 49), till the time was ripe. Nazareth (see view below) is today a town of 40,000 inhabitants and the capital of the Northern District of Israel.

A<small>ND</small> were baptized of him in Jordan, confessing their sins. (Matt. 3 : 6)

After telling the story of the birth and early life of Jesus, St. Matthew continues with a description of the stir caused by the Precursor of Jesus, St. John the Baptist. Masses of people flocked to be baptized in the Jordan.
The River Jordan is the principal water-course of the Holy Land, and flows through both Galilee and Judaea. It was therefore best suited for the baptisms of the masses moved by the preaching of John the Baptist. The exact position of the place of baptism referred to in the Gospels is disputed. St. Matthew seems to favour a site nearer to Jerusalem, Judaea and Peraea ("the region round about Jordan"), and is followed by St. Mark (1 : 5) and St. Luke (3 : 3). St. John (3 : 23), however, suggests Aenon, near Salim, south of Beth-Shean. Later Christian tradition has in general followed the former identification.
The view above, taken in the vicinity of Jericho and not far from the point at which the river enters the Dead Sea, shows the Jordan flowing peacefully between the green vegetation which lines its banks. The river is here fairly deep and the localities where it could be safely entered for immersion and baptism are none too numerous.

THEN was JESUS led up of the Spirit into the
wilderness to be tempted of the devil.   (Matt. 4 : 1)

Before the beginning of his mission, Jesus withdrew into the wilderness — from the context, and especially
Matthew 3 : 1, we can understand the text as referring to the Judaean desert. This area, which extends over
the eastern slope of the Judaean mountains from the watershed to the Jordan Valley and the Dead Sea, is a vastness
of arid hills, cut by deep canyons by which the occasional winter-floods find their way to the east. Situated close
to the settled parts of Judaea and yet accessible only with difficulty, it has been the immemorial refuge of the
outlaw (see Vol. II, p. 147), and of those troubled in spirit and disgusted with urban materialism. Towards the
end of the period of the Second Temple, the deep spiritual crisis which had afflicted Israel since the fall of the
Hasmonaeans led many people to seek a return to the pure ancestral religion by taking up their abode in the
wilderness. Among these there were many dissident sects, such as that which has bequeathed to us the Dead Sea
Scrolls. The view above shows a particularly savage part of the desert in the upper reaches of the Choziba Valley,
now called Wadi el-Qelt. The striated limestone rocks are deeply cut by canyons scoured out by the winter
rains. The many caves formed in the cliffs can serve as a shelter for seekers after solitude and contemplation.

THEN the devil taketh him up into the holy city, and setteth him on a pinnacle of the temple.   (Matt. 4 : 5)

The holiness of Jerusalem had taken deep roots in Jewish consciousness from the time of the Babylonian exile (Isa. 52 : 1, Neh. 11 : 1) and had become undisputed in the later part of the period of the Second Temple. The Gospel therefore uses the appellation "the holy city" as an obvious synonym for "Jerusalem". We find this appellation also on coins of the First Revolt against Rome (see coin on right). The Jewish authorities coined silver shekels to demonstrate their independence, for silver coinage had previously been reserved for the emperor. The shekels bear on the reverse the legend "Jerusalem the Holy" encircling three pomegranates or myrtles. This device has been interpreted either as a reference to the Aaronic priesthood, or as the arms of the city in ancient times.

The "pinnacle of the Temple" mentioned here is most likely the south-eastern corner of the Temple esplanade, as it was built by Herod and as it stands till this day (see view below). The walls of the esplanade are formed of huge ashlar blocks (see pp. 94-95). Even today the wall at this corner is fifty feet high; in the time of Jesus, however, it went right down to the slope of the rock in the Valley of the Kidron below, a sheer drop of over 130 feet. This dizzy height explains the nature of the temptation contained in the following verse.

H E came and dwelt in Capernaum, which is upon the
sea coast . . .   (Matt. 4 : 13)

Unable to make much headway in Nazareth (cf. Luke 4 : 16-30), Jesus descended to the shores of the Sea of
Galilee and settled in Capernaum, which is therefore occasionally called "his city" in the Gospels (Matt. 9 : 1).
Capernaum is the Greek form of the Hebrew name Kefar Nahum, "The Village of Nahum" — an unknown
personality. The locality is also mentioned by Josephus (*Life,* 399, 403; *War* III, 519) as a place on the border
of Galilee, near its sea and the Jordan. It has been identified with the ruin known to the Arabs as Tell Hum,
where the remains of a synagogue (see pp. 254, 274) have been excavated. Owing to the city's position on the Sea
of Galilee, with ready access to the Decapolis region and its Gentile inhabitants, it could be assumed that the people
of Capernaum would lend a readier ear to the new teaching than the inhabitants of landlocked Nazareth.
Matt. 11 : 23 implies that Jesus was somewhat disappointed by the response of Capernaum to the call, although
at least five of the apostles lived there. From Talmudic sources we learn of the existence of a Judaeo-Christian
community at Kefar Nahum in later days — proving that Jesus' teaching there had apparently not been entirely
fruitless.
Above is a view of the grove which now covers the remains of the village.

AND JESUS, walking by the sea of Galilee, saw two brethren, Simon called Peter, and Andrew his brother, casting a net into the sea : for they were fishers . . . he saw other two brethren, James the son of Zebedee, and John his brother, in a ship with Zebedee their father, mending their nets . . .   (Matt. 4 : 18, 21)

The Sea of Gennesaret is the largest sweet-water lake of the Holy Land and as such is very rich in fish, especially of the *chromis* and *hemichromis* species (see also p. 51). Hence the shores of the lake were populated by fishermen, who constituted a considerable proportion of the inhabitants of the various cities, such as Tiberias. It was from among these that Jesus began to call the first of the apostles; fishermen, who are exposed to the vagaries of storm and sea, are pious, if not by nature, at least by profession. The first to be called were Simon and his brother Andrew. Simon the son of Jonah, like many other Jews of Galilee, was surnamed *Kaipha* or "rock", in Greek Peter (from *petra,* "rock"); his brother's name (*Andreas,* i.e. "the manly one") is purely Greek and we do not know his Jewish name. The two were casting a net into the sea. This is one of the methods of fishing still used to this day on the shores of the Sea of Galilee (see illustration on p. 28). Fishing can be done with a rod (see p. 57), but then only a few fish can be caught; the better method is for the fisherman to wade into the shallow water by the shore and, with a skilful swing, to throw out a circular fishing net, nine to fifteen feet wide, so that it falls outspread on the surface of the water. It is subsequently drawn back by a rope attached to its centre. Other methods were the casting of a draw net from a boat (or from two boats — Luke 5 : 7) and dragging it to the shore; or plunging a deep-sea net into the water. A good place to fish was the vicinity of Capernaum, where warm springs issuing into the sea draw the fish to the shore. Of course, nets were often fouled on rocks or dirtied, and had to be mended (see illustration on p. 29). James and John, the sons of Zebedee, were thus employed when called.

אמרתי לגבורים שירי סתרתי אשר הייתי בוזי
פזרתי ... בשר עיר לרוחי ורוחי
אני ויהי ... למים לפנים עד ... ם
... ום

AND seeing the multitudes, he went up into a mountain . . . And he opened his mouth, and taught them, saying, Blessed are the poor in spirit: for theirs is the kingdom of Heaven. Blessed are they that mourn: for they shall be comforted. (Matt. 5 : 1-4)

Neither here, nor in the parallel account of St. Luke (6 : 20-23), is there any indication as to the exact place where Jesus pronounced the Blessings. However, Christian tradition has from early times located the spot on the Mountain of the Beatitudes, a hill 368 ft. high above Capernaum (owing to the depression of the Jordan Valley the hill is actually 312 ft. below sea level). This gentle elevation, with its extensive view over the sea and the mountains encircling it, has for centuries been regarded as a fitting background for the famous message of the Gospel (see view above).

Recently, the wording of the Beatitudes has been found parallelled to some extent in one of the Thanksgiving Hymns of the Dead Sea Sect (XVIII, 14-15, see illustration below). The Scroll text refers to the *meek, those that are of contrite spirit, them that mourn.* The parallel is however mainly formal, the message of the Beatitudes being in the main spiritual and religious, whereas that of the Sect is social and national.

NEITHER do men light a candle, and put it under a bushel, but on a candlestick . . .   (Matt. 5 : 15)

The ancients employed various methods of artificial lighting: torches, candles, but mostly lamps with wicks burning in oil. The latter were made from clay or metal. In Jesus' time the lamps had a rounded receptacle with an opening for the oil and a flared nozzle with a hole for the wick. As the light given by such an oil-lamp was comparatively weak, several lamps were sometimes grouped together, or one lamp was provided with several nozzles and wicks (polykandilia). Another way of increasing the quantity of light was to place the lamp (lykhnos) on a high stand or candelabrum (lykhnia) as described in this verse, which attests to Jesus' familiarity with the appointments of the usual Greco-Roman house. Several such bronze lamps, placed on stands of the same metal, were found at Pompeii (first century A.D.) and are exhibited in the Naples Museum. One of them is illustrated above. The placing of the lamp in an elevated position was the more necessary because of the feeble light provided by such oil-lamps.

FOR verily I say unto you, Till heaven and earth pass, one jot or one tittle shall in no wise pass from the law, till all be fulfilled.
(Matt. 5 : 18)

While the reference to lamps and candelabra on the preceding page shows Jesus' acquaintance with Greco-Roman usage, this verse is evidence of his close study of Hebrew writing. The text mentions the "jot" (*iota* in Greek) and the "tittle" (in Greek *keraia* = "horn") of the Law. The first refers to the *yod*, the smallest letter of the "square" Hebrew script, which was adopted in the Persian period and is still used to this day. In this alphabet the *yod* is a short stroke suspended above the line. The "horns" on the letters (in Hebrew *taggim*) are the little excrescences added to some Hebrew letters at their upper ends. In the illustrations, which are taken from the writing on ossuaries roughly contemporary with Jesus, we see these two special features of the Hebrew script. In one we find *Yehosef* (Joseph) written with a small *yod* at the beginning; in the other the wording reads *Yehudah ha-sofer* ("Judah the scribe") with "tittles" on the last three letters of the name. Their minuteness shows that Jesus did not intend to change even the smallest prescription of the Law.

AND if any man will sue thee at the law, and take away thy coat, let him have thy cloke also. (Matt. 5 : 40)

In order to illustrate the precept of loving even our enemies, Jesus again uses a parable from Greco-Roman custom. The Greco-Roman contemporaries of Jesus usually wore two garments. The lower one, called here "coat" (*khiton* in Greek, a word identical with the Hebrew *kuttoneth* "garment"), was a kind of shirt or under-garment worn next to the body. The upper garment or *himation* (here translated "cloak") was a woollen mantle draped over the other. In case of need a himation could serve as the only garment; and indeed it was worn as such by philosophers and other unworldly persons. The verse therefore indicates that if the less necessary garment is in dispute, the more vital one should also be sacrificed for the sake of peace.

The illustrations show, on the left, a Roman copy of a Greek statue of the Athenian tragic poet Sophocles (496–406 B.C.), clothed in a *himation*; and, on the right, a statue of the "smith god", Hephaistos, who is repre-sented wearing the short *khiton* of the artisans.

AND JESUS saith unto him, The foxes have holes, and the birds of the air have nests ...   (Matt. 8 : 20)

The tragic homelessness of a spiritual leader is here vividly portrayed in two parallel similes, one from animal-life, and the other from bird-life. Foxes live in pairs in deep holes, in rocky or wooded ground, approached by several passages leading to a central cavern about three feet in diameter; the whole system can be as much as 45 feet in circumference. In addition to this main lair, foxes usually have various small hideouts for use in time of need. The other simile is taken from a bird's nest, which has at all times been regarded as a symbol of happy domesticity and was specially protected by the Mosaic Law (Cf. Vol. I, p. 278). The illustration below shows a bird's nest at breeding time, with the eggs well protected among the leaves and stalks of a plant. The picture above is a typical foxhole, situated in rocky terrain.

ND, behold, there arose a great tempest in the sea, insomuch that the ship
was covered with the waves: but he was asleep . . . Then he arose, and rebuked
the winds and the sea; and there was a great calm.   (Matt. 8 : 24, 26)

On its way from its sources near Mount Hermon to the Dead Sea, the Jordan forms first the smaller Lake Huleh
and then the large Lake of Chinnereth, known in the Gospels as the Sea of Gennesaret, the "Sea of Galilee"
(Matt. 4 : 18) or the "Sea of Tiberias" (see p. 143); occasionally it is also called simply "the lake" or "the sea"
for short. This sea, which is 14 miles long and 8 miles wide, is situated 680 ft. below sea level; its maximum
depth is 156 ft. It was the centre of the activities of Jesus and the apostles in the first period of their ministry;
the first apostles were drawn from among the fishermen busy on its waters (pp. 28-29) and their comings and
goings in various parts of the sea are the framework for most of the events recorded in the first part of the Gospels.
Although the sea is usually calm, its waters presenting a lucid blue surface slightly ruffled by soft breezes (see
view above), it can occasionally become quite stormy, with high winds tearing across its surface and raising
waves which can be dangerous for the usually frail craft plying on it. In such cases the fishermen take up their
oars, furl their sails and try to get out of the path of the storm as quickly as possible. The wind is strongest and
the waves are highest on the eastern side of the lake. Usually the wind is higher at noon; but when a storm
rises at night, as described above, the situation can become very serious indeed.

Aᴺᴰ when he was come to the other side into the country of the Gergesenes, there met him two possessed with devils, coming out of the tombs, exceeding fierce, so that no man might pass by that way.   (Matt. 8 : 28)

The events recorded in this verse as occurring in the country of the "Gergesenes" are located in the region of the "Gadarenes" by St. Mark (5 : 1) and St. Luke (8 : 26). Those commentators who accept the version of St. Matthew identify the Gergesenes with the hamlet of Chorsi (the Arab Kursi) on the eastern shore of the Sea of Galilee; but the majority incline to accept the reading Gadarenes as referring to the city of the Decapolis Gadara (now Umm Qeis). Although this city was situated on a mountain peak south of the Yarmuk river and to the east of the Jordan (see map p. 131), its territory may have reached the shore of the Sea of Galilee. As their city was a famous centre of Greco-Syrian literary and religious life, the inhabitants of Gadara might well have flouted the religious prohibitions of their Jewish neighbours by keeping swine on the banks of the sea.

The rock-cut tombs which form a characteristic feature of funerary architecture in the Hellenistic and Roman period could — in view of the generally mild climate of the country — quite easily provide shelter for any kind of outcast, including the mentally deranged. The illustration on the left shows one such rock-cut tomb in the vicinity of the so-called "Tombs of the Judges" in Jerusalem. This and similar tombs are roughly contemporary with the events recorded in the Gospel. They consist of a vestibule and a hall, with chambers branching off from the latter. Such tombs made excellent hiding-places, especially as they were not often visited.

A ND he said unto them, Go. And when they were come out, they went into the herd of swine : and behold, the whole herd of swine ran violently down a steep place into the sea, and perished in the waters.

(Matt. 8 : 32)

Pig-breeding was a highly profitable business in antiquity; the pork was not only consumed locally, but could be salted and sold to the Roman army. The Gentile inhabitants of the Decapolis, therefore, raised large herds of pigs in their territories, each in charge of a swineherd (*suarius*). In view of the detestation of this animal expressed in the Mosaic law (see Vol. I, p. 186), the Jews living in the same district must have abominated this practice. A reflection of this attitude is still evident in the Gospel story, in which the pigs are made the abode of impure spirits and perish in the lake, the banks of which they had profaned by their presence.

The illustration on p. 36 (right) shows a bronze figurine of a jumping pig found at Pompeii; that on p. 37 below is the funerary stele of a swineherd from Bologna in Northern Italy. Both are roughly contemporary with the Gospel story. On the stele the deceased is seen following his herd of seven pigs. The view on p. 37 (left, above) shows the steep banks of the Sea of Galilee in the region where Gadarene territory presumably reached its shore. The steepness of the bank makes the story of the plunging herd more vivid and illustrates the evangelist's thorough knowledge of local topography.

37

AND, behold, they brought
to him a man sick of the palsy,
lying on a bed ... And he arose,
and departed to his house.

(Matt. 9 : 2, 7)

From the shore of Gadara Jesus returned to Capernaum and there healed a paralytic. Paralysis, i.e. the loss or impairment of the motor or sensory function of the nerves, may result from a variety of causes, some connected with organic changes, some with lesions, some with poisonous substances and some with virus diseases. In the state of medical knowledge in antiquity all these causes were lumped together and recovery from this disease was generally despaired of. The patient was kept on his bed till he regained the use of his limbs or died, the latter eventuality being the more likely. Hence the fact that in this particular case the paralytic was able to arise from his bed and take it up and carry it to his house made a strong impression on the people of Capernaum and on future generations. This miraculous healing was consequently a favourite subject of ancient Christian art. In the illustration above we see it depicted on the walls of the oldest known church (for its plan see p. 252), found in a private house in the city of Dura-Europus on the banks of the Euphrates, and dating to the first half of the third century A.D. In the painting (reproduced above) we see the formerly sick man, now healed, carrying on his back a typical bed (klinê), consisting of a metal or wooden framework and a mattress formed by a criss-cross of ropes.

AND as JESUS passed forth from thence, he saw a man, named Matthew, sitting at the receipt of custom: and he said unto him, Follow me. And he arose, and followed him.

(Matt. 9 : 9)

After the healing of the paralytic, the evangelist describes how Jesus recruited another apostle, probably St. Matthew himself, from the customs-house (in Greek *telonion*). The term *telonion* denotes two different kinds of fiscal activity: the collection of customs or tolls paid on merchandise passing from one country to another, and the collection of taxes due to the state. The common feature of both functions was that the customs or taxes were farmed out by the government to "publicans" (Matt. 9 : 10) who, in return for a fixed payment, obtained the right to collect as much as they could from the public. These publicans were therefore universally hated and are naturally lumped together with "sinners" in the next verse. St. Matthew seems to have been engaged in collecting customs dues rather than taxes, as Capernaum was not an important administrative centre, but was close to the frontier (which followed the line of the Jordan) between the territories of Herod Antipas and of his brother Philip. Although the Roman empire was economically one unit, it was nevertheless divided into customs regions, and dues were collected on goods passing from one area to another. The customs tariffs were sometimes quite complicated, such as the Palmyrene tariff of A.D. 137 which includes hundreds of items and the first lines of which are reproduced below the relief. The illustration above shows the interior of the office of a Pannonian business man of the third century A.D., as represented on a funerary stele. The deceased is seated at a table, ledger in hand, with a bag of coins — his daily takings — in front of him. Before him stands his clerk, reading from a large roll which represents the daily account book. A similar scene must have been enacted every day at St. Matthew's customs office.

Aɴᴅ when ᴊᴇsus came into the ruler's house, and saw the minstrels and the people making a noise . . .

(Matt. 9 : 23)

Another miracle performed at Capernaum was the bringing back to life of the daughter of Jairus, "the ruler of the synagogue" (see p. 87). The child had already been given up for dead and preparations for her funeral were in full swing.

It was a custom of great antiquity in the Orient, especially in Egypt (see Vol. I, p. 124; II, p. 168), for a great crowd (including professional wailing women) to accompany the funeral procession, "making a noise" of weeping and lamenting. We also find musical instruments in the representations of funeral processions. The employment of pipers who played dirges on flutes over the dead is mentioned at least twice in the Mishna, the codification of Jewish law and practice from the days of the Second Temple onwards (*Mishna Shabbat* 23 : 4, *Baba Meziah* 6 : 1). One representation of such practices, shown above, was found on the reliefs from the tomb of the Haterii in Rome, about one generation after Jesus. We see a dead woman on her bier, with the wailing women standing above her, a seated flutist playing at the right below, while the mourners of the family receive condolences.

AND JESUS went about all the cities and villages, teaching in their synagogues ...   (Matt. 9 : 35)

From Capernaum Jesus' activities branched out into the cities and villages of Galilee, of which there were — according to Josephus — no less than 204. His preaching naturally took place in the synagogues, of which there was at least one in every village, and where the men of the village would certainly be found on a Sabbath day. The synagogue *(beth ha-knesseth* in Hebrew, i.e. the "house of assembly") probably came into being during the Babylonian exile to take the place of the ruined Temple. It served as a place of meeting for the exiles, for exhortation and for the reading of the Law. With the Return to Zion the institution spread in the Land of Israel, till it became universal in Jewry. According to the rabbinical law, every community was bound to have a synagogue, usually built either on the highest point of the settlement or on the shore of a sea or bank of a river (see p. 27). The synagogues were used for congregational prayer, preaching, interpretation of Scripture and for other communal functions as well. They were therefore the natural place of resort for anyone wishing to persuade his fellow-Jews. Jesus preached in the synagogues at Capernaum (Matt. 12 : 9), Nazareth (Luke 4 : 16) and elsewhere. St. Paul regularly used the synagogues in the Diaspora as the starting point of his mission in every city (see pp. 176, 181). No remains of synagogues dating from Jesus' time have been found (except the inscription, p. 162), but the earliest surviving Galilean structures (second to fourth cent. A.D.) give a good idea of the external appearance of such buildings. Their ornate façades faced Jerusalem. The photograph above shows one of the best preserved Galilean synagogues, that of Kefar Bar'am.

Pʀᴏᴠɪᴅᴇ neither gold, nor silver, nor brass in your purses. Nor scrip for your journey, neither two coats, neither shoes, nor yet staves . . . (Matt. 10 : 9-10)

When sending the disciples to preach to "the lost sheep of the house Israel", Jesus ordered them to travel with the utmost simplicity. They should carry no money (neither gold nor silver minted by the imperial Roman government, nor even the copper coins of the local princes and cities). Normally such money was carried in a girdle (*zona* in Greek, translated "purse"), as was usual in antiquity. They were also forbidden to carry a wallet or leathern pouch for victuals (*pera* in Greek, here translated "scrip"). Nor were they to have two coats (*khiton* in the Greek original, i.e. tunics; of necessity they had to carry a *himation* or mantle, see p. 33), or sandals (*hypodemata* in Greek, i.e. soles attached to the foot), or even staves. The latter demands went beyond even the practice of the pagan ascetic philosophers. On the painting from Villa Boscoreale (1st cent. A.D.) we see a venerable sage, clad in the pallium of his class, but *with* sandals on his feet and leaning on a staff.

WHAT I tell you in darkness, that speak ye in light: and what ye hear in the ear, that preach ye upon the housetops.

(Matt. 10 : 27)

Continuing to instruct the disciples, Jesus advised them to proclaim their teaching openly, in contrast to the conspiratorial methods commonly adopted by the rebels against Rome in a country seething with discontent, as Judaea was. The warm climate of the oriental countries (including the Land of Israel) and the small number of rainy days (not more than fifty on the average), has led to the general adoption of flat-roofed houses. In this way an oriental village presents a striking difference at first sight from the settlements in northern countries with their steep and gabled roofs, intended to carry off the rainwater. The flat rooftops were either paved with stones, or protected with a special mixture of earth and stones which had to be repaired every year; if neglected it grew weeds (see Vol. IV, p. 55). The use of the housetops for talking, sleeping, and especially for walking in the fresh evening air, is mentioned several times in the Bible (1 Sam. 9 : 25-26; 2 Sam. 11 : 2). Of course, anything passing on a housetop would be visible and audible from afar; hence the allusion to "preaching upon the housetops" in the verse above. The illustration shows an Arab village in Israel today, with its characteristic flat roofs.

WOE unto thee, Chorazin, woe unto thee, Beth-
saida . . .   (Matt. 11 : 21)

Chorazin is generally identified with the ruins called in Arabic Khirbet Kerazeh, about two miles north of Capernaum. The site contains the remains of a synagogue, probably of the third century A.D. The synagogue is built
of black basalt stone, on the usual plan of Galilean synagogues of the early type. The façade faces Jerusalem
and the interior is divided into a central hall and three side-halls by rows of columns. The Chorazin synagogue
is remarkable for its sculptures, especially the frieze which includes images of human beings (grape-gatherers
etc.), as well as mythological figures taken from the Greeks (Hercules, Medusa, a centaur). Apparently these
were allowed by the local rabbis. Such a liberal attitude might have been traditional in the locality and have
raised hopes in Jesus which were later on to be disappointed. Chorazin is mentioned in Talmudic sources as
a place where wheat ripened early. In the fourth century the site was deserted. The "seat of Moses" (shown
on p. 63) was found in this synagogue.

TAKE my yoke upon you, and learn of me ... For my yoke is easy ...   (Matt. 11 : 29-30)

In the predominantly agricultural society of Jesus' time, as in that of the Prophets, figures of speech taken from the daily life of the villagers were of course the most easily understood. One of the most common of such symbolical expressions is that referring to any task of burden as a "yoke" — the wooden bar fastened over the necks of two oxen and attached to the plough they are to draw. This metaphor is often used to indicate either the servitude imposed on Israel by its enemies or — in the form of "breaking the yoke" — the liberation of the people from such a condition (Vol. III, p. 33). In the Gospels, however, the symbolic meaning is more frequently the self-imposed yoke of the disciples of Jesus (Acts 15 : 10; 1 Tim. 6 : 1); in one case St. Paul calls one of his helpers his "true yoke-fellow" (Phil. 4 : 3). Reproduced above is a group of Etruscan votive bronze figurines representing a peasant ploughing with a yoke of oxen. It was found near Arretium in Italy and is dated to the sixth century B.C.

FOR as Jonas was three days and three nights in the whale's belly; so shall the Son of man be three days and three nights in the heart of the earth. (Matt. 12 : 40)

The miraculous story of the Prophet Jonah (Vol. III, p. 250-254) has exercised a very strong influence on Jews and Christians alike. Thus we find this prophet mentioned, together with Abraham, Moses, Joshua, Samuel and Elijah, in the very early prayers quoted in the Mishna *(Taanith* 2 : 4) as one of the examples of God's mercy. As such he could be invoked on days of fasting when the rains did not come. Together with Moses' striking of water from the rock (see p. 226), the miracle of Jonah ranks among the most popular representations in the frescoes in the Catacombs (the underground cemeteries of the early Christians in the vicinity of Rome). This was a specially popular Christian motif, because Jonah's three days' sojourn in the belly of the fish and his rescue therefrom appeared as a "prefiguration" of Jesus' death and resurrection. The story of Jonah is usually represented in three parts: Jonah is thrown into the sea and swallowed by a dragon-like fish; then he is cast forth by the fish on dry land; and finally he lies under the "gourd" (see Vol. III, p. 254). The picture above is reproduced from the Catacomb of Sta. Priscilla in Rome (third century A.D.). It shows the prophet, his arms outspread in an attitude characteristic of prayer, issuing from the mouth of a fish. As usual in these paintings the "big fish" appears as a kind of maritime dragon.

BEHOLD, a sower went forth to sow; And when he sowed, some seeds fell by the way side, and the fowls came and devoured them up. Some fell upon stony places, where they had not much earth; and forthwith they sprung up, because they had no deepness of earth: And when the sun was up, they were scorched; and because they had no root, they withered away. And some fell among thorns; and the thorns sprung up and choked them. But others fell into good ground, and brought forth fruit, some an hundredfold, some sixtyfold, some thirtyfold.

(Matt. 13 : 3-8)

The famous parable of the fate of the seeds which fell on different kinds of ground and developed accordingly serves to illustrate the close knowledge of agricultural labour shown everywhere in the Gospels. The first seeds, which fell by the road-side, remained on top of the ground; for the users of the road had trodden its surface hard (see picture above on the left), and the grains were picked up by passing birds. The second group fell into shallow earth covering rock; they grew easily and before the others, because their roots encountered no resistance at first; but they could not develop to any depth and, when the summer heat began, they wilted easily (for wheat growing on rocky soil, see above on the right). The third cluster fell on good soil, but one too well watered and too favourable to the development of noxious weeds which ultimately destroyed the useful plants (see below on left, wheat growing among weeds). Only the fourth and last part fell on soil which was suitable in all respects. The resultant crops varied, of course, according to the richness of the soil; a thirtyfold yield is attested in antiquity for the mountain lands of Judaea, while crops of sixty to one hundred times the original sowing were obtained in the lands famous for their fertility, such as Babylonia and Egypt, and also occasionally in the most fertile parts of the Land of Israel, such as the plain of Gennesaret.

AGAIN, the kingdom of heaven is like unto treasure hid in
a field . . .   (Matt. 13 : 44)

The unstable political conditions in the Orient during the whole of the Hellenistic and the Early Roman periods,
with their frequent wars and revolutions, naturally led many people to safeguard their fortunes by converting
them into coins — which in any event would keep their value as metal — and to bury these in some place where
they could remain unsuspected till reclaimed. If, as often happened, the original owner of the treasure perished
suddenly, all knowledge of his treasure was lost, except for the few cases of accidental discovery at a much later
time. Such hoards of coins are among the archaeologically most valuable finds of antiquities, because they provide
us with first-hand information about the coins that were in circulation at that particular time, about trade routes,
and about the general state of economic development. Coins of good alloy and weight indicate prosperity;
coins of cheap metal, poorly struck, the reverse.
The picture above shows part of one such hoard found in 1960 on Mount Carmel; it consists of nearly five
thousand pieces, mostly Tyrian shekels (see p. 57), half-shekels and Roman coins, of the first centuries B.C.
and A.D. This great treasure "hidden in a field" was a lucky windfall for the man who chanced on it.

Is not this the carpenter's son?   (Matt. 13 : 55)

Returning to Nazareth, Jesus resumed teaching in a synagogue, but met with no response because of a question of status. In the fairly rigid social hierarchy of antiquity the artisans, who were engaged in manual labour, were regarded with little more respect than the peasants and the slaves; and indeed, much of the work done by free workmen was also done by trained slaves. The contempt expressed in this verse for a "carpenter's son" agrees well with what we know of ancient society, which reserved the higher activities in the political and intellectual spheres for "gentlemen of leisure". Only the Jewish community in the Talmudic period was an exception in this respect, most of the rabbis earning their living by handicrafts. However, despite the low opinion held of them, ancient carpenters were most skilful, as we see from the extant specimens of their work. In the illustration above (a gold-glass of the fourth cent. A.D. found at Rome) we see carpenters, dressed in the short tunic of their trade, sawing boards, cutting a piece of wood with a kind of axe, drilling holes with a bow-drill, working a plane and receiving instructions from Minerva, the goddess of arts and crafts, in the making of a waggon-axle and the fixing of the wheels. At the lower right, Daedalus, the first master-carpenter in Greek mythology, is shown building a ship; the other workers seem to be his assistants. The central personage probably represents a master-carpenter in whose memory the glass was made.

49

BUT when Herod's birthday was kept, the daughter of Herodias danced before them, and pleased Herod.

(Matt. 14 : 6)

The Gospel pauses in the story of Jesus for a brief account of the execution of John the Baptist and the circumstances surrounding this event. Herod Antipas, King Herod's son, had put John in prison, but feared to touch him. Some extraordinary stimulant was required to induce him to act against the prophet — and this was supplied by his step-daughter, the princess Salome, who agreed to dance before him and his guests. The two principal nations of antiquity, the Greeks and the Romans, differed fundamentally in their attitude to the dance. While the Greeks regarded it as one of the bodily exercises in which a free man might engage without shame, the Romans, with their customary gravity, judged it unworthy of a person of any social standing and left dancing to professionals of low class and lower reputation. This derogatory opinion of dancers and dancing can explain the extraordinary effect produced by a dance executed by no less a person than a princess of the royal house in honour of her stepfather's birthday. Among the realistic representations which appealed to the Hellenistic artist, we find the bronze statuette, which is reproduced here, of a dancer enveloped in her drapery (ca. 200 B.C.). It gives a fairly good idea of the kind of dance probably executed by Salome.

Aℕᴅ they say unto him, We have here but five loaves and
two fishes.   (Matt. 14 : 17)

Followed by great multitudes, Jesus preferred to teach in desert places, far
from the inhabited localities; there those listening would be more receptive
than when in the presence of the authorities, and would also better understand the parables drawn from nature. However, on one such occasion
evening came and the mass of Jesus' hearers were left without food, except
for five loaves and two fishes.

Loaves of bread and fish would be the most common kind of food carried by
the mass of people gathered on the banks of the Sea of Gennesaret; for it was
famous both for its rich hauls of fish (see pp. 28-29) and for the fertility of
its surroundings (see next page). The loaves of antiquity, which were baked
at low temperatures, resembled rather flat cakes than the loaves made today.
A good representation of them was found in a Pompeian painting (first
century A.D.) showing the shop of a seller of bread. Two men are buying
bread from the merchant, who stands behind a table piled high with loaves,
while a child stretches out his hand to one of them. The other picture shows
two mouth-breeding fishes (*Tilapia zillii*) found to this day in the waters
of the Sea of Galilee (Cf. Vol. I, p. 187).

AND when they were gone over, they came into the land of Gennesaret.   (Matt. 14 : 34)

The "Land of Gennesaret" referred to in this verse is the fertile plain extending southwards from the city of Gennesaret (Old Testament Chinnereth, Arabic Tell el-'Oreimeh) near the north-western shore of the lake, not far from Capernaum. It is known in the Talmud also by the name of the "Valley of Arbel", from another locality at its extreme southern end. The name Gennesaret, which has been interpreted as meaning the "Garden of the Prince", suggests that this area was a royal estate. Both the Talmudic sources and Josephus (*Jewish War* III, 506-521) praise its fertility in the most extravagant terms. The view above shows the part of the plain bordering on the lake, looking north-east.

The extremely rich alluvial basalt soil of the plain is brought down by three brooks issuing into it from the surrounding hills. Filling up a former bay with their silt, these brooks have created a shore-plain of considerable extent, famous for its palms, fig-trees, walnut-trees, olives, vine and citron. Neglected for a long time by the Beduin who once owned it, it has now been restored to its former fertility.

THEN JESUS went thence, and departed into the coasts
of Tyre and Sidon.   (Matt. 15 : 21)

After an acrimonious dispute with the Pharisees (verses 2-20) concerning the ritual ablutions before eating, in
which appeal was made to the authority of the prophet Isaiah (29 : 13), Jesus left Galilee and went northwards
into adjacent Phoenicia (see map, p. 131).
The "coasts of Tyre and Sidon" in this verse are a general term referring to the land of the Phoenicians, part of
present-day Lebanon. The country is called here by the name of its principal cities, both of which had territory
stretching far inland. The domains of Tyre reached as far as Cadasa overlooking the Huleh; while Sidon had a
common border with Damascus. In the time of Jesus, Tyre had recovered from the blows inflicted upon it by
Alexander (see Vol. III, pp. 182-3) and had again become one of the great commercial centres of the Mediterranean coast, especially famous for its purple (p. 177). Sidon, its rival for the leadership of Phoenicia, was
the centre of glass manufacture, and exported its products to the whole of the Roman empire. In both cities
the Phoenician population had become thoroughly Hellenized. Both had large Jewish communities.
The view of Tyre (top), taken from the north, shows the long peninsula occupied by the city and connected to
the mainland by the remains of Alexander's siege dam. The picture below it shows the harbour of Sidon, with
its boats. The castle (middle distance) dates from the time of the Crusaders.

Aᴎᴅ she said, Truth, ʟᴏʀᴅ: yet the dogs eat of the crumbs which fall from their masters' table.

(Matt. 15 : 27)

While sojourning in Phoenicia, Jesus was appealed to for help by a Gentile woman (see p. 89). Refusing at first, Jesus finally relented when the woman humbly compared her need to that of a dog fed by crumbs fallen from his master's table. Oriental people generally held the dog in great contempt (1 Sam. 17 : 43; 2 Sam. 9 : 8; Isa. 56 : 10 etc.), whereas the Greeks, and in particular Greek youths, had a very great affection for their hunting dogs; very often we find the dog represented on the grave-steles set over their tombs. No wonder, therefore, that the dogs shared their masters' repast, tied under the couches on which the ancients were accustomed to repose while eating. The illustration above shows such a scene. It is taken from a Corinthian krater (7th cent. B.C.), and represents the wedding of Heracles with Iole, the daughter of king Eurytios. Heracles is reclining on the right, Iphitos, a member of the royal family, on the left; Iole stands between them. Two dogs are tied up under the tables bearing the repast of which they are undoubtedly getting their share.

W HEN JESUS came into the coasts of Caesarea Philippi . . .   (Matt. 16 : 13)

After returning to Galilee (Matt. 15 : 29), and after another dispute with both Pharisees and Sadducees, Jesus again left Herod's domain for that of his brother, Philip. The city referred to in the Gospels as Caesarea Philippi (here and Mark 8 : 27) was originally, in the Hellenistic period, called Paneas, in honour of the Greek god Pan. Philip, Herod's son, rebuilt it and renamed it Caesarea in honour of Augustus Caesar (p. 104) to whom the great city-temple was dedicated. It was generally known as Caesarea Philippi ("of Philip"), to distinguish it from the larger Caesarea-by-the-Sea, which had been founded by Philip's father, Herod (p. 167). The Jews called it *Qisaryon* or "Little Caesarea". The most prominent feature of the region was the cave dedicated to Pan, the Paneion, situated in a high cliff near the city. The cliff is carved with niches which once contained statues and is inscribed with dedications to Pan and the nymphs (see illustration below). It has been suggested that the naming of Peter "the rock on which the church shall be built" (v. 18), which took place in this locality, was inspired by the sight of the great cliff of Caesarea Philippi.

AND behold, there appeared unto them Moses and
Elias talking with him.　　　　　　　　(Matt. 17 : 3)

The "high mountain" of verse 1 has been traditionally interpreted, since the third century A.D., to be Mount
Tabor, the most prominent mountain of Lower Galilee, celebrated in biblical history and song (Vol. II, p. 81).
In the vision of the three disciples Jesus appeared between the two great saviour figures of the Old Testament:
Moses, the leader of the people, a prophet the like of whom had never since arisen in Israel (Deut. 34 : 10),
and Elijah, who revived prophecy in Israel, saved the true religion from the cult of Baal, and was honoured
by being taken up to Heaven alive. Both these personalities figure prominently in Jewish and Early Christian art.
The illustrations shown here are taken from the fresco paintings of the synagogue at Dura-Europus (third century
A.D.). On the right is a representation of Moses reading the Law to the people of Israel (some scholars consider
this an image of Ezra). The leader is shown in the Hellenistic dress reserved at Dura for prominent Jewish heroes.
He is holding the scroll of the Law open in both hands; the receptacle at his feet was probably the container
for the scroll; the covering might be meant for the "vail" which Moses had to put on his face (Exod. 34 : 33).
The figure of Elijah on the left is a detail of the representation of the sacrifice on Mount Carmel in the same
synagogue (for full picture see Vol. III, pp. 298/9).

Go thou to the sea, and cast an hook, and take up the fish
that first cometh up; and when thou hast opened his mouth,
thou shalt find a piece of money; that take, and give unto
them for me and thee.   (Matt. 17 : 27)

The methods of fishing employed on the Sea of Galilee did not differ in the main from those of the ancient
Egyptians and other oriental nations (see Vol. III, pp. 44, 112). Normally the fishermen, who were interested
in catching plenty of fish, used nets (see pp. 28/29 and Luke 5 : 6); but in such cases as the present, when a few
fish had to be caught for personal needs, a rod, line and fishing-hook were used. The picture is a representation of a fisherman on an Early Christian sarcophagus (fourth cent. A.D.). He is standing on the shore of the
sea in which the miracle of Jonah is happening, with a basket (see p. 155) on his arm, and is just catching a big
fish, while a water-fowl is also fishing by his side.
The obligation which had to be discharged by the payment of the money found in the fish was the half shekel,
the tax paid by every Israelite for the maintenance of the Sanctuary (Exod. 30 : 13). For two persons this would
amount to one shekel, or a Tyrian *stater* (the word used in the Greek original and translated "piece of money")
or tetradrachm. There were two kinds of stater in antiquity: the one in common commercial use was the light
Attic stater of ca. 9 gm.; this however, was not regarded by the Temple authorities as the equivalent of the
Hebrew shekel. The "holy shekel" (see p. 26) was of heavier weight (ca. 15 gm.) and corresponded to the
Phoenician standard. The illustration shows a Tyrian stater, roughly contemporary with Jesus. The reverse side
shown here has the eagle, found on coins of Tyre from Ptolemaic times onwards, then the club, the emblem of
Hercules-Melkarth the great god of Tyre, a date and an inscription: "Of the Tyrians". As is proved by the coin
hoards (see p. 48), issues of Tyrian money circulated freely in Galilee in Jesus' day and later, up to the time of
the destruction of the Temple.

ᴀɴᴅ he went out about the third hour, and saw others standing idle in the marketplace.

(Matt. 20 : 3)

The "market place" (in Greek *agora,* in Latin *forum*) was the central square of most cities of Greece and Italy; it served not only for trade, but also for popular assemblies, and of course also for loiterers and persons seeking work. In the Hippodamian plan of the Greek cities in the Hellenistic period, the agora was a rectangular area set in the centre of the network of city streets intersecting at right angles.

The Roman plan was to place the forum — often several fora — at certain points along the main street of the city (*cardo*). The illustration shows one of the best preserved market-places in Palestine, that of the city of Gerasa beyond the Jordan, dating to the third cent. A.D. Contrary to earlier usage, it is ovoid in shape with a tetrapylon (building with four gates) in its centre. The plaza is beautifully paved with heavy blocks laid along lines which follow the curve of the porticoes. The row of Ionic columns following the ellipse supported a curving portico, with shops, taverns etc. behind it. The portico also served the workmen looking for jobs, who could in the meantime sit in its shade, waiting till someone came along to hire them.

The parable of the labourers working in a vineyard was uttered in "Judaea" beyond the Jordan (Matt. 19 : 1), which Jesus crossed on his way from Galilee to Jerusalem, i.e. not far from Gerasa. For the area referred to see map, p. 131.

THEN sent JESUS two disciples, saying unto them, Go into the village over against you, and straightway ye shall find an ass tied, and a colt with her: loose them, and bring them unto me. (Matt. 21 : 1-2)

Leaving the Jewish area beyond the Jordan (the "Peraea"), Jesus passed through Jericho. He then ascended the Mount of Olives from the east, by way of the Judaean desert, finally reaching the village of Bethphage. Preparations were made for a solemn entry into Jerusalem, and two disciples were sent to bring an ass to their master. The riding animals of antiquity were the horse and the donkey. The latter occurs earlier, already in the patriarchal period (Vol. I, p. 66). The horse, which was introduced into the Orient by the Hyksos, was at first used for drawing chariots rather than for riding (Vol. I, p. 145). The horse is the more suitable animal for covering large distances, as its movement is less tiring for the rider; also it can travel at much greater speed. However, for the purpose of a triumphal entry into the crowded, narrow streets of an oriental city, as here envisaged, an ass is far preferable; it is slower, does not endanger the passers-by and allows the rider to dismount easily whenever necessary. The ass bred in Palestine, *Equus asinus,* is a sturdy breed and far more intelligent than is popularly believed.

A<small>ND</small> J<small>ESUS</small> went into the temple of God, and cast out all them that sold and bought in the temple, and overthrew the tables of the money-changers . . .   (Matt. 21 : 12)

Most of the business of antiquity was conducted in the open; this was true also of money-changers and bankers. (The Greek word for "table", *trapeza,* is also used to mean a bank.) The manifold requirements of Temple worship necessitated a good many commercial transactions. One of the most important of these was the changing of money brought by the masses of pilgrims who made their way up to Jerusalem every year from all over the Jewish Diaspora. As we have seen (p. 57), the Temple authorities regarded only the Tyrian coins as equivalent to the "holy shekel" in which the Temple dues had to be paid. Hence the various currencies — Roman denars, Attic drachms, coins from Asia Minor, Egypt and beyond — had to be changed into "holy shekels" at the tables of the money-changers. These sat in the outer court of the Temple, which was considered less sanctified than the Inner Temple; near them were the sellers of doves, while the purchase of sheep for sacrifices went on north of the Temple area, near the Sheep Pool (see p. 142). The illustration below, taken from a funeral monument found at Neumagen in the Rhineland (third cent. A.D.), shows a Roman banker sitting at his table and dealing with a heap of coins spread before him. (For a similar representation see p. 39).

THERE was a certain householder, which planted a vineyard, and hedged it round about, and digged a winepress in it, and built a tower, and let it out to husbandmen, and went into a far country.

(Matt. 21 : 33)

The wording of this parable closely follows the Greek translation of Isaiah 5 : 1 (see Vol. III, p. 24-26) in the Septuagint version, though there is no reference to digging (lit. quarrying) a wine-press there. In spite of the verbal similarities, we must note that the economic techniques behind these two passages were quite different. In the time of Jesus, the Land of Israel, together with the other countries of the ancient Orient, had passed through a technical revolution, initiated by the Greek and Macedonian settlers established there by the Hellenistic kings and followed by the native cultivators. Thus vines were now to a large extent grown on high supports (see picture on the right); the wine-presses consisted of large square pressing vats connected with storage vats by channels (see picture on left); and, instead of the provisional huts constructed in Isaiah's time and occasionally still in use today, solid stone towers were constructed to protect the vineyards. At a still later stage, wine-presses were operated by machinery; this technique was already in use in Italy in the first century A.D., but spread only slowly in the East. Wine was one of the important export articles of Judaea and in Jesus' time viticulture was practised on a large scale.

SHEW me the tribute money. And they brought unto him a penny. And he saith unto them, whose is this image and superscription? They say unto him, Caesar's . . . (Matt. 22 : 19-21)

In order to confound the Pharisees, Jesus asked for a piece of "tribute money" (in the Greek original: "census money"). This represented the fixed poll-tax paid as tribute by every native of a Roman province (such as Judaea had become after the deposition of Archelaus in A.D. 6). The payment corresponded to a Roman silver denarius, the equivalent of a day's wage (Matt. 20 : 2). Like all silver and gold currency, these coins were struck by the imperial mint only, while the cities and local rulers were restricted to coining in bronze. Therefore, although the emperor's head could be found also on coins of the cities and those of most of the Herodian rulers, the reference here is undoubtedly to a denarius of the then reigning emperor Tiberius (see picture above). On its obverse we see a head of the emperor with, surrounding it, the Latin inscription (beginning on the right): "Tiberius Caesar, son of the deified Augustus, Augustus"; and on the reverse the figure of Peace holding an olive branch. The inscription around it reads: "The High Pontiff." It was such a coin that Jesus must have taken to show the Pharisees the "image and superscription" of Caesar.

THE scribes and the Pharisees sit in Moses' seat.   (Matt. 23 : 2)

The "seat of Moses" (in Greek: "the *kathedra* of Moses") was a special chair of honour, set up in the synagogues for the principal teacher of the Law or any other person whom the community intended to honour; the word "kathedra" in Greek means specifically the seat (with arm-rest and a high back) occupied by a professor when teaching (see p. 209). Such chairs have been found among the remains of several ancient synagogues; the one illustrated here was found at Chorazin (see p. 44). On its front there is a Judaeo-Aramaic inscription commemorating the benefactions of a certain Yudan son of Ishmael in donating various parts of the synagogue. It reads: "Remembered for good be Yudan the son of Ishmael who made the portico and the steps of the gate. May his share be with the Just". The arm rests and the back are ornamented in relief with traditional Jewish motifs. To occupy such a seat was the ambition of every aspiring rabbinical student.

FOR ye compass sea and land to make one proselyte . . . (Matt. 23 : 15)

The decline of the ancient Greek and Roman religions, which had already begun in the Hellenistic period, created a spiritual vacuum which left the way open for the influx of various oriental faiths. Both Judaism and Christianity were able to attract many highly intelligent people whose religious longings remained unsatisfied by the prevailing types of philosophy, whether Stoic or Epicurean. In consequence we find large numbers attracted to the Jewish religion, which, before the destruction of the Second Temple, was not yet bound up with a defeated and despised nation. The proselytes were of various kinds: some adopted the tenets of Judaism to the full, while others (the "proselytes of the gate") only followed the moral precepts of a religion for which they felt sympathy, without fully adopting it. To the latter category belonged the "devout and honourable women" of Antioch of Pisidia, who were influenced by the local Jews against Paul (Acts 13 : 50); Greek expressions similar to the word used here *(sebomenai)* have been found used in inscriptions to denote such sympathizers with Judaism. In the illustration above we see the tombstone and epitaph erected in a Jewish catacomb on the Via Appia, Rome, by one Mannacius to his "sweetest sister" Chrysis, a proselyte.

Such full proselytes went on pilgrimage to Jerusalem and are mentioned in the Acts (2 : 10, see p. 160) as members of the throng which crowded the Holy City on a Pentecost festival.

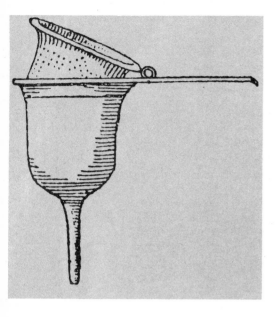

YE blind guides, which strain at a gnat . . . for ye make clean the outside of the cup, and of the platter . . .

(Matt. 23 : 24-25)

After reproaching the Pharisees with ambition and bigotry (see the preceding pages), Jesus attacked their ritualistic attitude. The rules for ritual cleanness set out in the Book of Leviticus (chapters 11-15) had been worked into a most intricate system of regulations through the development of the Oral Law by the scribes and rabbinical scholars. Uncleanness could be conveyed by touch, by carrying, by being in the shadow of an object, by entering an unclean house, and the like. Anyone who intended to keep himself ritually clean had to avoid as far as possible all contact, direct or indirect, with unclean people or things, otherwise he had repeatedly to undergo an elaborate ritual of sacrifice and purification. This explains the care with which the members of the Pharisee sect, who went furthest in their striving for ritual purity, cleaned their vessels and strained their wine. Illustrated above are a platter and a jug from the Herodian period (on the right); and a drawing (on the left) showing the use of a strainer in Roman times. Because there were no good corks, the contents of the containers used in antiquity were exposed to all kinds of insects and other impurities, which had to be removed by straining.

BECAUSE ye build the tombs of the prophets, and garnish the sepulchres of the righteous.

(Matt. 23 : 29)

The custom of commemorating important personages by elaborately built and decorated funerary monuments dates to Old Testament times (Vol. II, p. 189 and Vol. III, p. 48). In the Jerusalem of the period of the Second Temple, the valleys surrounding the city were filled with rock-cut sepulchres, some of which were subsequently venerated as the burial places of various prophets and kings. The custom persisted after the destruction of the Temple. Thus we find in the Jewish necropolis of Beth Shea'rim, established in the third and fourth centuries A.D. around the sepulchre of the Patriarch Judah I of the house of Hillel (died c. A.D. 217), a series of monumental tomb façades, intended to make the "sepulchres of the just" more imposing. The facade shown above is that of catacomb No. 20 at Beth Shea'rim, which was the burial cave of several prominent rabbinical families related to the Patriarch. The vault had one main entrance with double doors, and two side entrances, with a row of three arches built along the rock face. Inside the cave over two hundred stone coffins have been found, many decorated with reliefs of animals and plants (and in one case even a human face); such representations were apparently allowed by the rabbis. A place of prayer under the open sky is cut in the rock above the facade of the grave; it points to Jerusalem and has steps all round it.

WHEN ye therefore shall see the abomination of desolation, spoken of by Daniel the prophet, stand in the Holy place . . .

(Matt. 24 : 15)

The sins of the people will finally result in the end of the world, as prophesied by Daniel and others. The Book of Daniel (9 : 27; 12 : 11) refers to the "abomination of desolation" to be erected in the Sanctuary. By this was meant the pagan altar put up by Antiochus IV Epiphanes during the religious persecution which caused the Maccabean revolt. When Judaea became a Roman province, the term was transferred to other obnoxious manifestations of the pagan cult, and in particular to the standards of the legions which were decorated with images of the emperors and of Roman gods, as well as the to imperial statues in general — above all, of course, to the statue of himself which the emperor Caligula intended to have erected in the Temple. The prophecy of Jesus that the "abomination of desolation" would stand in the holy place was fulfilled within forty years, when the victorious Roman army stood on the ruins of the Temple and sacrificed to its gods. The picture above represents such a sacrifice. It is taken from one of the reliefs now on the triumphal arch erected in honour of the emperor Constantine I at Rome in 312. However, the reliefs were originally made for some monument in honour of Marcus Aurelius (163-181) and only the head of the emperor was changed. We see him here standing in the midst of the standard-bearers of the various legions and burning incense on an altar, while slaves bring an ox, a pig and a sheep for sacrifice (the so-called *suovetaurilia*). In the background are the eagles and flags (*vexilla*) of the various detachments of the victorious army.

Now learn a parable of the fig tree; When his branch is yet tender, and putteth forth leaves, ye know that summer is nigh.

(Matt. 24 : 32)

The fig is one of the most common kinds of fruit trees growing in the Land of Israel, and as such was included in the "seven species" characterizing the Promised Land (Vol. I, pp. 260/1). In prophetic literature it is also often described with a wealth of details showing an exact knowledge of the tree and its development. In the Gospels, too, the fig tree appears frequently (see also p. 110 and Luke 13 : 6). The fact that the fig is among the earliest trees to put forth its leaves (see illustration above) and thus serves as a harbinger of the warm season is used in this parable as a symbol of the approaching kingdom of heaven, foreshadowed by the tribulations mentioned in verses 29-31 of this chapter. The "messianic woes" which are to precede the final redemption were a standard assumption of the period preceding the destruction of the Second Temple. The people felt that it had been purged of the sin of disobedience of the Law by being punished in an earlier generation by the Babylonian Exile. If, nevertheless, it was subjugated by the Romans, this could only be as an indication that the Kingdom of Heaven would be preceded by a period of turbulence and suffering, and that the coming of the Saviour could not be long delayed.

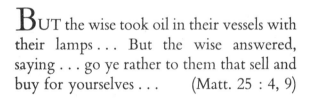

BUT the wise took oil in their vessels with their lamps... But the wise answered, saying... go ye rather to them that sell and buy for yourselves...   (Matt. 25 : 4, 9)

In the parable of the five wise and the five foolish virgins allusion is made to the manner of obtaining and distributing oil in antiquity. Oil was the principal cooking fat of the time, as well as the essential element in unguents, which were used instead of soap, and finally the main source of light. The oil was extracted by a complicated process requiring strong presses which only the large landowners or farmers could afford. The common people, especially the inhabitants of the cities, had therefore to apply to oil-sellers. The relief reproduced above on the right is the monument of one such merchant; it was found in Roman North Africa. The deceased is seen standing full face; he is ladling oil from an open vessel with his right hand, while in his left he is holding a funnel for filling a vase. After the oil had been brought home, it had to be poured from its container into the narrow opening of the pottery lamps common at the period (see p. 31). For this purpose special receptacles (lamp feeders) were used, such as the one shown on the left. It dates from the third century B.C. and is decorated with the relief of a Nike sacrificing a bull.

THERE came unto him a woman having an alabaster box of very precious ointment, and poured it on his head, as he sat at meat.   (Matt. 26 : 7)

Jesus was dining at a house in Bethany, a village on the Mount of Olives and at that time the temporary habitation of the disciples. His head was anointed during the feast by "a woman" who is by some identified with St. Mary the Magdalene. The unguents in general use in antiquity (because of the greater exposure of the body to sunlight and the non-existence of soap) were of various kinds. The most expensive ones — of the kind called "precious" here — were prepared from plant ingredients brought from distant lands, the spices of Southern Arabia, India and the Far Eastern Isles. Some of them were imported by way of Ceylon, the Red Sea and the Nabatene. Heavy duties levied on these expensive commodities rendered their price to the consumer many hundreds of times dearer than their original price. Because they were so very costly (cf. Mark 14 : 5), such unguents were carried in vessels with very narrow openings, from which they were decanted drop by drop. Of this kind were the vessels called *alabastron* (translated here "alabaster box"). They were elongated drop-shaped juglets, usually made of alabaster, a translucent whitish stone consisting of calcite (calcium carbonate). The illustration shows a pottery imitation of such a stone vessel, also called *alabastron*.

AND he took the cup, and gave thanks . . . (Matt. 26 : 27)

Returning to the city, Jesus and the disciples sat down to the Passover meal, consisting of unleavened bread and the flesh of a roasted lamb (probably in the dish mentioned in v. 23). At least four cups of wine had to be drunk at this meal. The drinking vessel used by Jesus during the Last Supper is described by the three Gospels (here, Mark 14 : 23, and Luke 22 : 17) as a wine cup *(poterion* in Greek). The "giving of thanks" over wine was one of the blessings prescribed by Jewish Law before drinking wine. Drinking cups in antiquity were either flat bowls on a high stand *(kylix)*, or deep rounded bowls; the latter were the more usual in the Orient. Such bowls, great quantities of which have been found in the Greco-Roman strata of the cities of the Holy Land, were made of pottery, metal or glass. The first kind were the most common. As we read, however, in Mark 14 : 15 and Luke 22 : 12 that the supper took place in the large upper chamber, "furnished and prepared", we can assume that the appointments on this occasion were of the best available. In the case of cups this would indicate glass ware. The art of blowing glass had been invented about the time of Jesus and was practised mainly in the coastal cities of Palestine and Phoenicia, partly also by Jewish makers. A fine glass cup of this period is illustrated above; its handles show it to have been used for drinking.

T HEN cometh JESUS with them unto a place called Gethsemane . . .　　　(Matt. 26 : 36)

After the Last Supper, Jesus and the disciples went out from the city of Jerusalem on to the Mount of Olives, and came to a place called Gethsemane. This name is derived from the Hebrew *gath shemanim*, meaning an oil-press. The position of the place so called is not indicated here or in the parallel verse in Mark 14 : 32; however, two other verses, in which Gethsemane is not expressly named but which clearly refer to the same event, speak of the "Mount of Olives" (Luke 22 : 39) and a garden by the "Brook Cedron" (John 18 : 1). All these indications, taken together, have led to the traditional identification of Gethsemane with an area still planted to this day with olive trees, situated in the Valley of Kidron at the foot of the Mount of Olives, opposite the Temple Mount (see view above). The olive groves which gave the Mount of Olives, or the Ascent of Olivet (2 Sam. 15 : 30; see also Vol. III, p. 294), its name, supplied the raw material for the presses situated at the foot of the mount. This area would usually be deserted, except in the days of the year immediately following the olive-gathering, and would thus, at the time of Passover, have been suitable for the contemplative gathering described here.

T HEN began he to curse and
to swear, saying, I know not
the man. And immediately the
cock crew.   (Matt. 26 : 74)

The domestic fowl was introduced into Egypt and
Greece in the middle of the second millennium
B.C. It is not mentioned in the Old Testament,
and a fighting cock first appears on a Judahite seal
only in the sixth cent. B.C. (Vol. III, p. 139). In
the Greco-Roman period poultry had become
quite common; poultry-raising in Jerusalem is
mentioned in the Talmudic sources. The cock was
esteemed as the announcer of the morning ("cock-
crow" is mentioned in Mark 13 : 35 as a precise
moment of time between midnight and morning);
for the same reason its early morning crowing was
thought to put to flight the demons of darkness
rampant in the night. The illustration below shows
a bronze figurine of a cock, found at Lyons and
dating to the Roman period.

W<small>HEN</small> he was set down on the judgment seat . . .
(Matt. 27 : 19)

Arrested at Gethsemane, Jesus was led first before the high priest Caiaphas, who — under the Romans — exercised supreme jurisdiction over Judaea. The high priest's council found Jesus guilty of blasphemy but, not being allowed to sentence anyone to death, transferred the prisoner to the Roman governor, Pontius Pilate, to stand trial on political, and not religious, grounds. A Roman provincial governor, even of the low rank of procurator, like Pontius Pilate, had the right to pronounce judgment in civil and criminal cases brought before him, including sentence of death. As he personified the "majesty of the Roman people", the exercise of his judicial functions was surrounded with ceremonial forms intended to evoke awe and respect. He had to pronounce judgment seated, and his seat was placed on a raised dais high above the crowd of litigants in front. Such a dais was called in Latin *tribunal,* a name applied to the court of justice as a whole; the Greek term used here is *bema.* As the magistrate had to be ready to pronounce judgment in any place besides his usual residence, his seat of judgment was of a special kind, called *sella curulis.* It was a portable chair with legs which could be folded together. The right to such a chair was equivalent to high office in the Roman commonwealth. In the relief above we see the emperor (who was the chief magistrate of the republic) distributing largesse from a *sella curulis* set up on a tribunal (from the Arch of Constantine at Rome, see p. 67).

WHEN Pilate saw that he could prevail nothing, but that rather a tumult was made, he took water, and washed his hands before the multitude . . .   (Matt. 27 : 24)

Since it was the general custom in antiquity to eat with one's hands, these had to be washed at the conclusion of a meal; washing one's hands thus became the sign of the conclusion of any kind of business. Among the Jews, washing the hands was also a preliminary purification before approaching the altar (Ps. 26 : 6) or engaging in any other ritual act indicating innocence (Deut. 21 : 6). This, however, could hardly apply to Pilate, who more likely wanted to show by washing his hands that his part in the judgment of Jesus was completed. The vessels used for washing the hands were brought by a servant; they consisted of a jug, among the richer classes usually of bronze, which contained the water, and a basin of the same material (see illustration above) over which the hands were held and into which the water was poured. The servant also held a towel for drying the hands after they had been washed. The examples chosen for illustration were among the booty taken from the Romans by the Jewish rebels under the leadership of Bar Kokhba (A.D. 132-135). Later, when the tide turned against the rebels, they took these vessels with them to their caves of refuge near the Dead Sea, where they were found in 1960.

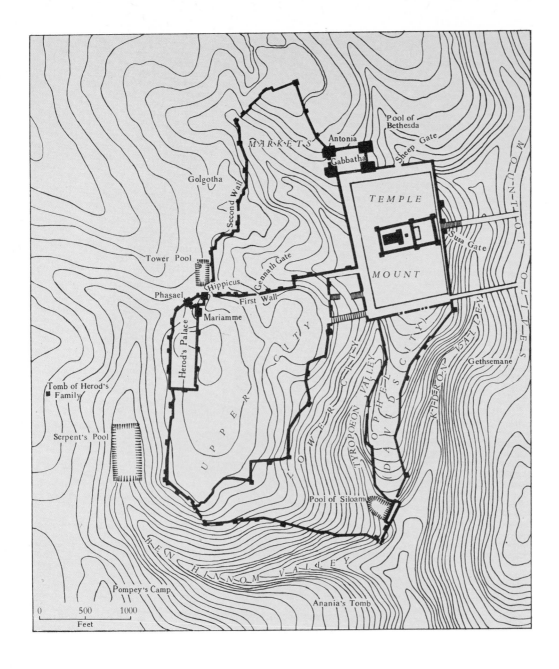

Condemned by Pilate to be crucified, Jesus was led into the hall of the governor's residence (*praetorium*) and thence to the place of execution at Golgotha. Such a place is not mentioned in Jerusalem by any source outside the Gospels. It is traditionally identified with an area now enclosed within the Church of the Holy Sepulchre. Executions in antiquity were public and the place selected was, as far as possible, outside the city gates, where passers-by could be impressed by the spectacle of justice being done. As there was no suitable flat surface to the west, south and east of the walls of Jerusalem, we may assume that Jesus was crucified somewhere outside the then existing north wall. In this connection we may disregard the Third Wall of Jerusalem, which was built by King Agrippa I (A.D. 41-44), i.e. about a decade after Jesus. The two earlier walls (see plan) are described by Josephus in his *Jewish War* (Book V, chapters 4-5). The First Wall connected Herod's Palace (roughly on the site of the present Citadel), in the North-West corner of the Upper City, with the Temple Mount, and encircled the Upper and Lower Cities to the south of it. The Second Wall began at the Garden Gate in the First Wall, close to the towers of Herod's Palace, and followed a semi-circular line protecting the commercial quarters of the city, till it reached the castle Antonia (see p. 190). It was outside this wall that Jesus was crucified; but as its course is still subject to dispute, no certain location of Golgotha can be made in the present state of our knowledge.

 And they crucified him, and parted his garments, casting lots . . .

(Matt. 27 : 35)

The possessions of those condemned to death were usually confiscated by the state. In the case of those who were almost destitute they were usually appropriated by the executioners and guards. To ensure a fair distribution, lots were cast for what could not be divided.

The ancients had various methods of deciding by chance. One way known to the Romans was by the toss of a coin; those wagering cried *caput* or *navis* ("head" or "ship", according to the two images appearing on the two sides of the common *as* coin). As we have to presume, however, that the casting of lots for Jesus' garment was between several persons, it is probable that dice, shaken in a beaker, were used (for a pair of dicing gamesters see p. 251). In the illustration on the right, a painting on a vase signed by the Attic vase-painter Exekias (c. 550-540 B.C.), another form of gambling is shown. The legendary heroes Achilles and Ajax are portrayed playing a game of draughts for a stake.

AND laid it in his own new tomb, which he had hewn out in the rock : and he rolled a great stone to the door of the sepulchre, and departed.

(Matt. 27 : 60)

After Jesus' body had been delivered by permission of Pilate to Joseph of Arimathea, it was wrapped in clean linen and taken to a new tomb, hewn in the rock and intended for Joseph himself and his family. As a councillor (member of the Sanhedrin), Joseph seems to have moved from his native Arimathea to Jerusalem, and to have also prepared himself a tomb in his new home.

The desire to protect the graves of one's family from robbery, a form of crime very common in antiquity in view of the valuable objects left with the deceased (see next page), led to the creation of more or less elaborate devices to guard the entrance of the tomb-caves which were the common form of burial among the Jews of Jerusalem in the time of Jesus. One such device, of which several examples are still extant, was the rolling stone. This was a heavy cylindrical block, placed in a rock-cut grove across the entrance of a tomb. It was usually poised on a slightly sloping track, in such a way that it remained closed by force of gravity and had to be rolled upwards and secured with a wedge, before the grave could be entered. One such stone has been found in the Tombs of the Kings of Adiabene in Jerusalem; another (see picture) in the Tomb of Herod's Family, a monument mentioned by Josephus as situated opposite the Upper City (see plan, p. 76).

AND when they were assembled with the elders, and had taken counsel, they gave large money unto the soldiers, Saying, Say ye, His disciples came by night, and stole him away while we slept.

(Matt. 28 : 12-13)

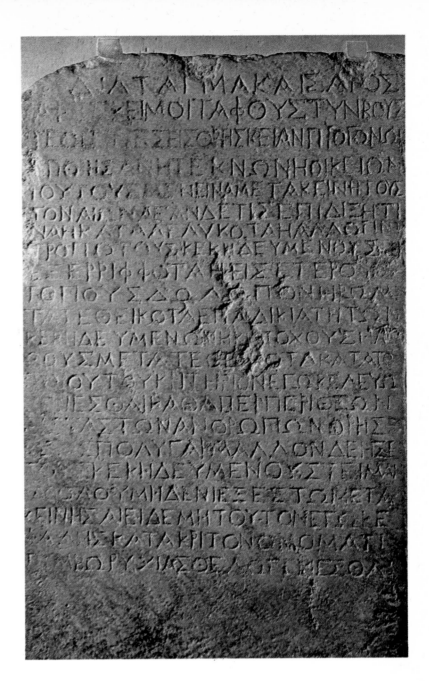

The suggestion made in this verse that a body might be stolen from a grave has been singularly confirmed by the text of an inscription from Palestine (according to one theory, from Nazareth). This is a decree in Greek (see illustration) issued by Augustus Caesar. The Greek is apparently the translation of a Latin original. In this decree the emperor denounces those who damage tombs, exhume the dead, transport the dead from one tomb to another, or remove inscriptions or other parts of the sepulchre. Such evildoers have committed an offence against the gods. In particular, those changing the place of entombment are to be punished with death. Although this decree was in all probability issued long before the death of Jesus, it shows the frequency with which bodies were removed from their tombs (usually to enable other people to use the ready-made grave) and the plausibility of the explanation given for the disappearance of Jesus' body from its sepulchre.

ST. MARK

THE beginning of the gospel of JESUS CHRIST, the Son of God, as it is written in the prophets, Behold, I send my messenger before thy face, which shall prepare thy way before thee.

(Mark 1 : 1-2)

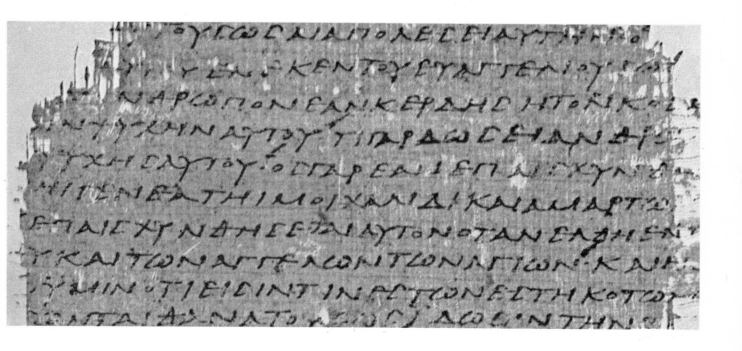

St. Mark, to whom the second Gospel is traditionally attributed, is usually identified with the John mentioned in Acts 12 : 12 who bore the Roman surname Marcus (Acts 15 : 37). According to Acts his mother, presumably well-to-do, owned a house in Jerusalem which served as a Christian meeting place. A cousin of Barnabas (Col. 4 : 10), St. Mark accompanied St. Barnabas and St. Paul on Paul's first missionary journey (Acts 13 : 5), but left them in the course of it (Acts 13 : 13), under circumstances which later led to a temporary breach between St. Paul and St. Barnabas (Acts 15 : 37-39). Ultimately, however, St. Paul evidently reached an understanding with St. Mark and they became trusted associates (Philem.24). According to a credible tradition, St. Mark, who was, of course, not one of the twelve apostles and not an eyewitness of the events he records, based his Gospel upon the reminiscences of St. Peter. Since he probably wrote it for the Church in Rome, the Gospel is much less Jewish in tone than that of St. Matthew; it contains relatively few quotations from the Old Testament and the author is careful to explain for the benefit of his readers the geography and customs of the Holy Land, with which he supposes them to be unfamiliar. St. Mark's chief concern is with the events in the life of Jesus rather than with his teaching. The shortest of the Gospels, St. Mark is believed by very many present-day scholars to be the oldest. If this is true, it was presumably used by both St. Matthew and St. Luke as a principal source for their narrative sections. The order of events is chronological; without any preliminary material, St. Mark begins with the story of the precursor St. John the Baptist, and introduces the ministry of Jesus in 1 : 14. At least one third of the book is taken up by the story of the passion.

The illustration above shows the Chester Beatty papyrus fragment of the Gospel of St. Mark, the earliest remaining Ms. of the book. The fragment contains the verses 8 : 34 — 9 : 1; it dates to the third century A.D.

AND preached, saying, There cometh one mightier than I after me, the latchet of whose shoes I am not worthy to stoop down and unloose.

(Mark 1 : 7)

The common footwear of the Hellenistic Orient was the sandal, i.e. a leather sole attached to the foot by leather latchets (see p. 42). High shoes were worn only by persons engaged in work which was performed in rough ground, such as shepherds, hunters or soldiers. The sandal, which was adopted by the Romans from the Greeks and which was for a long time regarded as highly informal wear, was tied to the foot in a variety of ways; sometimes the latchets passed between the toes, and sometimes the foot was protected by a net bound across the ankles. Reproduced above is the sandal of a statue of a male deity, dating to the second century A.D., which was found at Caesarea.

A guest's sandals were loosened by a servant as soon as the guest entered the house of his host; it is to such a lowly service that the above verse refers. In the banquet scene (p. 120) we see, on the left, a servant removing the shoe of one of the guests.

84

FOR the earth bringeth forth fruit of herself; first the blade, then the ear; after that the full corn in the ear. But when the fruit is brought forth, immediately he putteth in the sickle, because the harvest is come.   (Mark 4 : 28-29)

The parables of Jesus were suited to the work and life of his hearers, who were predominantly members of the lower classes. Many of them must have been farmers, since agriculture was at that time, and for centuries afterwards, the main occupation of the Jews of Galilee. Hence the various stages in the development of the wheat crop were quite familiar to Jesus' audience: the blade which protrudes from the earth after the winter rains; then the ear which sprouts as soon as the blade has reached a certain height; and finally the full ear with its grains, when the time is ripe and the weather favourable. Two of these stages are illustrated above from fields of wheat growing in the Land of Israel as it grew in Jesus' time. When the grain is ripe, it is harvested. The illustration below of the ancient method of harvesting with a sickle is taken from reliefs of the third century A.D. found at Ghirza in Libya.

ND when they had sent away the multitude, they took him even as he was in the ship:
and there were also with him other little ships.
(Mark 4 : 36)

Sailing and fishing even in the waters of an inland lake such as the Sea of Galilee involved the use of various
kinds of vessel, some large and able to stand the storms on the lake (see p. 35), others small and more suitable
for going to and from the big ships. In general the ancients developed a multitude of ship types, adapted to the
various purposes of navigation. On a mosaic found at Althiburus in Africa no less than twelve different kinds
of ships and boats were represented, each designated by its proper name. They include heavy cargo boats,
light transport ships, and fishing and river craft. The illustration above is taken from a Pompeian painting
showing on the left a large ship with rowers, approached on the right by a small sailing boat.

ND, behold, there cometh one of the rulers of the synagogue, Jairus by name . . .

(Mark 5 : 22)

The Jewish communities in the Land of Israel and in the Diaspora were organized around their synagogues, which served not only as places of worship, but as communal centres as well (see pp. 41 and 162). At the head of each community was a group of officials with various titles, headed by a chief most commonly entitled *archisynagogos*. As indicated here, there could be several officials with such a title in one place; on the analogy of the similar term *archihiereus* or high priest (in the plural), we can assume that such "rulers of the synagogue" served for a stated period and kept their title even after their term of office. In the Diaspora each of the synagogues of a big city had its own chiefs, but sometimes there was one archisynagogos for a whole province. One such personage was brought to be buried at Beth She'arim (see p. 66), the central Jewish necropolis of the third and fourth centuries A.D. The tablet shown below commemorates one "Jacob from Caesarea, archisynagogos of Pamphylia. Peace". As we learn from the Acts of the Apostles (2 : 10), Pamphylia, a province of Asia Minor, contained many Jewish communities, united apparently in one provincial organization presided over by an archisynagogos.

AND immediately the king sent an executioner . . .
(Mark 6 : 27)

In describing the official who was ordered to behead St. John the Baptist, the Gospel uses the Latin word *speculator*. This is a Roman military term, originally denoting the soldiers who were entrusted with reconnoitring and in general with the collecting of intelligence. As such they were in daily contact with the commander-in-chief or provincial governor, and gradually assumed the functions of his bodyguards and confidential servants. They were entrusted with delicate tasks, such as the conveying of imperial orders to commit suicide. The petty princelings of Rome's vassal states, like Herod Antipas, naturally aped the institutions of the imperial court and had their own *speculatores*. The illustration above is a detail from the reliefs on the column erected at Rome in honour of the emperor Marcus Aurelius (163-181); it shows an imperial *speculator* standing on guard at the entrance to the emperor's tent.

THE woman was a Greek,
a Syrophenician by nation...
(Mark 7 : 26)

The woman who fell at Jesus' feet is described in the Gospel as a Greek, but Syro-Phoenician by race. Obviously the author intended to indicate that she was thoroughly Hellenized, although not of Greek origin; in fact her familiarity with such Greek customs as having dogs under the tables at banquets (a custom repugnant to the true Orientals who despised dogs — see p. 54) shows the extent of her Hellenization. It was one of the cardinal principles of the Hellenistic period that the adoption of Greek culture (including, of course, Greek religion) made a person a Hellene, whatever his racial origin; and it was owing to this liberal attitude that Hellenism could spread in the Orient. Of course this Hellenization was only possible in polytheistic nations whose gods could be amalgamated with the Greek deities; it failed in the main with the monotheistic Jews. The woman here is described as being of Syro-Phoenician origin. From the time of Herodotus, the Greeks, following Persian usage, extended the term "Syria" (originally "Assyria", Persian *Athura*) from Assyria proper to the whole of the Mediterranean coastland. In order to distinguish between the various nations inhabiting this area they added a qualifying epithet to the general name "Syrian". Thus Herodotus calls the Philistines "Palestinian Syrians". In a similar way this woman is called a Phoenician Syrian; and indeed the Phoenicians were among the most Hellenized of the oriental nations. The illustration shows one of the women mourners from the Sarcophagus of the Weeping Women, found in the Royal Tombs of Sidon in Phoenicia and dating to the fourth century B.C. The style and workmanship of the sarcophagus is Greek, but in type and conception the mourning woman is Phoenician.

ND there was a cloud that overshadowed them: and a voice came out of the cloud, saying, This is my beloved Son; hear him.

(Mark 9 : 7)

The association of the deity with clouds can, in the Orient, be traced back to ancient Mesopotamia, where the gods were thought to dwell in the mountains and the moisture-laden clouds brought their blessed rain to man. In Assyrian reliefs the hand of a god appears from a cloud-shaped rosette. Traces of this belief can still be found in various passages of the Bible: God appears in a cloud (Ex. 24 : 15 etc.), the cloud is His chariot (Ps. 104 : 3) and He speaks in a cloudy pillar (Ps. 99 : 7). In Jewish and Early Christian art a hand appearing out of a cloud is the common symbol of God. Reproduced above is a detail from the sacrifice of Isaac as represented on the mosaic pavement of a synagogue found at Beth Alpha in Israel (early sixth cent. A.D.). Abraham, who is about to lift the knife to slay Isaac, turns his head as he hears a voice calling out: "Lay not (thy hand)". The words are accompanied by the drawing of a cloud, with the sun's rays shining from behind it and a hand stretched forth out of it.

I T is better for him that a millstone were hanged about his neck, and he were cast into the sea.　　(Mark 9 : 42)

In the Greek original the words here translated "millstone" are *mylos onikos,* a "donkey millstone". The use of blindfolded animals to provide the rotatory motion necessary to turn millstones was common in ancient times, after the invention of turning mills. It is still common in Arab countries, as can be seen from the picture of an oil-press on the right; the upright millstone was turned on the lower stone by means of a horizontal rod to which an animal was harnessed; in turning it crushed the olives. A true "donkey mill" is represented in the Roman relief on the left. It consists of an upper and lower millstone, the one set upon the other. A rod attached to the upper stone is connected with an elaborate yoke carried by the ass.

BLIND Bartimaeus, the son of Timaeus, sat by the highway side begging.   (Mark 10 : 46)

It is characteristic of the close-knit social framework of Israel in biblical times that, although the poor are frequently mentioned in the Scriptures, and special provisions are made for their relief and their rights are protected, there is no reference to beggars in the streets. The poor or disabled were taken care of by their family or tribe. It is only in the social disintegration of the Hellenistic period that begging in public places is referred to, and even then it was not regarded as anything but shameful ("To beg I am ashamed", Luke 16 : 3). Almsgiving is first mentioned in Jewish sources in Ecclesiasticus (4 : 2). Representations of beggars are not common in Greek art; it is only with the realistic and social tendencies of Hellenistic times that we find such images as the humpbacked beggar of Alexandria (c. 100 B.C.) in the illustration above.

ᴀɴᴅ ᴊᴇsᴜs sat over against the treasury, and beheld how the people cast money into the treasury . . . And there came a certain poor widow, and she threw in two mites, which make a farthing.   (Mark 12 : 41-42)

Apart from the Temple dues (see p. 57), which had to be paid regularly as a tax, pilgrims and visitors to the Temple were encouraged to make donations for various purposes, a custom dating back to the times of the First Temple (Vol. II, p. 279). According to the Mishna (*Shekalim* 6 : 1, 5), there were in the Temple thirteen chests each shaped like a *shofar* (ram's horn), marked respectively for shekel dues, bird offerings, wood, frankincense, gold for the Mercy-seat, and six for "free will offerings". The widow's donation probably belonged to the last class. Her offering consisted of two *lepta* ("mites") which together made up a *quadrans* (the Latin word is used in the Greek text, and is translated "farthing") or the fourth part of an *as,* the twelfth part of a silver *denarius.* The lepta thus represents the smallest coin in circulation, the Hebrew *perutah,* a small bronze coin of about 2 gr. The illustrations on the left are of two of such coins which were current in the time of Jesus, one struck by the procurator Pontius Pilatus in A.D. 29, and the other by his predecessor Gratus in A.D. 22. They do not display the emperor's head, in deference to Jewish objections (see also p. 67), but only the title of the emperor ("Of Caesar") and the name of his mother "Julia" (Livia), together with such symbols as the *simpulum* (ladle for purifying water — on the right) or the palm branch (on the left). The inscribed box (on the extreme right) is a collecting chest used by the worshippers of the Syrian goddess Atargatis. It shows that the custom of collecting for the temples was a general one in antiquity.

ᴀɴᴅ as he went out of the temple one of his disciples saith unto him, Master, see what manner of stones and what buildings are here.

(Mark 13 : 1)

On leaving the Temple, Jesus and the disciples passed through the outer wall of the Temple esplanade, which had been built by Herod from huge blocks of stone (see illustration). Some of these can still be seen, for example those used in the Western (or Wailing) Wall or in the Southern and Eastern walls of the Temple Mount. The ashlar blocks measure on the average 9-15 ft. in length and are 3-4 ft. high; the largest one is 36 feet in length and the heaviest (21 × 6 ft.), which is set in the south-eastern pinnacle wall (see p. 26), weighs nearly a hundred tons. The stones are dressed in the manner typical of Herodian times, with a rough boss in the centre and a margin around it; as a special refinement the margin is repeated around the bosses. No wonder the massive wall and the splendid buildings (see p. 139) evoked general admiration among Jews and Gentiles alike.

ᴀɴᴅ as he sat upon the Mount of Olives over against the temple ...   (Mark 13 : 3)

The Mount of Olives (see also p. 72 and Vol. III, p. 294) is the most conspicuous landmark in the vicinity of Jerusalem; from inside the city it seems to overlook the Temple Mount, as the low-lying Kidron Valley separating the two is invisible (see view above). As it was the custom of pilgrims from Galilee to approach Jerusalem from beyond the Jordan and by way of Jericho (so as to avoid passing through the Samaritan territory separating Galilee from Judaea), their last station before reaching the city was the Mount of Olives. There too Jesus stayed during the days preceding the crucifixion in the village of Bethany (modern el–Eizariyeh), the home of Lazarus, Mary and Martha (see p. 146), going into the city every day and returning in the evening (Luke 21 : 37; John 8 : 1-2). Jesus' lamentation over Jerusalem (Matt. 23 : 37) was uttered on this Mount, and the Ascension (see p. 133) also took place there.

G O ye into the city, and there shall meet you a man bearing a pitcher of water . . .
(Mark 14 : 13)

In the absence of cheap metal receptacles, most of the liquids used in ancient house-keeping (water, wine and oil) were carried on the shoulder in big pottery vessels. In this case the jar was used to bring water to the chosen house for the Last Supper. As it was a well appointed house (see p. 71) and thus probably provided with a cistern, we can only assume that the water carried to it was of superior quality, possibly from the aqueduct which Pontius Pilate had made to bring water to the Temple Mount. This aqueduct (see plan, p. 76) encircled the Upper City where, according to tradition, the Last Supper took place. Piped water was common in ancient Rome, but not usual in provincial cities like Jerusalem. The illustration above, taken from a Byzantine mosaic of the sixth century found at Beth-Shean, shows a man, symbolizing the month of September, who is carrying a cock in his left hand, while with his right he steadies a ribbed water pitcher, typical of the period from Herod to the Byzantines, on his shoulder.

A<small>ND</small> he answered and said unto them, It is one of the twelve, that dippeth with me in the dish. (Mark 14 : 20)

In accordance with our assumption that the Last Supper took place in a well appointed house (see p. 71), the "dish" (*tryblion* in Greek) could well have been one of fine imported ware, large enough for all the meat and its gravy to be served up in it. All the diners then partook of the meal by dipping their hands into the common dish. The dish illustrated above was found in Samaria, in the precincts of the temple erected by Herod in honour of the emperor Augustus (30-20 B.C.), close enough to the times of Jesus. It is covered with red glaze, and has designs stamped on its surface. (The name *terra sigillata* given to such ware is derived either from *sigillum,* "stamp", or from their wax-red colour.) Such dishes were imported from pottery centres in the Aegean, Samos or Pergamon. The dish measures nearly a foot across, and should thus have sufficed for several persons dining together.

AND when the sabbath was past, Mary Magdalene, and Mary the mother of James, and Salome, had bought sweet spices, that they might come and anoint him.   (Mark 16 : 1)

Ointments and spices were used in antiquity not only to freshen the living but also to embalm the dead. Owing to their great price (see p. 70) they had to be kept in small containers with very narrow orifices, and had to be poured carefully from one container into another. By their very nature, such materials were handled by women, who could perform both the cosmetic and funerary functions connected with anointing. In the illustration we see a young woman, dressed in long violet robes and modestly veiled, who is decanting perfumes from a round *aryballos* into a narrow *alabastron*. The fresco was found near the Villa Farnesina in Rome, in the ruins of a patrician home situated on the right bank of the Tiber; the paintings were probably executed by a Greek artist named Seleucus. They date to the late Augustan period, i.e. to the time of Jesus.

ST. LUKE

F ORASMUCH as many have taken in hand to set forth in order a declaration of those things which are most surely believed among us . . . And he asked for a writing table, and wrote, saying, His name is John . . .

(Luke 1 : 1, 63)

St. Luke was a Gentile by birth; his name is a Greek version or diminutive of the Roman appellation Lucius. He was a physician by profession and accompanied St. Paul when he first crossed from Asia into Europe (as is evident from the "we" which first appears in the narrative of Acts 16 : 10-17), as also on a later journey (Acts 20 : 5-21 : 17). He was with the apostle during his long imprisonment at Caesarea (Acts 24 : 23-26 : 32) and later in Rome (Acts 27-28). The Gospel is addressed to one Theophilus, probably a Gentile interested in Christianity and possibly a high Roman official. Since the Gospel was written by a Gentile for Gentile readers, less stress is laid on Jesus' relationship to the Law and on other specifically Jewish elements in the background. St. Luke seems to have used the Gospel of St. Mark for the narrative outline of his book, enlarging it with stories derived from other sources, and with an account of Jesus' teaching, based in part, perhaps, upon the same source used by St. Matthew, and in part upon sources peculiar to himself. Since St. Luke was also the author of Acts (compare Luke 1 : 1-4 with Acts 1 : 1-2), this Gospel, in contrast with the other three, must be viewed as only the first volume in a two-volume history of the early Christian movement. Beginning in the temple at Jerusalem, the spiritual center of the Jewish world (Luke 1 : 9), St. Luke's story reaches its climax with the arrival of the great missionary to the Gentiles in Rome, the capital of the Gentile world (Acts 28 : 14). St. Luke's profound sensitivity of spirit, his obvious sympathy with women, with the poor and social outcasts, combined with his literary talents, give a uniquely attractive flavor to his Gospel, which for many Christians is "the most beautiful book ever written."

The illustration on top is of the earliest extant papyrus with part of the Gospel of Luke 3 : 8-20; it was purchased by A. Chester Beatty from a dealer in Egypt in 1930, and dates to the beginning of the third century A.D. The name written by Zacharias, and translated John, or *Ioannes* in the Greek, is derived from the Hebrew Yohanan, a shortened form of the original Yehohanan ("The Lord has been gracious"). The illustration above shows it written out in full in square Hebrew letters on an ossuary from the time of the Second Temple. The name as written by Zacharias must have looked just like this, or very similar.

EM·QVAR·EDACTA·INPO
AVGVSTI·POPVLIQVEROMANI·SENAT
SVPPLICATIONESBINASOBRESPROSP
IPSI·ORNAMENTA·TRIVMPI
PRO·CONSVLASIAM·PROVINCIAM·CT
DIVI·AVGVSTITERVMSYRIAM·ET·PI

AND it came to pass in those days, that there went out a decree from Caesar Augustus, that all the world should be taxed. (And this taxing was first made, when Cyrenius was governor of Syria).

(Luke 2 : 1-2)

The evangelist St. Luke twice attempts (here and in 3 : 1, see p. 106) to indicate an exact chronological framework for his story by naming the various persons in authority at the time of the events narrated. Here he refers to a decree issued by Caesar Augustus, ordering that a census be taken of the whole Roman world. The emperor Augustus was born Gaius Octavius, in 63 B.C. His mother was the sister of the dictator Julius Caesar, who adopted his nephew by testament; as Caesar's adopted son he was called Gaius Iulius Octavianus. In the turbulent times after Caesar's assassination he succeeded in making himself sole ruler of the Roman empire (30 B.C.—A.D. 14) and as such received the appellation Augustus ("The Venerable"). By restoring peace to the Roman empire he was instrumental in preparing the conditions favouring the rapid expansion of Christianity. The reproduction on the right is a statue of Augustus in full military panoply; it was found at the Prima Porta in Rome. "Cyrenius", the governor of Syria, is identical with the Roman senator P. Sulpicius Quirinius, who was governor of Syria from 11 to 8 B.C.; according to the Gospel he took a census in the time of his rule. The inscription shown on the left refers to some Roman who governed Syria twice, and has been attributed on good authority to Quirinius, although this attribution is by no means undisputed. If this identification is accepted, the census referred to by St. Luke would have taken place in the time of his second governorship.

AND there were in the same country shepherds abiding in the field, keeping watch over their flock by night. (Luke 2 : 8)

Bethlehem stands on the edge of the wilderness of Judaea, where an area of scanty vegetation separates the desert from the sown. The land around it was specially suitable for sheep-rearing; David, for instance, was a shepherd in this region; and there were many others like him in the centuries following. As the sheep were far away from settlements and passed the nights in the open, huddled together for warmth, they were in danger from the many beasts of prey roaming the desert in the dark. The shepherds had therefore to keep good watch in the small hours. That was the time when they might also observe remarkable phenomena, such as those which, according to the Gospel tradition, attended the birth of Jesus. The illustration shows a group of shepherds with their flock near a well in the Judaean desert.

NOW in the fifteenth year of the reign of Tiberius Caesar, Pontius Pilate being governor of Judaea, and Herod being tetrarch of Galilee, and his brother Philip tetrarch of Ituraea and of the region of Trachonitis, and Lysanias the tetrarch of Abilene. (Luke 3 : 1)

After indicating the date of Jesus' birth with great chronological precision, St. Luke employs other points of reference to fix the year in which John the Baptist began his activity. He starts with the regnal year of the Roman emperor, Tiberius Caesar, the adopted son and successor of Augustus (see the picture on the left above). Tiberius officially calculated his reign from the time he was appointed co-regent by Augustus in A.D. 4, but the unofficial dating of his reign from Augustus' death in A.D. 14 is probably used here. This would place the beginning of the events related in this Gospel in A.D. 29. St. Luke then proceeds to name the rulers of the three areas into which the kingdom of Herod had been divided: Pontius Pilate, the procurator of Judaea (A.D. 26-36); Herod Antipas, Herod's son, who ruled Galilee from 4 B.C. till his deposition in A.D. 39; his brother, Philip, who ruled the Herodian lands in the Gaulan, Bashan and Hauran from 4 B.C. to his death in A.D. 34. An inscription in Nabataean, set up in the temple at Seeia in the Hauran (see picture on the left of p. 107), commemorates this popular ruler. Lysanias, the fourth ruler mentioned, was in charge of the principality of Abilene, north of the Hermon. He is probably mentioned here because, at a later time, his territory formed part of the domain of the Herodians Agrippa I, Agrippa II, and his brother Herod. The inscription on the right, which was found near Damascus, is a votive offering for the salvation of the emperors dedicated by a freedman of Lysanias the tetrarch, in connection with the erection of a sanctuary.

AND the soldiers demanded of him, saying, And what shall we do?
And he said unto them ... be content with your wages. (Luke 3 : 14)

From the time of Marius (second century B.C.) the Roman army was no longer recruited from citizens mobilized for the duration of a campaign, but was composed of regular soldiers. Usually they came from the poorest classes of the population, and served for their pay and what they could lay their hands on in the course of a campaign. They also looked to their leaders to furnish them with a livelihood at the conclusion of their service. This dependence of the army on its leaders gave the generals of the Republic the power to subvert the legitimate government and to fight for dominion amongst themselves. With the advent of the empire, the soldiers depended on the emperor only; but as they soon became conscious of their power to make and unmake emperors in time of unsettled succession, they were allotted an ever-increasing portion of the state revenues. In the time of Tiberius this process was only just beginning; but even then the soldiers stationed in the provinces were easily tempted to use their power to oppress and plunder the provincials, to accept bribes, and to enrich themselves in other unlawful ways. St. John the Baptist asks them to renounce all such sources of ill-gotten wealth, and to be satisfied with the modest wage of 10 *as* (ten twelfths of the denar, less than the wage of a labourer, see Matt. 20 : 2). The picture below is a reproduction of a relief from the later period of the Roman republic. It shows soldiers being paid off at the end of a campaign and resuming their civilian garb and their family life.

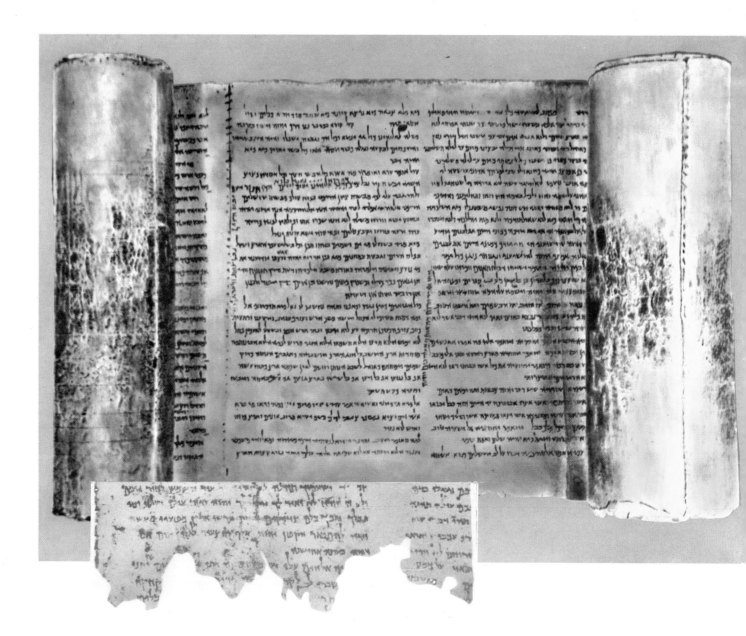

AND there was delivered unto him the book of the prophet Esaias. And when he had opened the book, he found the place where it was written, "The Spirit of the LORD is upon me, because he hath anointed me to preach the gospel to the poor; he hath sent me to heal the brokenhearted, to preach deliverance to the captives, and recovering of sight to the blind, to set at liberty them that are bruised."

(Luke 4 : 17-18)

The above verse is one of the earliest proof-texts for the custom of *haphtara* ("conclusion" after the reading of the Law), i.e. the reading of parts of the prophetic books of the Bible on Sabbaths and holidays (other references to this custom occur in the Mishna — Tractates *Rosh ha-Shana* 4 : 6 and *Megilla* 4 : 1-5). To this day the *haphtara* is read by a member of the congregation, whereas the Law is customarily intoned by a precentor. Jesus, who was a member of the Nazareth congregation (see p. 23), entered the synagogue and was handed the scroll of Isaiah by the "minister" (the Greek *hyperetes* "servitor", i.e. beadle) to read the verses 61 : 1-2. Because of Isaiah's messianic visions, the book of this prophet was the favourite reading matter of the various sects in Judaea; they cherished the prophetic ideals and interpreted them each in their own fashion. In the recently discovered library of the Qumran sect (the Dead Sea Scrolls), manuscripts of Isaiah are more numerous than any other books of the Bible. The finds include the earliest known complete scroll of this book (see illustration above). The picture below reproduces from this scroll the verses which were read by Jesus and quoted by St. Luke. The scroll used in Nazareth must have looked similar to the one shown here.

AND rose up, and thrust him out of the city, and led him unto the brow of the hill whereon their city was built, that they might cast him down headlong.

(Luke 4 : 29)

Nazareth is situated near the escarpment by which the mountains of Lower Galilee descend into the Valley of Esdraelon. One high hill in the vicinity of the town has been designated by tradition as the place where the attempt was made on Jesus' life. It is a prominent elevation due south of Nazareth, rising to a height of 1200 ft. above the Mediterranean, and 750 ft. above the plain. Its southern face (see view above, on the left) is a steep cliff from which a person could well be cast headlong. The hill is called in Arabic Jebel Qafzeh ("The Mountain of the Leap"), in commemoration of the tradition mentioned above. It contains caves with remains of prehistoric man dating to the Palaeolithic Age.

FOR every tree is known by his own fruit. For of thorns men do not gather figs, nor of a bramble bush gather they grapes. (Luke 6 : 44)

In order to illustrate the rule that "a good man bringeth forth that which is good; and an evil man . . . that which is evil", men are here compared to good and bad trees, each of which brings forth fruit according to its kind. For the purpose of this analogy, Jesus chose two pairs of sharply contrasted examples from the plant world. The first plant in the first pair is the thorn (*akanthos* in Greek), a term which includes any kind of spiky species. The best known of these is the *Acanthus spinosus,* the leaves of which, with their pointed folioles, served as a model for the Corinthian order of Greek capitals. Thorns are plentiful in the Land of Israel, both on waste and cultivated land (Vol. III, p. 216 and p. 47), and are mentioned many times in both the Old and the New Testament. The second plant, in contrast to the useless thorn, is the fig (*Ficus carica, L.*), which was highly prized for its sweet and tasty fruit (See Vol. III, p. 121 and p. 68). The first plant in the second pair is the bramble bush (*Rubis ulmifolius, L.*) which is also fairly common, especially in the coastal plain. Some of the fruits of the bramble family are edible, and in general it is less of a useless plant than the thorns; brambles with their sharp spikes can also be used as hedges. No bramble fruit can, however, compare with the grape, the fruit of the vine, another of the "seven kinds" of trees with which the Promised Land has been blessed. The vine produces good fruit and provides the raw material for wine, "that makes glad the heart of man" (Ps. 104 : 15; also Judg. 9 : 10-14).

FOR he loveth our nation, and he hath built us a synagogue.
(Luke 7 : 5)

Capernaum, like most of the Jewish villages in Galilee (see p. 41), boasted a synagogue. This one however, was, distinguished from the others by being the gift of a non-Jew, the centurion commanding the local garrison. As the Galilean synagogues of still later times were built according to the prevailing style of Greco-Roman architecture, they could quite well have been erected with the active participation of Gentiles. In fact, when these synagogues were first studied and their ornamentation, including the pictorial representation of animate beings, was recovered, some scholars, acting on the mistaken belief in the hostility of Talmudic Judaism to such decoration, assumed that all Galilean synagogues were the gift of the Roman emperors and had been built according to their taste. We know now that this is not the case and that most of these edifices were erected by Jewish donors. Of the synagogue visited by Jesus at Capernaum nothing is visible; but another synagogue, which is one of the finest and best preserved of the Galilean synagogues of the early type, was erected on its presumed site in the second century A.D. (see photograph).

AND it came to pass the day after, that he went into a city called Nain . . .   (Luke 7 : 11)

Nain, which is here called a "city", was apparently a large village at the eastern end of the Valley of Esdraelon, on the slopes of the "hill of Moreh" (Vol. II, p. 87); its successor is the present-day village of the same name 5 miles SSE. of Nazareth (see photograph). After being for many centuries merely one of the larger villages of the district of Sepphoris, one of the chief cities of Lower Galilee, Nain was in the fourth century A.D. detached from it and became the headquarters of a special district, which it remained till the Arab conquest in the seventh century A.D. The village was situated on a hill slope and had a gate, and presumably also a wall (Luke 7 : 12). Below it there is a spring, which irrigates plantations of olives and figs. The gate gave on to a road branching off from the *via maris,* the great highway from Damascus to Egypt. The crags by the wayside served for rock-cut graves.

MY head with oil thou didst not anoint . . .   (Luke 7 : 46)

Living mostly in the open air and exposed to the drying effects of the strong sunshine of the Eastern Mediterranean lands, the Jews in the time of Jesus had to anoint themselves with oil to protect their skin. Moreover, as soap was unknown in antiquity, oil to some extent took its place as an emollient of the dirt adhering to the body (see also p. 70). The hair in particular, which was worn rather long, required regular anointing with oil or perfumes containing fats. To anoint the hair of a guest was a mark of honour; to refuse to do so was an act of discourtesy towards those invited. The picture above, from an Etruscan vase of the fourth century B.C., shows Eros anointing the head of Ariadne, the consort of the god Bacchus-Dionysus. The winged god is holding a striated alabastron in his left hand, and is applying the oil to the hair with a long stick, presumably of metal, with a rounded end. Similar sticks have often been found with glass vessels in Palestinian tombs of the time of Jesus and later, and they presumably served the same purpose as the one seen here.

AND JESUS said unto him, No man, having put his hand to the plough, and looking back, is fit for the kingdom of God.

(Luke 9 : 62)

The predominantly agricultural character of the Judaean economy in the time of Jesus is illustrated by this parable, in which persistence in a task is illustrated by the example of a farmer who, having once started to plough, refuses to look back as long as his task remains uncompleted and the furrow has not been made to the very end. The plough used at that time was still, in the main, that of the Bronze and Iron Ages: a pole with the yoke attached at one end, and a beam, sheathed in iron (the cutting edge), at the other. The ploughman guided the share by a handle attached to the pole. Certain improvements were made in the Roman period so as to fit the share for deeper ploughing; but in the light soil of the Land of Israel the old type of plough was still efficient enough. The illustration below is from a second century A.D. mosaic found at Cherchel in Algeria (Roman Africa); it shows a ploughman putting all his strength into drawing a furrow.

AND went to him, and bound up his wounds . . .
(Luke 10 : 34)

Ancient medical practice was developed scientifically by the Greeks. It was based, first of all, on the necessities of treating the wounded in war. As such, it had reached a high surgical standard already in the Homeric period. The extant representations of the binding up of wounds are usually connected with fighting; the methods are similar to those used today. Reproduced here is a vase-painting of the early fifth century B.C. by the Athenian vase-painter Sosias. It shows Achilles binding up an arrow wound in the arm of his friend Patroclus. The concentration of Achilles on his task and the pain of Patroclus, who averts his head and braces his leg against the wall, are very vividly rendered. The bandage is applied cross-wise as it would have been today. The fact that the good Samaritan bound up the wounds of the robbed man himself shows that the principles of first aid were well understood in that time even among laymen.

ARE not five sparrows sold for two farthings?
(Luke 12 : 6)

The version of the same saying in Matt. 10 : 29 is: "Are not two sparrows sold for a farthing?" (*assarion*, from Latin *assarius nummus* or *as*, the twelfth part of a silver denarius); here five sparrows are sold for two *as*, probably because a reduction was made for the larger quantity. Sparrows were a very common article of food, and were sold in the market either in pairs (as in Matthew), which was the smallest quantity needed for a meal, or in fives. The details given in the Gospels are confirmed by the contents of the Price Edict of the Emperor Diocletian, in which he fixed the maximum prices of all kinds of goods and services (end of the third century A.D.); copies of this edict have been preserved in inscriptions. In line 35 of Part IV we find the maximum price of ten sparrows — the cheapest of the edible birds — fixed at 20 denarii (see illustration); if we take into account the devaluation of Roman money between the first and third century A.D., this corresponds roughly to the price stated in the Gospels.

A ND he said, This will I do: I will pull down my barns, and build greater . . .
(Luke 12 : 18)

The scientific methods of agriculture adopted in the Hellenistic period throughout the Orient, as well as the peaceful conditions in the early days of the Roman empire, led to a great extension of the cultivated area in Palestine, especially — under the impetus given by the Herodian kings — in the Hauran region. The increase in the yield of the fields, and the necessity of storing as much grain as possible in order to meet the demands of the government for taxes in kind, obliged every landowner to provide all the storage place he could, while at the same time safeguarding it within the walls of his estate. Thus, in African mosaics representing the houses of the big landowners of the district, barns are shown inside the same enclosure as the dwelling-house. The illustration above is the reconstruction of a Syrian estate of the fourth century A.D. at Mujeba, based on a survey of its remains. Opposite the living house and behind it, two low barns are visible along the outer walls of the court-yard.

A ND he said also to the people, When ye see a cloud rise out of the west, straightway ye
say, There cometh a shower . . .   (Luke 12 : 54)

Having been brought up in a small provincial town, and living in close communion with the tillers of the soil
and with fishermen — the two classes of the common people most vitally affected by the weather — Jesus
was very well acquainted with the signs of impending climatic changes. In Matt. 16 : 2 the red evening sky is
taken to portend fair weather for the next day; here a cloud in the west indicates rain (see illustration above).
As the colder regions, and in particular the Mediterranean Sea, the great reservoir of moisture in the area, are
situated to the west of the Land of Israel, a barometric depression to the east, with the consequent incursion of
cool, moisture-laden air from the west, usually leads to cloud formation and to precipitation. Therefore, in the
rainy winter season the peasants carefully watch the western sky, looking for the signs of clouds which will
bring the much needed rain to their fields. Red skies, on the other hand, are a sign that the atmosphere is laden
with fine particles of dust blown in from the desert — a sign of easterly winds and fair weather.

WHEN thou art bidden of any man to a wedding, sit not down in the highest room; lest a more honourable man than thou be bidden of him.

(Luke 14 : 8)

The usual way of dining in ancient times was on couches arranged on three sides of a rectangle (see the reproduction above of a Pompeian painting). In this picture, the diners are reclining on the couches, while their servants move to and fro within the space left between them. A late arrival on the left is having his shoes removed by a slave. Of the three couches (see diagram) that in the middle (*in medio*) was regarded as the most honourable; of the three places on it that on the left (the *summus*) was assigned to the guest of the highest rank, as no one was reclining on a couch behind him. The couch to his left (*in summo*) was the next in dignity; that on the right (*in imo*), being held in the lowest esteem, was occupied by the host and his family. These arrangements explain the necessity of refraining from occupying the highest place, which had perhaps been reserved for a "more honourable man".

AND another said, I have bought five yoke of oxen . . .   (Luke 14 : 19)

In the absence of any other source of power, any work requiring muscular force in antiquity was done either by men or by draught animals. Horses could be employed for some of the lighter work, and donkeys for turning millstones (see p. 91); but the main animal power was supplied by oxen, normally working in pairs. As these were joined together under one yoke (see p. 45), they were called "a yoke" for short. The "yoke" was thus both the unit of power and also a unit of land; the Romans employed a unit of measurement called *iugum* (a yoke), i.e. the area of land which one pair of oxen could plough in a day. The figurines of the two bulls attached to a plough, shown above, were found, together with other models of livestock and farm implements, at Civita Castellana in Italy and probably belong to the Hellenistic period. The purchase of five yoke, i.e. of ten oxen, was thus a very serious business, like purchasing land or taking a wife; in this parable it is used by worldly people as an excuse for shunning the kingdom of heaven.

FOR what king, going to make war against another king, sitteth not down first, and consulteth whether he be able with ten thousand to meet him that cometh against him with twenty thousand? Or else, while the other is yet a great way off, he sendeth an ambassage, and desireth conditions of peace.   (Luke 14 : 31-32)

Although the subject nations of the Roman empire were excluded from any active participation in politics, and especially in foreign affairs, and although their share in waging the wars of the Empire was limited to furnishing auxiliary troops, they were nevertheless very much interested in such matters. One of the proofs of such interest are the "Parables of Kings" found in the Talmudic sources, which are a thinly disguised comment on the vicissitudes of Roman politics. In the Gospels, too, the same interest in and understanding of political events is shown. The Roman practice of consultation before engaging in warfare is exemplified by a detail of the reliefs from the column of Trajan (98-117) commemorating the two Dacian wars of this emperor. He is seen surrounded by his advisers and presiding over a council of war (see illustration above). The picture below is a reproduction of the reliefs found on a gold cup discovered with other treasures at Boscoreale in Italy, showing the emperor Augustus receiving a Parthian embassy. The Parthians kneel at the feet of the emperor, who is flanked by his advisers and a body-guard.

ND not many days after, the younger son gathered all together and took his journey into a far country, and there wasted his substance with riotous living.　　(Luke 15 : 13)

Hellenistic and Roman literature, and especially the writers of comedies and satires, have left us detailed accounts of the ways in which young men, amply equipped with money but devoid of any serious purpose in life, spent their substance. These usually took the form of gambling, drinking and keeping company with women of loose morals, such as abounded in the great cities of the Greco-Roman world. As Greek maidens and married women of good family were kept in strict seclusion at home, removed from contact with anyone not of their own family, they were limited in their outlook. The only way, therefore, for a man to enjoy the society of women of wit and education was to frequent the society of *heterae*. The picture above, reproduced from a wall painting found at Herculaneum, shows a youth banqueting with a woman. Various dishes and jugs are set on the table in front of them, while a servant brings them a box (presumably a jewel-box) to which the lady is pointing in a suggestive manner; the youth however seems to be pre-occupied with catching the wine flowing from the lower end of a rhyton held by him at some distance from his lips.

AND he would fain have filled his belly with the husks that the swine did eat: and no man gave unto him. (Luke 15 : 16)

The original word here translated "husks" is the Greek *keratia,* "little horns", a reference to the form of the pod of the carob tree (*Ceratonia siliqua, L.*). This tree, which grows on very dry soil, reaches a height of 24–30 feet. The pods, up to a foot long, are green at first, but turn brown when ripe; they can also be dried in the sun, and are very rich in sweet syrup (up to 50%). They were used in antiquity, and to a certain extent are still used even now, as food for fattening cattle; they are also quite fit for human consumption. The original habitat of the carob tree seems to have been in Asia Minor; but it spread to Cyprus, the Lebanon and to the Judaean mountains, penetrating deep into the drier parts of the country, including even the Central Negeb. By Roman times its area had extended all over the Eastern Mediterranean and had probably reached Italy as well.

AND the LORD said, If ye had faith as a grain of mustard seed, ye might say unto this sycamine tree, Be thou plucked up by the root, and be thou planted in the sea; and it should obey you.   (Luke 17 : 6)

The mustard plant (*Sinapis nigra*), one of the most common weeds in Palestine, is sometimes also cultivated as a garden herb which produces tiny seeds used as condiment; it is therefore referred to here and in Matt. 13 : 32; 17 : 20, as the smallest and most insignificant of plants, which nevertheless can become important to the true believer (picture on right). The sycamine (*Morus nigra, L.* or black mulberry) is a handsome tree (see illustration on left) growing to a height of 20–30 feet. Its red or black fruit was much appreciated in antiquity. It was used to colour wine, and to excite elephants for battle (1 Macc. 6 : 34). Among the ancient Greeks the sycamine was sacred to Pan and was supposed to confer wisdom. The contrast between the tiny mustard seed and the large sycamine is emphasized here to give point to the power of faith.

AND he ran before, and climbed up into a sycamore tree to see him . . .

(Luke 19 : 4)

The sycamore (*Ficus sycamorus, L.*; see Vol. III, p. 241), which is common in the lowlands and is also found in the mountains of Judaea and in the Jordan Valley, grows to a height of up to 25-50 feet and has a spread of as much as 60 feet; it was therefore especially valued for its shade and was planted along the roads. Its sweet fruit is similar to that of the fig tree, but much smaller, and is therefore not marketed today; children, however, still find it very tasty. Owing to its size and the spread of its branches it was most suitable for a small man to climb, if he wanted to see what was happening on the road (see illustration above). The Jericho which Jesus entered and passed through (v. 1) was situated neither on the site of the Old Testament Jericho near Elisha's fountain (see Vol. II, p. 254), nor on that of the present-day city, but was the Herodian town of that name, near the Herodian palace which has recently been excavated at a site called in Arabic Tulul Abu el-Alayiq, close to the point at which the Wadi el-Qelt issues into the Jordan Plain. As the centre of the rich royal estates in the Jordan Valley, it was the proper place for the residence of a head tax-gatherer ("chief among the publicans", v. 2).

AND he called his ten servants, and delivered them ten pounds, and said unto them, Occupy till I come . . . LORD, behold, here is thy pound, which I have kept laid up in a napkin. (Luke 19 : 13, 20)

The "pound" of this verse is the Greek *mna* or mina, a word derived from the Semitic *mneh* "to count" (see Vol. IV, p. 204) and indicating a unit of weight, or a quantity of silver of that weight. The Greek *mina* was the sixtieth part of a talent, and equal to 100 drachmae or denarii (see p. 62). It thus represented 67.5 grains of silver in the time of Alexander, but only 55 grains in the time of Jesus, owing to the general devaluation of money. Such a quantity of silver could not be coined, and the mina therefore appears only as a unit of reckoning. Weights of a mina are quite commonly found in the Holy Land; the one reproduced above is a round weight ornamented with cornucopias, an ear of wheat and the mask of a satyr. The inscriptions read "Year Four", "Public Mina". Such standard weights were issued by public authorities and their accuracy was controlled by a special official, the *agoranomos* or overseer of the market.

The term rendered "napkin" in the Greek original is the Latin word *sudarium,* a handkerchief used for wiping away sweat and dirt from the face. Owing to the nature of ancient dress, with its flowing draperies, the hem of a garment would usually be employed for this purpose; but naturally this would be repugnant to more refined persons who would use a sudarium. Representations of such kerchiefs are correspondingly rare; the one reproduced here is a drawing of a statue of a Roman lady of the imperial period who is holding one in her left hand. The use to which the napkin is put in our verse here also becomes clear if one considers the absence of pockets in the dress of the Greeks and Romans. The wearer of a toga could tuck money away in the girdle which held its voluminous folds in place; but a servant had to be content with a simple *khiton,* or at the most with a *himation* (see p. 33), neither of which provided any possible receptacle for coins. The servant here therefore put the coins (weighing a mina, or about half a pound of silver, see above) in a *sudarium* and bound them round his neck or body for safe-keeping. Larger sums were carried in special bags (see p. 42).

F OR the days shall come upon thee, that thine enemies shall cast a trench about thee, and compass thee round, and keep thee in on every side. (Luke 19 : 43)

The verse above describes the normal beginnings of a siege in ancient times. The enemy's first step was to surround the beleaguered fortress with a "trench" (or rather, following the Greek, an earthen wall or *charax*), thus sealing it off and preventing the escape, provisioning or reinforcement of the troops inside. This task completed, the siege-dam could be thrown up and the siege-engines brought to bear on the defences. The photograph above shows the fortress of Masada on the shores of the Dead Sea, the last stronghold of the Jews in their First War against the Romans, A.D. 66-73. Built by Herod on an almost inaccessible rock, 1000 feet high, it was besieged by the Romans for several months in A.D. 73. They first threw a siege wall (*circumvallatio*) around the fortress at the foot of the rock (see the lower edge of the pictures) and put up camps (see upper left). Then a tower was brought up along a siege-dam to the fortress wall, which the battering ram then breached. The besieged committed suicide rather than fall into the hands of the Romans.

Owing to the dry desert climate and the isolated position of the site, the siegeworks around Masada have been wonderfully well preserved till this day.

128

AND they shall fall by the edge of the sword, and shall be led away captive into all nations: and Jerusalem shall be trodden down of the Gentiles, until the times of the Gentiles be fulfilled. (Luke 21 : 24)

The horrors of ancient warfare are graphically described in this verse. According to the prevailing practice (abandoned in the more humane Hellenistic period but revived by the Romans), the vanquished became the property of the victor, to dispose of as he saw fit. He might kill them (the usual fate of the warriors, and all the old and useless); he might sell them into slavery; and he might settle other peoples in their cities and on their land. All these disasters befell the Jews after the First Roman War, a generation after Jesus. The reproductions illustrate the practices enumerated in our verse here: a Roman and a Dacian fighting on a relief from the time of Trajan (above right); a relief on a Roman sarcophagus showing the bringing in of prisoners; and a coin of Hadrian (above left) picturing the emperor, or his representatives, using a plough-share to draw the line of the walls of a newly-founded Roman colony, in this case the colony called Aelia Capitolina which was set up in A.D. 135 on the ruins of Jerusalem.

A<small>ND</small> he said unto them, The kings of the Gentiles
exercise lordship over them; and they that exercise authority upon them are called benefactors.   (Luke 22 : 25)

The title "Benefactor", in Greek *Euergetes,* was conferred in the Hellenistic period on princes and other prominent
personages for real, imaginary or prospective benefits. Among the rulers thus honoured were e.g. Antigonus,
one of Alexander's generals, the emperor Trajan, and many others. On coins the term appears as the honorific
title of two kings of Syria, Alexander Balas (150-145 B.C.), and Antiochus VII Sidetes (138-129 B.C.). One of
the prominent personages thus honoured was Gaius Stertinius Xenophon, the physician of the emperor Claudius,
a native of Cos. The illustration above reproduces the dedicatory inscription of the Jewish synagogue at Nitria,
an oasis in the Libyan desert, SW. of Alexandria. It is addressed to the kings Ptolemy VII (143-116 B.C.) and
his Queen Cleopatra, who are called the "Benefactors" at the beginning of line five. Ptolemy was officially
entitled *Theos Euergetes,* "Beneficent God", but this form of appellation could hardly be used on a synagogue
inscription.

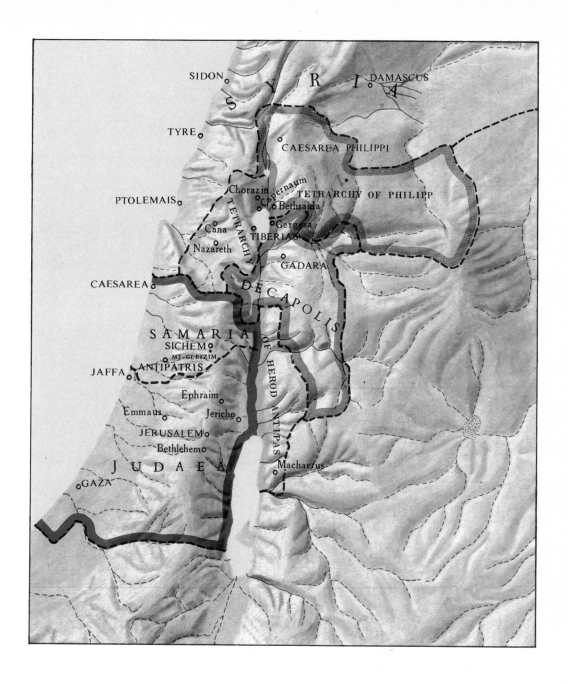

AND as soon as he knew that he belonged unto Herod's
jurisdiction, he sent him to Herod, who himself also was
at Jerusalem at that time.   (Luke 23 : 7)

The map given here illustrates why Pilate regarded Jesus as falling under the jurisdiction of Herod Antipas.
Herod the King had, as a Roman vassal and with Roman support, united under his sceptre most of the Holy
Land, except the Negeb and Southern Trans-Jordan (which belonged to the Nabataeans), the coastal cities
Ascalon and Ptolemais (Accho), and most of the Decapolis, a league of cities established by Pompey in 63 B.C.
After Herod's death, Gaza and the Trans-Jordanian cities of Gadara and Hippos were attached to the province
of Syria, and the remainder of Herod's kingdom divided among his sons: Archelaus received Judaea and Samaria
(see p. 23); Herod Antipas — Galilee and Jewish Trans-Jordan (the Peraea; see p. 58); and Philip — the Gaulan,
Bashan and Hauran (see p. 106). When Archelaus was deposed, his territory became a province directly adminis-
tered by a procurator (governor). Pontius Pilate was one of those governors. As Jesus was a citizen of Nazareth
(in spite of the designation of Bethlehem as the traditional birthplace), and this locality lay within the dominions
of Herod Antipas, Herod was supposed to have jurisdiction in this case. The map illustrates the political division
of the Holy Land in A.D. 30, the probable date of the events recounted here.

AND, behold, two of them went that same day to a village called Emmaus, which was from Jerusalem about threescore furlongs.

(Luke 24 : 13)

The distance indicated in this verse would place the Emmaus of the New Testament at the Mozah of the Old Testament, the Ammaus of Josephus (*Jewish War* VII, 217), in which Vespasian's veterans settled after the fall of Jerusalem in A.D. 70. The place has ever since been called *Colonia* (Arab Quloniyeh, a village four miles west of Jerusalem). Other scholars, however, following ancient authorities, adopt a manuscript reading "a hundred and sixty stadia" (furlongs), and identify Emmaus with the place of the same name which was an important strategic centre in the Maccabean and Roman wars (now called Imwas). The latter view is adopted here, and the illustration above shows the site of this Emmaus, in the foothills of the Judaean mountains, on the ancient road connecting Jerusalem with Jaffa and the coastal plain.

AND it came to pass, while he blessed them, he was parted from them, and carried up into heaven.

(Luke 24 : 51)

The traditional site of the Ascension is a small mosque, built within the remains of a Crusader church (and on the foundations of an older Byzantine structure). It stands on the Mount of Olives near its summit, not far from the ancient site of Bethphage (et-Tur). In 375 A.D. a pious woman by the name of Poemonia erected a church there called *In Bomon* ("On the High Place"), with a set of steps leading up to it. The church was in the form of an octagon, 57 feet in circumference, inside which there was a rotunda on columns, open to the sky in its centre. The Crusaders restored the building, adding arcades and small columns. Although it became a mosque in about the year 1200, the Christian communities in Jerusalem have kept the right to perform divine service there on certain days of the year.

ST. JOHN

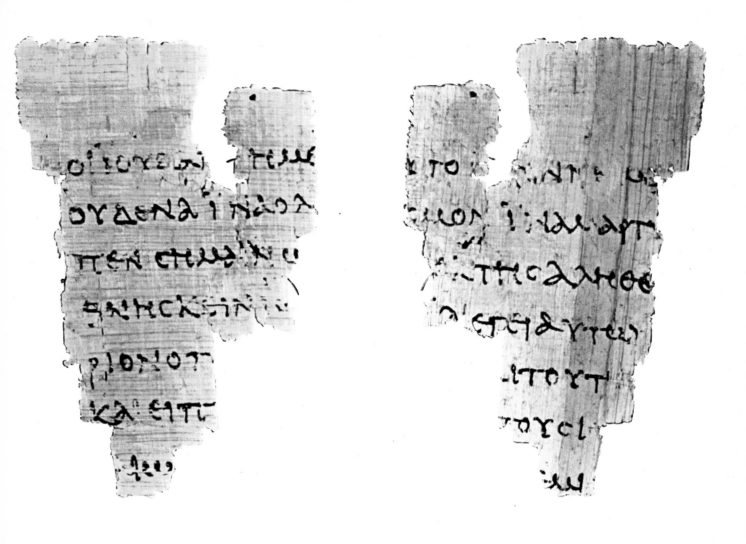

IN the beginning was the Word, and the Word was with God and the Word was God.

(John 1 : 1)

Traditionally the fourth Gospel is attributed to John the son of Zebedee (Matt. 4 : 21), identified with the disciple "whom Jesus loved" (John 13 : 23). It is believed by many, however, that the Gospel is more likely the work of an unknown writer, who was familiar with the Synoptic Gospels but wished to produce another Gospel which would be less concerned with the external facts of Jesus' life and teaching than with their inner meaning. Consequently some of the incidents in his Gospel are rearranged for dramatic effect, and he includes long discourses, quite unlike those of the Synoptic Gospels, which seem rather to be free meditations upon great spiritual themes than literal transcripts of addresses actually given. The opening words "In the beginning . . .", which are intended to suggest the opening words of Genesis, give to the whole of the following story a cosmic and transcendent setting, while the Greek philosophical word, *logos* ("word"), introduced in the same sentence, is evidence of the author's intention to interpret the significance of Christ in mystical and speculative terms. The order of the narrative, with its account of three visits of Jesus to Jerusalem (John 2 : 13; 5 : 1; 7 : 10) instead of the one visit recorded elsewhere, is so different from that of the other Gospels that they cannot really be compared. In view of its differences from the Synoptic Gospels and its flavour of philosophical thought, it has often been supposed that the Gospel must have been written at a very late date and probably in Asia Minor, but recently-noted similarities with the terminology and thought-forms of the Dead Sea Scrolls have increased the plausibility of the view that it was composed in Palestine and at a relatively early date.

The illustration shows two papyrus fragments from the first half of the second century A.D., containing vv. 18 : 31-33, 37, 38 of the Gospel of St. John. It was acquired by B. P. Grenfell for the John Rylands Library in Manchester in 1920 and is the oldest existing manuscript of any part ot the New Testament.

A ND the third day there was a marriage in Cana of Galilee . . .　　　　　(John 2 : 1)

The traditional site of Cana in Galilee (so called to distinguish it from another Cana in Coelesyria) is Kefr Kanna in the vicinity of Nazareth. However, modern scholarship derives the name from the Hebrew *qaneh* (reed), and identifies the place with a ruin called Khirbet Qana in the hills bordering on the plain of Netophah in the heart of Lower Galilee (see view). This plain was apparently part of the royal domain of the Herodians and was worked by their tenants, supervised by royal officials. This would explain the presence there of a "king's man" (*basilikos* in Greek — John 4 : 46, translated "nobleman" in the A.V.).

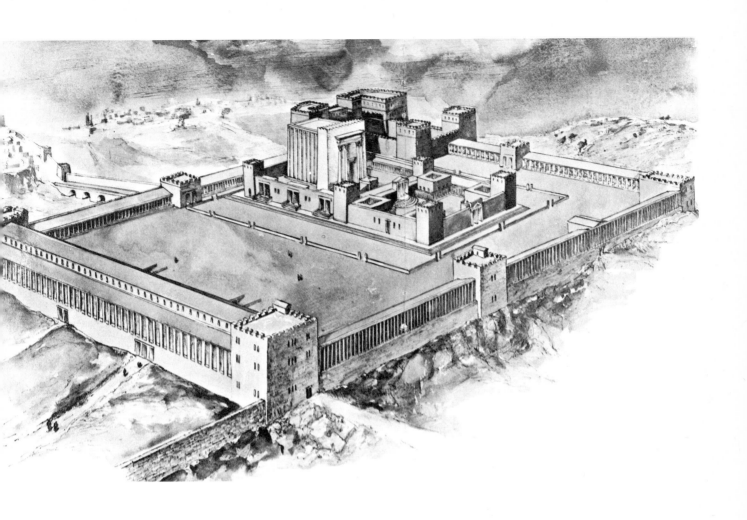

T HEN said the Jews, Forty and six years was this temple in building, and wilt thou rear it up in three days?

(John 2 : 20)

According to Josephus, the rebuilding of the Temple was begun by King Herod in the fifteenth (or possibly eighteenth) year of his reign (22 B.C.). It was completed, according to the verse above, in A.D. 24. Josephus states that the last decorations were not finished till the time of the governor Albinus, A.D. 62-64, a few years before its destruction. The building was famous for its magnificence: Josephus compares its wide expanses of marble and the profusion of its gold ornaments to a "mountain of snow glittering in the sunlight". Even the rabbis, who were no friends of Herod, had to admit that "he who had never seen the Temple of Herod, did not see beauty in his days". The drawing here is a reconstruction of the Temple in the time of Jesus. It shows Herod's esplanade, 1590 × 1030 feet in area, with porticoes running round it. Beyond it was the Outer Court which ended at a balustrade; this the Gentiles were not allowed to pass (see p. 188). Within this was the Inner Temple, with its two courts: the Court of Women on the east, and the Inner Court on the west. In the latter stood the great altar of burnt offerings. Behind it rose the Temple itself, a huge edifice 300 feet wide in front, 300 feet long and 300 feet high. The fortress of Antonia (see p. 190) can be seen behind it. The Temple was a fortress and a place of worship combined; it was the heart of Jerusalem and the focal point of the whole Jewish Diaspora.

THEN cometh he to a city of Samaria, which is called Sychar, near to the parcel of ground that Jacob gave to his son Joseph. Now Jacob's well was there. JESUS therefore, being wearied with his journey, sat thus on the well: and it was about the sixth hour. There cometh a woman of Samaria to draw water ...   (John 4 : 5-7)

According to Gen. 33 : 19, Jacob bought a plot of ground near Sichem, which later on served as the burial place for his son Joseph (Ex. 13 : 19; Josh. 24 : 32). Jacob's well is traditionally located in the plain where the Sichem valley branches out to the north and south, east of Mounts Gerizim and Ebal. (Some commentators correct the reading Sychar above to "Sichem"; while others identify it with the modern village of Askar east of Nablus, which is also mentioned in the Mishna as En Soker, *Menahot* 10 : 2.) The well is very deep (75 feet according to some measurements) and its water is cold and good; it was once choked with rubbish but has been cleared, and a church is being built on the foundations of an earlier Byzantine church. The "woman of Samaria" referred to in v. 7 is not an inhabitant of the city of Samaria, which is many miles to the north, but a Samaritan. In Jesus' day, this nation, which had split off from the Jews in Persian times (Vol. IV, p. 241), occupied the Plain of Sichem near their sacred mountain, Gerizim, and the mountains of Ephraim around it.

The drawing of water from wells and carrying it home is till this day the woman's task in Arab villages and Beduin encampments. The picture below shows two Beduin women drawing water in the Negeb.

Our fathers worshipped in this mountain . . .   (John 4 : 20)

Gerizim, the "Mountain of the Blessings" of Deut. 27 : 12 (see Vol. I, p. 289), was chosen by the Samaritans as the site of their sanctuary after their break with Jerusalem (see Vol. IV, p. 241). In Hellenistic times king Antiochus Epiphanes turned the Samaritan sanctuary into the temple of Zeus Horkios ("The Guardian of Oaths"), but the Samaritans continued to worship on another peak of the mountain where they had an altar of their own. The sanctity of Gerizim in the eyes of the Samaritans made the mountain obnoxious to the rabbis who transferred the biblical mountains of Gerizim and Ebal to the vicinity of Jericho. In this they were followed by some Christian interpreters and the Madaba Map (a mosaic map of the Holy Land made in the sixth century A.D. — see Vol. III, p. 257). Samaritan worship at Mount Gerizim continued till the time of the emperor Zeno A.D. 479; and to this day the surviving Samaritans still perform their Passover sacrifice on the mountain with the full biblical ritual. The view above shows the city of Nablus (Roman Neapolis), with the peak of Mount Gerizim on the right.

NOW there is at Jerusalem by the sheep market a pool which is called in the Hebrew tongue Bethesda, having five porches.
(John 5 : 2)

According to various sources, the principal market for the sale of sheep in Jerusalem was to be found north of the Temple Mount (see plan, p. 76). Sheep constituted the principal offering for sacrifices; but, as it was not convenient to have the sheep market in the Temple Court itself, it was held in a valley adjoining the Temple Mount on the north. After purchasing his sheep, an Israelite wishing to make a sacrifice could take the offering through the Tadi Gate into the Outer Court of the Temple and then by the "Gate of the Offering" (*Shaar ha-Qorban, Mishna Middot* 1 : 4) to the Inner Temple, and deliver it there into the hands of the sacrificing priests. For this reason we find the Sheep Gate of Nehemiah (Vol. IV, p. 233) in this vicinity, as well as the Sheep Market of Josephus and the Sheep pool mentioned here. It is interesting to note that the sheep market of Arab Jerusalem is still held outside Herod's Gate in the present city wall, in the same area as in ancient times. The Pool is called Bethesda in the translation above; some scholars, however, prefer the MS version Bethezatha or Beth Zeitha ("The House of Olives"), which is probably the name of the suburb of Jerusalem enclosed by Agrippa I by the Third Wall (Josephus, *Jewish War* II, 149).

The photograph shows the remains of the walls of one of the five porches of the Pool (below), with (above) the apse of a medieval church erected on the spot.

A FTER these things
JESUS went over the sea
of Galilee, which is the
sea of Tiberias.
(John 6 : 1)

The Sea of Galilee, or Lake Gennesaret, is undoubtedly the geographical centre of Jesus' activity in Galilee (see also p. 35). Here another of its names is mentioned: "Sea of Tiberias", after the principal Galilean city situated on its shores. This is the name preserved in Jewish tradition (*Yamma shel Tiberya — Tosephta Sukka* 3 : 9) and by the Arabs, who call the lake *Bahr Tabariyeh*, the Sea of Tiberias.

Tiberias is one of the few cities in the Holy Land which have kept their Roman name; this happened because the city was founded in Roman times and entirely superseded the previously existing village of Rakkath (Josh. 19 : 35). Tiberias was founded by Herod Antipas the tetrarch (see p. 131), in honour of the emperor Tiberius, most probably in A.D. 18. In the time of Jesus' mission it was therefore quite a new city. The Herodian town was situated south of the present-day Old City of Tiberias; part of its area is shown in the photograph. The line of walling in the background is the 18th cent. southern wall of Tiberias, which was built on the foundation of the northern wall of the Roman city. Constructed on a lavish scale and inhabited by a mixed population of fishermen and artisans, Tiberias soon became one of the largest and most prosperous cities on the lake; and it has retained this position, owing to the decline of its only rival, Taricheae-Migdal. As the other cities bordering the lake (Gadara, Susitha-Hippos) are at some distance from its waters, it rightly took its name from Tiberias.

NOW the Jews' feast of tabernacles was at hand.

(John 7 : 2)

The proper observance of the "feast of ingathering" (Ex. 23 : 16; 34 : 22), held in the autumn at the end of the year's harvest, had been laid down in detail in Lev. 23 : 42. It was to be celebrated for seven days, from the fifteenth day of the seventh month (counting from Passover), with the boughs of various trees (Vol. I, p. 196) and by dwelling in booths (Ibid., p. 197). After being neglected, together with many other religious observances prescribed in the Law, during the period of the Monarchy, the feast was revived with great splendour in the days of Nehemiah (Neh. 8 : 14-18) after the return from the Babylonian exile. The Talmud devoted to this festival a special treatise called *Sukka* ("The Booth"), in which the building of this structure is minutely dealt with. From the days of Nehemiah onwards, the Feast of Tabernacles has been regularly observed by the Jews of the Holy Land and of the Diaspora. (See illustration above, showing a tabernacle erected in present-day Jerusalem.) In the time of the Second Temple, the last day of the feast (the so-called "Rejoicing of the Well"), when libations were poured on the altar amid great popular gladness and the whole of Jerusalem was bathed in light, symbolized the agricultural character of the festival and the close connection of the religion of ancient Israel with the cultivation of the Land of Israel.

ND it was at Jerusalem the feast of the dedication, and it was winter. (John 10 : 22)

The "Feast of Dedication", or *Hannuka,* is the only Jewish festival without an Old Testament basis. It was instituted by Judas Maccabaeus as leader of the Jewish forces which revolted against Antiochus IV Epiphanes, king of Syria. In 165 B.C., having freed the Temple Mount from foreign domination, he removed the altar which had been polluted by heathen sacrifices, cleansed the Temple and restored the sacrifices (1 Macc. 4 : 52-59). It was subsequently decreed that the ceremony of dedication, which lasted eight days, should be commemorated annually at the same period of the year (25 Kislev—2 Tevet). Already in the time of Josephus (*Ant.* XII, 325) the name given to this Festival was "the Feast of Light", from the fact that the Jews had regained their religious freedom in what seemed their darkest hours. Rabbinical tradition, as found first in a commentary on the *Megillat Taanit* ("Scroll of the Fasting", i.e. a list of days of rejoicing on which fasting was forbidden) and in the Babylonian Talmud, *Shabbat* 21b, tells of the discovery in the desecrated Temple of a single jar of oil which burnt miraculously for eight days, hence the eight days of the festival. The Gospel, however, by using the Greek term *enkainia* ("dedication"), here recalls the historical origin of the feast. It is still observed in Israel and the Diaspora by the lighting of eight lights, one on the first day and one more on each succeeding day. The picture shows a torch procession held at night in Israel at the time of Hannuka.

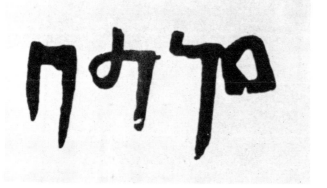

ΜΑΡΙΑΑΛΕΞΑΝΔΡΟΥΓΥΝΗ
ΑΠΟΚΑΠΟΥΗ⊂

Now a certain man was sick, named Lazarus, of Bethany, the town of Mary and her sister Martha. (John 11 : 1)

The family of Lazarus lived at Bethany (Beth Hanania), a village in the vicinity of Jerusalem, close to Bethphage where Jesus lodged during the days preceding the crucifixion. (Matt. 21 : 17; 26 : 6; Mark 11 : 1; Luke 19 : 29; John 12 : 1). It is now called el-Eizariyeh in commemoration of Lazarus. Of the names of the three members of the family, one is Hebrew, one Aramaic and one Greek. This mixture was typical of the end of the period of the Second Temple. Lazarus is a shortened form of Eleazar (Hebrew *El'azar* "God is help", which appears also in the form *Eli'ezer* "My God is help"). It is the name of the third son and successor of Aaron, from whom the high priests of the house of Zadok were descended. The top plate shows an inscription on an ossuary (see p. 20) reading "the Sons of Eleazar"; it is thus that Lazarus would have written his name. His sisters have common Aramaic and Greek names. The Aramaic one (Martha "Lady", feminine of *mar* "Lord") also occurs on an ossuary (see reproduction below). Her sister Mary, a Greek form of the Hebrew Miriam, was particularly attached to Jesus, who commended her (Luke 10 : 42) for her devotion; it was she who brought the perfume for anointing (John 12 : 3, and by analogy Matt. 26 : 7; Mark 14 : 3 where Mary is not named). The Greek form of the name (Maria) appears on the ossuary inscription (middle illustration) which reads in full: "Maria the wife of Alexander, from Capua".

IT was a cave, and a stone lay upon it.   (John 11 : 38)

Archaeological surveys in the vicinity of Jerusalem have given us a clear idea of a well-to-do family tomb from the time of Jesus. Scores of such tombs have been found in the slopes of the valleys to the east and south of Jerusalem. In order to keep the stench of putrefaction away from the city, tombs were rarely allowed on the side of the prevailing winds, the north and the west, although here too there were exceptions. As the making of a tomb-cave required a vertical rock-face for the entrance, the sites chosen were often disused quarries, where the removal of blocks had created just the surface needed. The cave cut out of the rock usually consisted of a main hall, with a smaller vestibule. The bodies of the deceased were laid in a pit in the hall for the first year, till only the bones remained. Afterwards these were collected and placed in small stone boxes, the ossuaries (see p. 20). These miniature coffins were then placed in loculi (horizontal niches cut into the rock). The caves were closed by a stone door; for additional security a rolling stone was sometimes provided (see p. 78). Cases of illegal burial, or the removal of the mortal remains of the owners of the tomb and of their family, were frequent (see p. 79). Disused tombs, which were left open, became the refuges of outlaws and the mentally deranged (p. 30). Shown in the photograph here is a row of tomb-caves excavated at Beth-She'arim, where the Jerusalem tradition of burial in tomb-caves was continued; the stone closing the upper cave is clearly visible.

TOOK branches of palm trees, and went forth to meet him . . .　　　　　(John 12 : 13)

The palm, one of the "seven kinds" of trees with which the Promised Land has been blessed (see Vol. I, p. 260), was a biblical symbol of righteousness (Ps. 92 : 12). Its immense, branch-like leaves were waved on festive occasions, the movement lending a solemn note to the rejoicing. Thus we read in 1 Macc. 13 : 51 that, when the Acra, the enemy fortress in the heart of Jerusalem, fell to Simon the Hasmonaean, it was entered with hymns of praise, the waving of palm branches and the playing of instruments. Among the Greeks palm branches were given to the victors in athletic contests and chariot races (see p. 280). It was natural, therefore, that the triumphal entry of Jesus into Jerusalem should have been accompanied by the waving of palm branches held by the multitude crowding both sides of the road. A more difficult problem is to find where the palm branches came from. Although the palm grows in the vicinity of Jerusalem, it is by no means common there; possibly the solemn occasion warranted the stripping of the trees in and around the city. Palm leaves (the term "branch" is botanically incorrect) are easily obtained, as there are generally a few young shoots growing out of the main stem of the tree. The illustration above shows one of the numerous palm groves still standing on the shores of the Sea of Galilee.

Aᴼᴿᴷᴱᴿ that he poureth water into a basin, and began to wash the disciples' feet...

(John 13 : 5)

The warm climate of the Holy Land, the dusty roads, and the general habit of walking in sandals (see p. 84) which left the foot uncovered, made washing the feet a necessity whenever a person passed from the street on to the comparative cleanness of a house-floor. When guests arrived after a long and tiring journey, the first duty performed by an attentive host, or his servants, was to arrange for their feet to be washed. Water for this purpose was provided by Abraham for the three visiting angels, by Lot for the two angels, by Laban for Eliezer, and by Joseph for his brethren (Gen. 18 : 4; 19 : 2; 24 : 32; 43 : 24). Usually this courtesy took the form of providing the water and letting the guests do the washing themselves; an exception is the humble Abigail who asked David "to let thine handmaid to be a servant to wash the feet of the servants of my lord" (1 Sam. 25 : 41). This metaphorical expression undoubtedly describes the practice in rich houses with plenty of maid-servants. The same custom was common among the Greeks; the painting on a skyphos (see below), found in Etruria (Attic pottery, late fifth cent. B.C.), shows the returning Odysseus having his feet washed by his old nurse Eurykleia (Od. 19 : 386 ff.).

IN my father's house are many mansions . . .   (John 14 : 2)

The Greek word here translated "mansions" is *monē* (from *monos* "alone, single"), i.e., a dwelling apartment for one person, many of which were combined to form a rich man's villa. The conception of a house composed of many separate units originated among the Persians, who dispersed their pavilions in the gardens of their royal palaces. This design was followed by the Hellenistic kings, and was later adopted by the Roman aristocracy. Pliny and others have left descriptions of sumptuous Roman villas, consisting of many terraces and buildings, situated among shady gardens with plenty of trees and flowing water. The various apartments were connected by cryptoporticoes, underground passages which provided a covered walk in all kinds of weather. The illustration above, taken from a Pompeian landscape painting, shows such "mansions" along the sea-shore. The houses vary in size; some are of one storey, others of two; all have cool porticoes facing the water while trees of many kinds screen the houses on the land side, towards the hills seen in the background. Jesus no doubt had this kind of extensively planned villa in mind when he used this parable. Such a type of Greco-Roman house must have been familiar to his listeners, perhaps from the Herodian Palaces in Jerusalem, Tiberias and Jericho. The first of these is described by Josephus (*Jewish War* V, 176, ff.) as a complex of halls and bed-chambers with gardens all around them.

A<small>ND</small> the soldiers platted a crown of thorns and put it on his head . . .　　　　　　(John 19 : 2)

The Roman way of executing condemned persons differed considerably with the social status of the sufferer. In the case of persons of low degree, such as Jesus was supposed to be, and especially where the condemnation had a political and social background, the death penalty was aggravated by scourging and other ways of inflicting pain. In the case of Jesus, who was condemned for an alleged usurpation of the title of a "King of the Jews" this procedure developed into a parody of royal pomp. A purple robe, a reed imitating a sceptre, and a crown of thorns were used by the brutal soldiery for this purpose. The Greek texts referring to the crown (here and in Matt. 27 : 29 and Mark 15 : 17) use the term "a wreath — *stephanos* — of acanthus". The latter is either a plant of the acanthus family (one of which is known as the *Acanthus spinosus,* a thorny plant) or the sharp-thorned acacia, which is also often called acanthus. Tradition however identifies the thorns used with the *Zizyphus spina Christi* Willd., a bush or small tree which grows from tropical Africa to Southern Asia. Like all plants of its family, the Zizyphi, it has sharp thorns on its branches, which can be easily twisted and plaited into a wreath. A branch of this species is illustrated above.

W HEN Pilate therefore heard that saying, he brought JESUS forth, and sat down in the judgment seat in a place that is called the Pavement, but in the Hebrew Gabbatha.

(John 19 : 13)

The identification of the locality described in this verse depends on our conception of the residence of the Roman procurator in Jerusalem (his permanent official residence was at Caesarea). Some scholars consider that Pilate resided at Herod's Palace in the north-western corner of the Upper City (see map, p. 76) and that the "pavement" (Greek *lithostroton*, a term used also for mosaic pavements; in Aramaic *gabbatha* or "ridge"), was a space in front of the palace, facing the market. Tradition, however, places the residence of the procurator in the Antonia fortress, situated in the north-western corner of the Temple esplanade (see p. 190). In this area excavations have brought to light a courtyard paved with stone slabs (see the illustration above; the vaults above the pavement are modern). The pavement shown here could have corresponded to the open courtyard which occupied the centre of the fortress. Marks cut in the stones of the pavement are of the same type as those used by Roman soldiers elsewhere when playing various games of chance (see inset photograph). The courtyard of the Antonia would have been a convenient and safe place for the procurator to sit in judgment (see p. 74), but it is doubtful whether the Jewish multitude would have been allowed inside the fortress, as is implied in the following verses.

ישוע דמן נצרת מלכא דיהודיא

JESVS · NAZARENVS · REX · JVDAEORVM

IHCOYC · O · NAZΩPAIOC · O · BACIΛEYC · TΩN · IOYΔAIΩN

 AND Pilate wrote a title, and put it on the cross. And the writing was, JESUS OF NAZARETH THE KING OF THE JEWS. This title then read many of the Jews: for the place where JESUS was crucified was nigh to the city: and it was written in Hebrew, and Greek, and Latin.

(John 19 : 19-20)

In the time of Jesus the language mostly spoken by the Jews in Palestine — and to some extent used also in written texts — was a Judaean variant of Aramaic known as Judaeo-Aramaic; this is the language referred to in the Gospels as "Hebrew" (John 5 : 2; Acts 21 : 40 etc.). The rabbis continued to use Hebrew proper as a written language, and it was also spoken to some extent by the educated classes even in later periods. Aramaic would naturally have been used in the inscription set up over the cross specifying the crime for which the condemned man had suffered, because it was the one language understood by all of the population on whom the punishment was intended to make an impression. The second language would be Greek which became the language of cultured people throughout the Eastern Mediterranean in Hellenistic times, and remained so under the Romans. It was the language understood by most of the Jews in the Diaspora, who thronged Jerusalem at Passover; the Temple inscriptions warning Gentiles against entering the Inner Temple (see p. 188) were written mainly in Greek; and so were the Gospels themselves. The third language mentioned here is Latin, the language of the Roman army and administration. It may be presumed, however, that the actual order of the languages written on the inscription over the cross would have been different from that set out here: Latin, as the language of Rome, would have taken first place, followed by Greek and Aramaic. When Pilate is said to have "written" the inscription this does not necessarily mean that he wrote it with his own hand; probably it was dictated to a scribe. The scripts shown in the reconstruction above are the Hebrew of the Dead Sea Scrolls, and the current Greek and Latin script found in public notices painted on the walls at Pompeii and elsewhere.

BUT one of the soldiers with a spear pierced his side . . .

(John 19 : 34)

The weapons used by the Roman army were mainly two in number: the short sword for close combat, and the javelin or lance for attack from a distance. The Roman lance or pilum was about 3½ feet long, and consisted of an iron point on a long stem (with a length of two feet) which was joined to a shaft of light wood. The iron in the tip of the lance was left soft so as to bend easily on striking a hard object, such as an enemy shield, thus preventing it being pulled out and used again against the Romans. The pilum was employed in the following manner: the Roman legionaries approached the enemy's ranks, till they reached about the right distance for throwing the lance; after throwing it, they drew their swords and attacked the cowed enemy at the run. The lance was thus one of the standard pieces of personal military equipment and as such would naturally have been in the hands of the Roman soldiers guarding the cross. The illustration shows the tomb-stone of Publius Flavoleius, the son of Publius, a native of Mutina, a soldier of the 14th legion Gemina, who died at the age of 43 in Germany, after serving for 23 years. The deceased is shown in his fatigue dress, with an oval shield on his back. His tunic is girt with the *cingulum* or military girdle, with the sword attached to it; he holds a spear in his right hand.

154

Now when Simon Peter heard that it was the LORD, he girt his fisher's coat unto him . . .

(John 21 : 7)

Working in the heat of the sun, in ships far from the shore, the fishermen busy on the Sea of Galilee would be dressed as simply as possible. The term "fisher's coat" (in Greek *ependytes,* a "robe or garment worn over another") indicates that the following words "for he was naked" — *gymnos,* need not be taken literally. *Gymnos* means rather "lightly clad in the undergarment only". When fishing, St. Peter wore only the short tunic of the Greek workman, such as is shown on the Hellenistic figure, reproduced above, of a fisherman offering his wares (in the basket held in his left hand) to the passers-by in the streets of Alexandria. This statue belongs to the series of realistic Hellenistic representations of the common people. It serves to show the decline of the classical striving after the idealized image of man and the newly awakened interest in the individual and the characteristic qualities naturally found among the teeming thousands of the big cities of the Hellenistic East rather than on Olympus. It was over a tunic like this fisherman's that St. Peter hastily drew an upper garment, probably a *himation* (see p. 33), when he noticed Jesus' coming.

THE ACTS
OF THE
APOSTLES

THE former treatise have I made, O Theophilus, of all that JESUS began both to do and teach, Until the day in which he was taken up, after that he through the Holy Ghost had given commandments unto the apostles whom he had chosen.　　　　　　(Acts 1 : 1-2)

As is shown by the preface to the Book of Acts, this history of the early Christian novement is a sequel to the Gospel of St. Luke. Both are dedicated to a man named Theophilus, and are written in the same skilful literary style. As its title suggests, here is the very beginning of the story of the Church in action, set down by an eye-witness of at least some of the events and a participant in the transformation of a small Palestinian sect to a world religion, spreading across the Orient until it reached Rome herself. At first the story is concerned with events in Jerusalem: the replacement of Judas to reconstitute the Twelve; Pentecost; the emergence of St. Peter as the leader of the Christian community in its early days; and the martyrdom of St. Stephen, the leader of the new "deacons", for his ardent public preaching. Then the scope broadens: St. Philip is dispatched and converts a eunuch of the queen of Ethiopia on his southward journey home. But it is with the conversion of Saul of Tarsus that the appeal to the Gentiles begins in earnest. Geographic expansion was accompanied by internal problems within the Jerusalem Church, with attendant discussions about the validity of the Jewish Law, as regards both converted Jews and Gentiles who adopted Christianity. Starting with ch. 16, where St. Luke apparently joins St. Paul's missionary team, the chronology becomes firmer; many scholars believe that the second half of Acts is in effect based upon St. Luke's travel diary. More and more the narrative concerns itself with the mission to the Greeks and the Romans, of which St. Paul was the agent, and with his activities: his arrest at Jerusalem, transfer to Caesarea, his appeal to the emperor as a Roman citizen, and his voyage to the imperial city. There the story ends. The account can be well fitted into the general historical framework of the period; and, despite certain discrepancies with St. Paul's own account of certain events, as found in his Epistles, can be confirmed to a large extent from exterior sources. The illustration is from a third century papyrus of the Acts, containing vv. 23 : 11-16, 24-29; it was found at Oxyrrhynchus, Egypt, and is now in the Laurentian Library, Florence.

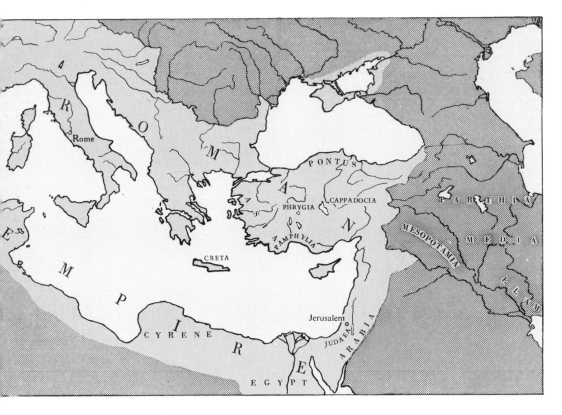

PARTHIANS, and Medes, and Elamites, and the dwellers in Mesopotamia, and in Judaea, and Cappadocia, in Pontus, and Asia, Phrygia, and Pamphylia, in Egypt, and in the parts of Libya about Cyrene, and strangers of Rome, Jews and proselytes, Cretes and Arabians, we do hear them speak in our tongues the wonderful works of God.

(Acts 2 : 9-11)

The Acts begin with the description of the first step of the Christian brethren after the final disappearance of Jesus from this earth: the descent of the Holy Ghost upon the apostles, empowering them to speak to the multitude of pilgrims from many nations collected at Jerusalem for the Pentecost, each in their own different tongue. The enumeration of the peoples assembled gives a bird's eye view of the Jewish Diaspora at that time, which is confirmed by other sources (see map). The description begins with the easternmost nations: the Parthians, the successors of the Persians, with their ancient allies, the Medes; to these are added the people of Elam, the region around Susa, and of Mesopotamia. All these were outside the Roman Empire. The rest of the list refers to nations subject to the Romans: beginning with Judaea, we pass to Cappadocia in Eastern Asia Minor, Pontus on the shores of the Black Sea, and Asia proper (the Roman province of Asia which included Ionia and Lydia, the western part of Asia Minor). Phrygia lay to the east of Asia and Pamphylia was a small province to the south. Egypt was populated by a million Jews in the time of Jesus, some of them living in Cyrene. The Arabians must be Jews living in the Nabataean Kingdom. Crete was a separate province in Roman times. Finally come the strangers from Rome, the heart of the Empire; they include both Jews (mostly descendants of captives brought by Pompey to Rome) and proselytes (see also p. 64). Characteristically, no Jews from countries west of Rome are mentioned, since the Diaspora did not extend so far in the first century A.D. The presence of proselytes in Jerusalem is attested by the ossuary inscription shown above, commemorating one "Judas son of Laganios, a proselyte". It was found in Jerusalem.

A ND sold their possessions and goods, and parted them to all men, as every man had need.

(Acts 2 : 45)

The Acts continue with the story of the organization of the Christian community in Jerusalem, the members of which shared all their property. The social ideals of the Prophets had stressed that part of the Mosaic law which favoured the poor and needy. With the final establishment of Roman power and the consequent creation of a firm political basis for a system of unabashed plutocracy, these humanitarian ideals began to fade even in Judaea. Here both the court and government of King Herod, and the aristocratic families of high-priests dependent on it, were more and more interested merely in enriching themselves. At the same time, those who were disgusted with the existing social system turned to the other extreme of strict equality in property. The first signs of this development can already be observed in the order of the Rechabites in the time of the Prophets; and, indeed, the nomad tribal life led by them and their like was based to a great extent on the use of the common funds of the tribe for the good of every one of its members. Similar attempts at creating an egalitarian state were made in the Hellenistic world. In Judaea, the Essenes followed this system; and we find it unequivocally propounded in the "Manual of Discipline" of the Dead Sea Sect: a novice who is accepted has "to bring with him all his property and the tools of his profession which are to be committed into the custody of the community's 'minister of works' ". After entering the community, the new member shares in the common fund with the others. (For the relevant passage in the Manual of Discipline, see above.) The early Christian community also practised a similar sharing of goods, which had already been envisaged by Jesus (Matt. 19 : 21).

ר שאלני בר רבי ל

ρΔΒΙΓΔμΔΛΙΗΛ

Ｔｈｅｎ stood there up one in the council, a Pharisee, named Gamaliel, a doctor of the Law, had in reputation among all the people . . .   (Acts 5 : 34)

The successful activity of the apostles aroused the suspicion of the Jewish authorities in Jerusalem. They were arrested and brought before the Sanhedrin, where opinions were divided. The Gamaliel who advised moderation, and who was also the teacher of St. Paul (Acts 22 : 3), was the son of Hillel the Babylonian, one of the founders of the Pharisee sect. Although their opponents, the Sadducees, were the official leaders of the people, the family of Hillel were nevertheless the acknowledged heads of the Sanhedrin, as they enjoyed the support of the masses. The tradition of humility and leniency in the application of the Law, first established in the school of Hillel, was traditional with his descendants; we see it here inspiring his son to counsels of moderation. After the destruction of the Temple and the disappearance of the high priestly aristocracy, the descendants of Hillel became the acknowledged leaders of Jewry, with the title of Patriarch. Gamaliel's grandson, Gamaliel II, was president of the Sanhedrin at Yavneh; *his* grandson was Judah I the Patriarch, the famous editor of the Mishna, who was buried at Beth-She'arim (see p. 66). Rabbi Judah's son, who succeeded him in the presidency of the Sanhedrin, was Gamaliel III. The inscription reproduced below, which was found in the Tomb of the Patriarchs (Catacomb No. 14) at Beth She'arim reads in Hebrew and Greek: "This (tomb) is of Rabbi Gamaliel"; the last two words are repeated in Greek.

Ｔｈｅｎ there arose certain of the synagogue which is called the synagogue of the Libertines . . .

(Acts 6 : 9)

Although the council (Sanhedrin) had refused to condemn the apostles, the zeal of St. Stephen the deacon caused the congregation of one of the numerous synagogues of Jerusalem to prosecute him for blasphemy and to execute him by stoning, as prescribed in the Law (Lev. 24 : 14).

The institution of the synagogue naturally took root last of all in Jerusalem, where the Temple sufficed for religious needs. It was mainly strangers who needed such centres. This explains the reference to a synagogue of the Libertines (i.e. freed slaves, probably repatriated captives who had been carried away by Pompey in 63 B.C.), and groups of Diaspora Jews from Alexandria, etc. (see also p. 160). Another parallel piece of evidence is the inscription reproduced above, which was found in the Ophel excavations in 1914 and has been dated to the time before the destruction of the Temple. It records the foundation of a synagogue, with a hospice, study rooms and a water installation, by one Theodotus, son of Vettenius (i.e. a freedman of the Roman family of the Vettii), who, like his father and his grandfather before him, held the office of head of the synagogue.

162

ᴀɴᴅ when forty years were expired, there appeared to him in the wilderness of Mount Sina an angel of the ʟᴏʀᴅ in a flame of fire in a bush.　　　(Acts 7 : 30)

Before his execution, St. Stephen answered his adversaries in a speech in which he reviewed the whole history of Israel from the Christian point of view. Among other episodes he mentioned the miracle of the burning bush (Ex. 3 : 2, ff.). As this led to the revelation of the God of Israel to Moses (ib. 14) and in particular to the revelation of the Divine Name of four letters (the Tetragrammaton), it was regarded as the beginning of the chain of events which continued with the Exodus, culminated in the Revelation on Mount Sinai and the Covenant with God, and ended with the Conquest of the Promised Land. It was thus endowed with special sanctity. Moreover, the bush which burned with fire but was not consumed was regarded as the fitting symbol of Israel, always attacked and in danger, but always surviving by divine grace. This symbol was transferred by the Christian interpreters to the Church, in their eyes the inheritor of the true Israel. Among the many pictorial representations of the scene, the earliest is that found in the Dura Europus synagogue (middle of the third century A.D.). It shows Moses standing barefoot (Ex. 3 : 5) with his shoes beside him and stretching out his hand in a gesture of veneration towards a bush, from whose green leaves red flames are shooting. The artists have represented Moses in the Hellenistic dress (white tunica with dark stripes and upper pallium in white) which was regarded by them as appropriate for the leaders of Israel.

A ND he arose and went: and behold, a man of Ethiopia, an eunuch of great authority under Candace queen of the Ethiopians, who had the charge of all her treasure, and had come to Jerusalem for to worship, Was returning, and sitting in his chariot read Esaias the prophet.

(Acts 8 : 27-28)

From Jerusalem the nascent Church began to spread out in all directions. The apostle St. Philip was sent down from Jerusalem by the south-western road which leads to the Elah Valley (Vol. II, p. 137), to the vicinity of Mareshah, and then to the cities of the southern coastal plain, Ascalon and Gaza. The reference to "Gaza the desert" does not mean that the city was a desert at the time; on the contrary, Gaza flourished in the Early Roman period. It is simply a reminder that Gaza stood on the site of the ruined Hellenistic city, which had been besieged, captured and destroyed by Alexander Jannaeus. The eunuch, who was a proselyte, is described as the treasurer of Queen Candace of Ethiopia (i.e. Nubia, the region above Egypt on the Nile). The word "Candace" was not a personal name, but a title, borne by a succession of reigning queens in Nubia. The one ruling in the time of Jesus was called Amanitere. The illustration on the left, taken from a relief on the walls of a temple in Naga (1st cent. A.D.) shows one of these queens, depicted, like Pharaoh, as of superhuman size, holding her enemies by their hair (cf. Vol. IV, p. 28) with her left hand and preparing to dispatch them by the sword in her right. As the eunuch was reading Isaiah while travelling, he must have been using one of the open Roman vehicles called *rhedae,* in the rear part of which a seat was provided for the passenger (illustration on the right). If the going was not too hard nor the pace too rapid, a scroll written in the large capitals of the period could probably have been read and understood on the move.

AND the LORD said unto him, Arise, and go into the street which is called Straight, and inquire in the house of Judas for one called Saul, of Tarsus: for, behold, he prayeth.

(Acts 9 : 11)

The Acts continue with the story of Saul of Jerusalem, a rabid persecutor of Christians, who saw a vision on his way to Damascus and was thereby transformed into Paul, who became a Christian saint. Damascus, the ancient capital of the Aramaean kingdom (see Vol. II, p. 261), was entirely reconstructed in the Hellenistic period (after the planning method of Hippodamus of Miletus, a famous town-planner of the fifth cent. B.C.). Traces of this Hippodamic plan are still visible in the Old City of the Damascus of today. It involved the use of straight streets, crossing each other at right angles, with modifications to suit local conditions. In Damascus the city was given the form of a rectangle, the long side parallel with the river Barada. The royal palace and citadel were situated in the north-west corner, with the great temple of Jupiter Damascenus (formerly a temple of Haddad, the Aramaean god, later the Cathedral of St. John and now the Ummayad mosque) to the east of it. As a result of this rectangular design, the east-west streets of the city were longer than the north-south streets which they crossed at right angles. The longest of them all was the "Street called the Straight", which to this day serves as the main commercial thoroughfare of the Old City (now called the Darb el-Mustaqim — see view above). Like most of the principal thoroughfares of the Roman cities, this street was bordered by two colonnaded porticoes, which provided shade and protection from rain for the passers-by, while at the same time leaving space for the shops lining the streets. When Paul was blinded on the way to Damascus, his companions took him into the centre of the city, to the house of one Judas, where the disciple Ananias called for him.

T HEN the disciples took him by night, and let
him down by the wall in a basket.   (Acts 9 : 25)

St. Paul began his missionary activity in Damascus with such success that his enemies among the Jews finally
resolved to get rid of him by denouncing him to the Nabataean governor of the city (see p. 234). To prevent
his escape they set watch at the gates of the city, where surveillance was easy. Although Damascus itself was
situated "beside many waters", it lay on the borders of the desert and was always hreatened by marauding
tribes. In the time of Augustus, Damascene caravans were regularly plundered by the Hauranites, till King Herod
put a stop to these depredations. Like most of the Oriental and Hellenistic cities of the East — but in contrast
to the Roman cities which were built in more peaceful times — Damascus was therefore surrounded by a wall
enclosing the rectangular space occupied by the city. The north side of this wall followed the Barada river,
which thus served it as a moat. The present wall of Damascus still contains large stretches of Roman work, with
round and square towers and massive stone masonry. The Eastern Gate at the end of the "Street called Straight"
has preserved its Roman aspect to this day. 300 yards south of it there is another Gate, called Bab Kisan (now
closed — see photograph above). According to tradition it was here that the disciples lowered Paul in a basket
through a window in the wall.

THERE was a certain man in Caesarea called Cornelius, a centurion of the band called the Italian band.

(Acts 10 : 1)

The Acts continue with an account of St. Peter's break with his old background in the matter of the prescriptions of Jewish Law, prompted by his vision at Jaffa. Thereupon he accepted the call of the centurion Cornelius to Caesarea. Caesarea-on-the-Sea (see view above) was the capital city of the Roman province of Judaea after the deportation of Archelaus (see p. 23). This was the normal residence of the Roman governor (he visited Jerusalem from time to time only — see p. 152), and here were the troops under his command, including a cohort called "the Italian". Although Caesarea was founded on the site of an earlier harbour town called the Tower of Straton by the Jewish King Herod, it had from the first a mixed population of Jews and Gentiles. Conflicts between these two disparate elements sparked the first War between the Jews and Romans. At the time of the Acts the population was evenly divided; so that the transition from the preaching of the new faith to Jews to the apostolate to the Gentiles could be most easily effected here. The centurion Cornelius belonged to the group of Roman non-commissioned officers who were entrusted with the training and command of the troops raised among the allies of the Romans. As in the legions, these old soldiers formed the backbone of the Roman army; they were strict disciplinarians (cf. Matt. 8 : 9) and wielded a stick made from a vine tree with which they are represented on surviving Roman monuments. Reproduced below is the tombstone of one Marcus Favonius Facilis, a centurion of the Twentieth Legion, stationed in Britain. He holds the stick in his right hand and a sword in his left.

AND when he had found him, he brought him unto Antioch. And it came to pass, that a whole year they assembled themselves with the church, and taught much people. And the disciples were called Christians first in Antioch. (Acts 11 : 26)

From chapter 11 onwards, the Acts are almost exclusively concerned with the activity of St. Paul, from the moment St. Barnabas brought him to Antioch to his arrival in Rome. Antioch was founded in 301 by Seleucus I Nicator, the first king of the Seleucid dynasty, and was so called in honour of his father Antiochus. It remained the capital of the kingdom of Syria till its annexation by the Romans, and continued to be the capital of the Roman province of Syria. The site was most judiciously chosen, in the broad valley of the river Orontes, with mountains protecting the city on the south. Nearby was the famous pleasure-resort of Daphne. In the period with which the Acts deal, Antioch was the third largest city of the Roman empire and was famous for its luxury and the mordant wit of its population. A Jewish community had existed there since the foundation of the city; in the time of Demetrius II the Jews helped to suppress a local rising. The large Jewish community in Antioch in Roman times served as the base for the preaching of St. Barnabas and St. Paul, who laboured there for a long time; it was here that the community for the first time adopted the name "Christians", i.e. followers of *Christos,* the "Anointed One" or Messiah. In later times Antioch was the seat of a Patriarch, the head of all the churches in the Orient. The present town of Antioch (Antakiye, in the Turkish province of Hatay) is a small place situated within the vast enclosure of the ancient walls. Excavations have so far uncovered only a small part of the city's rich remains.

WHEN they were past the first and the second ward, they came unto the iron gate that leadeth unto the city... (Acts 12 : 10)

Tradition places the arrest of St. Peter (told in Acts 13 which relates Agrippa I's persecution of Christians) at Caesarea, although the place is not mentioned in the text. In order to ensure the safety of the city founded by him Herod must have encircled Caesarea with a wall; but as the city grew in the peaceful period that followed, its buildings spilled over outside this wall, and it was not until the late Roman or Byzantine period that the larger circuit of walls was completed, forming a curving line from sea to sea. Like most Roman cities, Caesarea was divided into quarters (here called "wards") which had their own administration and police. The entrances to the city would have been protected by iron gates and closed at night time, to prevent undesirables from entering or escaping. The Romans did not adopt the elaborate devices for protecting the gateway that had been common in earlier times (see Vol. II, p. 262). The gates of their cities were simple openings in the wall, arched over, with statues of deities placed over the arch to protect the city. The engines stationed on the wall and towers were considered effective enough to keep attackers at a distance; and indeed any assault was usually made through a breach and not through the gate, the latter being considered only a provision for peaceful exit and entry. The illustration reproduces the gate of the "City of Egypt" in the fresco representing the Exodus at Dura-Europus. It is a typical Roman gate, with a statue of a city-god and two Victories placed over it. The two portals are shown open; they were often studded with nails or covered with metal sheets, and hence could be described by the epithet "iron".

Aɴᴅ upon a set day, Herod, arrayed in royal apparel, sat upon his throne, and made an oration unto them.

(Acts 12 : 21)

Chapter 13 ends with the story of the death of "Herod the King" who persecuted St. James and St. Peter. The personage called Herod in the Acts here was Marcus Julius Herodes Agrippas, known in history as Agrippa I, king of the Jews. He was a grandson of Herod and his Hasmonaean wife Mariamne, and the son of Aristobulus, Herod's son and victim. Agrippa was born in 10 B.C. and was educated at Rome, at the court of Tiberius. He incurred the aging emperor's suspicions, because of his friendship with the heir designate, Caius (Caligula), and was imprisoned; but when Caligula succeeded to the empire, he gave Agrippa first Philip's tetrarchy (see p. 106) and then that of Herod Antipas (A.D. 39). Upon Claudius' accession Agrippa received also Judaea and Samaria (A.D. 41) and thus united under his rule almost all of Herod the Great's former kingdom. After a wild youth, Agrippa I returned devoutly to his ancestral faith and, as king of Judaea, became very popular with his Jewish subjects and correspondingly unpopular with the Gentiles and the Christians. His sudden death at Caesarea in A.D. 44 has been variously attributed to illness or poison. The illustration on the left shows a coin of Agrippa I with the king's image. It is characteristic of his popularity with the Jews that he could permit himself such a liberty with the traditional ban on images of living persons; even his grandfather Herod had never dared to go so far (see p. 21).

On the right is a view of the theatre of Caesarea, now being excavated, in which Agrippa I fell suddenly and fatally ill (see verse 23 here and Josephus, *Antiquities,* XIX, 346-350).

SO they, being sent forth by the Holy Ghost, departed unto
Seleucia; and from thence they sailed to Cyprus. (Acts 13 : 4)

From Antioch St. Paul started on his first missionary journey by going
down to Seleucia, the port of Antioch. Seleucia was built at the same time
as Antioch, from which it was 16 m. distant, to serve as a harbour for the
capital of the Seleucid empire. Its plain was the only point at which a city
could be built along this strip of coast (and even so it was called Seleucia
Pieria, "the Stony"). From Seleucia St. Paul and his companions set out on
their journey, going first to Cyprus, where they landed at Salamis and
proceeded to Paphos (see map). From Cyprus they visited Perge in Pamphylia, on the south coast of Asia Minor, then went on to Pisidian Antioch
further inland, and various cities of Lycaonia and Galatia (see the following
pages). Returning to Perge, they re-embarked at Attalia and returned by
sea to Antioch.

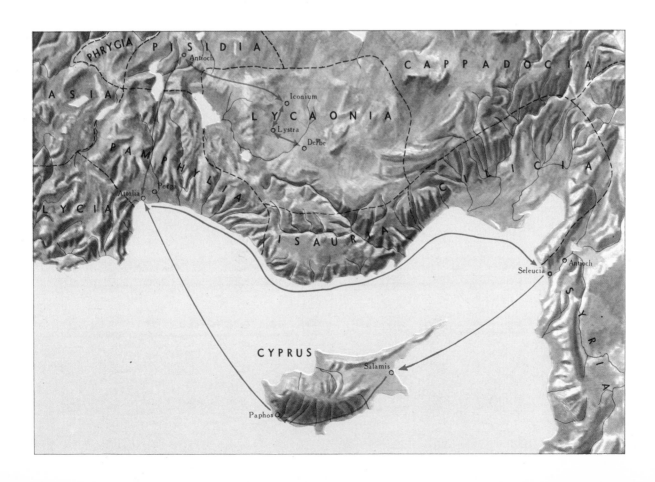

BUT when they departed from Perga, they came to
Antioch in Pisidia, and went into the synagogue on the
Sabbath day, and sat down.   (Acts 13 : 14)

The city of Antioch mentioned here was situated in Phrygia in Asia Minor, but so close to the border of Pisidia
that it was called "Pisidian Antioch" to distinguish it from the greater city of the same name in Syria (see photograph). There was a Jewish community in this city with its synagogue, frequented by the "Men of Israel" and
those "that fear God" (Acts 13 : 16). The latter belonged to a class of proselytes who were prepared to follow
the Jewish Law, but not to the full extent (see p. 64). The Acts (13 : 16-41) have preserved the text of the sermon
preached by St. Paul in the synagogue at this Antioch, the first one to be so recorded. At first St. Paul had some
success with both the Jews and the Gentiles, but the former mostly soon turned away from the new teaching and St.
Paul continued to address himself to the Gentiles alone. The pattern of events thus established at Pisidian Antioch
was soon followed in other places. The "God-fearing" Gentiles, who were half-prepared to abandon paganism
but wavered on the brink of Judaism, were obviously the most susceptible to the teaching of Christianity and
most capable of forming a bridge between it and the pagan world in general. By stirring up the "devout and
honourable women", i.e. the "God-fearing" (seboumenai in Greek) section of the local matrons, the leaders of
the Jewish community succeeded in having the missionaries expelled from Antioch; but they returned later on
(Acts 14 : 21-23) and founded a church there.

THEY were ware of it, and fled unto Lystra and Derbe, cities of Lycaonia, and unto the region that lieth round about.

(Acts 14 : 6)

From Antioch St. Paul and his company proceeded south-eastwards towards Iconium, Lystra (see view above) and Derbe, cities of the Roman province of Galatia, in the district of Lycaonia. Their activity followed the same pattern as described at Antioch: first they preached in the synagogue, and, after rejection by the majority of the Jewish community, they went on to form a Christian group among the Gentiles. The leaders of the Jewish community, fearing a split in their ranks and difficulties with the Gentile authorities, persuaded the latter to expel the newcomers; but ultimately means were found to ensure the survival of the nascent churches. Lystra, which was the most important of the cities visited, was a Roman colony. Its remains are situated at a place called Khatyn Serai, 18 miles south-west of Iconium.

AND they called Barnabas, Jupiter; and Paul, Mercurius, because he was the chief speaker. Then the priest of Jupiter, which was before their city, brought oxen and garlands unto the gates, and would have done sacrifice with the people.　(Acts 14 : 12-13)

After the miraculous healing of a crippled man at Lystra, the people of the city reacted in accordance with their views of the supernatural, i.e. they accepted St. Paul and St. Barnabas as gods visiting their city in human disguise. Many stories of such peregrinations of the Olympian divinities of the Greeks have been preserved in mythology and literature; indeed the intervention of a god *(deus ex machina)* was the standard dénouement of a Greek drama. Acting on this supposition, the Lystrians regarded St. Barnabas, who probably had the more imposing presence and was, moreover, St. Paul's senior, as the incarnation of Zeus-Jupiter, the chief Olympian deity. The illustration on the left above is a reproduction of the Jupiter Verospi, now at the Vatican; it is a Roman copy of a Greek original based on the image of Zeus created by Phidias in the fifth cent. B.C. for the great temple at Olympia. The god is shown seated, holding a thunderbolt in his right hand and a sceptre in his left (cf. also p. 223). St. Paul, being the more eloquent of the two apostles, was identified with Hermes-Mercurius, the herald of the gods. On p. 175 opposite is shown a statue of Hermes orating, a copy of a Greek original of the fourth cent. B.C. The presence of the gods naturally involved the sacrifice of animals, which were first garlanded, as was customary, before being offered up to the deities (see illustration on the right above, from a relief found at Rome, showing a sacrificial slave leading a garlanded bull).

THAT ye abstain from
meats offered to idols . . .
(Acts 15 : 29)

After their return from the first journey, St. Paul and St. Barnabas took part in a discussion in Jerusalem concerning the validity of the ritual prescriptions of the Jewish Law as regards circumcision and the purity of food. The assembly decided in the negative, allowing all meat save that offered in sacrifice to pagan gods. In common with most religions of the ancient world, the Greco-Roman type of worship involved the sacrifice to the gods of the choice animals from the worshipper's livestock, so as to ensure divine protection for the rest. Very soon, however, the sacrifice became only partial; some portions of the animal were burnt before the god, while the remainder was consumed either by the priests or by the person offering the sacrifice and his family. Sacrifices of whole animals were a rarity. To the Jews and Christians meat from sacrifices offered to idols was, of course, polluted and anyone eating of it was committing a heinous sin. The Jewish religion in any case excluded many animals offered in sacrifice (such as the pig or wild animals) from permitted foods. The early Christians — after some hesitation, cf. Acts 10 : 10-16 — abandoned these distinctions, forbidding only the meat offered to idols, blood, and animals that had been strangled. The animals sacrificed varied according to the various deities; a full Roman sacrifice (see p. 67) included a bull, a sheep and a pig. The illustration at the right above — a detail from a second cent. A.D. Roman sarcophagus — shows the sacrifice of a cock on an altar in front of the statue of the bearded god Dionysus.

A ND from thence to Philippi, which is the chief city of that
part of Macedonia, and a colony . . .   (Acts 16 : 12)

In his second missionary journey, St. Paul extended his activity to Europe; crossing over from Troas in Asia
Minor, he reached the harbour of Neapolis, and proceeded thence over ten miles of the Egnatian Road to the
Roman colony of Philippi, the first place where the Christian gospel was preached in Europe. Philippi was
founded in 357 B.C. by Philip II of Macedonia, the father of Alexander the Great. It was established on the site
of an older settlement called Krenides, after the numerous springs (*krene* in Greek) in its vicinity. Owing to the
presence of gold mines in the nearby Strymon valley, the town prospered till it became the chief city of the district (although not its political capital). In 42 B.C. Cassius and Brutus, who had conspired against and slain
Julius Caesar, were defeated there by the army of Caesar Octavianus (the future emperor Augustus) and Mark
Antony. In gratitude for his victory Augustus endowed Philippi with the privileged status of a Roman colony.
The city had a Jewish community, with a place of prayer situated — in accordance with Jewish Law — near
the river. After a series of conversions and healings, St. Paul and his companions were accused before the magistrates, illegally beaten (being a Roman citizen St. Paul was exempt from the rougher justice reserved for natives),
and imprisoned. Freed from prison by an earthquake, they left the city. Their return to Philippi (Acts 20 : 3-6)
and the letter to the Philippians (see p. 236) prove that Christianity had taken root in the city at that time. The
photograph shows the ruins of the market place of Philippi, as they appeared after excavation.

AND a certain woman named Lydia, a seller of purple, of the city of Thyatira . . .

(Acts 16 : 14)

Lydia of Thyatira is here called simply a "seller of purple" *(porphyropolis)* without any indication whether she sold the actual colour itself, or only garments dyed in it; the latter seems the more likely. Purple was an expensive colour, being obtained from the secretions of a tiny gland situated in the neck of the shellfish *murex trunculus.* Very little colour could be extracted from each shell, and in consequence the amount of labour necessary to produce a quantity of dye sufficient for a garment was enormous. Purple garments were therefore highly priced, and were regarded as the prerogative of kings and rulers (Luke 16 : 19; Rev. 17 : 4). Of the cities producing purple, Tyre was the most famous; but heaps of shells found at Ugarit and other coastal cities show that the making of purple was not confined to this city. The Talmud *(Bab. Shabbat* 20 a) mentions the "collectors of purple" between Haifa and the Tyrian Ladder in Palestine. The Phoenicians are presumed to have settled Dor because of the presence of the murex there. Great quantities of shells (from which the specimen shown on the left was taken) were found recently in the Hellenistic strata of Tel Mor near Ashdod (Azotus)-by-the-Sea. The ancient purple produced a crimson colour, as is shown on the standard of a Roman company *(vexillum),* reproduced here, from a third cent. A.D. fresco found at Dura Europus (picture above).

NOW when they had passed through Amphipolis and Apollonia, they came to Thessalonica . . .

(Acts 17 : 1)

Proceeding from Philippi along the Egnatian Road in the direction of Thessalonica, St. Paul passed through Amphipolis. This city was founded by the Athenians in 437 B.C. on a loop of the Strymon river in Thracia (hence its name, which means "city encompassed by a river") as a base for their rule in this region. The Spartans took it in 424 B.C., but the Athenians regained their control, till it was finally taken from them by Philip of Macedonia in 358 B.C. In Roman times it was the capital of Macedonia Prima. The lion monument (see lower photograph) was set up to commemorate Philip's victory in the fourth century; it must still have been visible in Paul's time. The next city on the Egnatian road was Apollonia, twenty-eight miles west of Amphipolis. Finally Paul and his companions reached Thessalonica (modern Saloniki), the great harbour city of Macedonia (for a general view of the city see p. 240). The top illustration here reproduces one of the principal monuments of the town, the arch, adorned with sculptures and dedicated to the emperor Galerius (fourth cent. A.D.). From Thessalonica Paul proceeded to Beroea and then sailed, probably from Pydna the nearest harbour, to Athens.

AND they took him, and brought him unto Areopagus . . .
(Acts 17 : 19)

Although the Athens visited by St. Paul was but a shadow of its former glory, it was still the intellectual capital of Greece, distinguished by its splendid monuments (see the view below showing the Acropolis, the rock in the heart of the city, with its famous temples, — the Parthenon on the right and the Erechtheion in the centre, with the steps leading up to the monumental entrance, the Propylaea, to the left), and its schools of philosophy and of art. It was no longer even the capital of the province of Achaia (Greece, see p. 181). Near the Acropolis was the rocky "hill of Ares" (Areopagus); according to Greek legend Orestes was here tried for and acquitted of the crime of matricide (see also p. 272); in classical times the supreme court of Athens sat here. It seems however probable that what St. Paul addressed on the Areopagus was an informal meeting of philosophers, curious to hear the new teaching, rather than a formal session of a court; the Acts do not refer to any charge brought against the Apostle during his stay at Athens. The philosophical tone of his discourse fits this supposition. The Areopagus (see photograph above) rises 60 feet above the valley encircling the Acropolis; traces of altars, seats and staircases leading up the hill are still visible.

FOR as I passed by, and beheld your devotions, I found an altar with this inscription, TO THE UNKNOWN GOD . . .

(Acts 17 : 23)

The polytheistic beliefs of the ancient world involved a host of gods, some of them universally known deities residing in their heavenly abode, others personified forces of nature or moral qualities, and still others associated with certain places or natural objects. All these supernatural forces had to be propitiated by offerings or prayers; according to the primitive magical conception which persisted even among the sophisticated Greeks and Romans, the pronouncing of the right name of a god or goddess in prayer gave the worshipper power over the deity and made it amenable to his wishes. It was, therefore, very important to know the right names of the god from among the plethora of appellations handed down by tradition. In order to avoid any possibility of omission of the right name deities were addressed in such general and comprehensive terms as "whether thou be god or goddess", or "the unknown god". No remains of the altar inscription referred to here by St. Paul have so far been discovered, but an identical inscription on an altar was found during the excavations of the city of Pergamon (see p. 271) in Asia Minor (see illustration on the left). Several altars dedicated in Latin to anonymous gods have also been discovered throughout the Roman empire.

AFTER these things Paul departed from Athens, and came to Corinth . . . And he reasoned in the synagogue every Sabbath . . . (Acts 18 : 1, 4)

From Athens St. Paul proceeded to Corinth, then the capital of the Roman province of Greece, called Achaia. Corinth owed its eminence among the Greek cities to its unique geographical position on the isthmus, the narrow tongue of land which connects the Peloponnesian peninsula with the rest of Greece. It had two harbours, one, Lechaion, on the west of the isthmus, and the other, Kenkhrai, on the east. After contesting the commercial and maritime hegemony of the Greek world with Athens, Corinth became the principal Macedonian stronghold in Greece, and then, in the second century B.C. the first city of the Achaian League. As such it was taken, plundered and razed to the ground by the Roman general Lucius Mummius, in 146 B.C. It was restored as a Roman colony by Julius Caesar and made the capital of the province, and soon again became populous and rich. As the principal harbour and trading city of Greece it attracted a Jewish community, who built themselves a synagogue. An inscription reading "(Syn)agogue of the Hebr(ews)" (see the drawing on p. 180) was found in the excavations in the city. The picture above shows the ruins of the sixth cent. B.C. temple of Apollo which was still standing in St. Paul's day, and behind it the rock of Acrocorinth, the principal fortress of the city area.

AND when Gallio was the deputy of Achaia, the Jews made insurrection with one accord against Paul, and brought him to the judgment seat. (Acts 18 : 12)

As in the other places where St. Paul's missionary zeal led to a schism in the Jewish community, the dispute at Corinth ended before the civil authorities; but in this case, seeing that Corinth was the capital of the province, the final arbiter was the proconsul (*anthypatos* in the Greek, here translated "deputy") Gallio himself; his famous answer: "If it be a question of words and names and of your law, look ye to it; for I will be no judge of such matters" is a reflection of the prevailing Stoic philosophy of the Roman administration. The full name of the Governor was Junius Annaeus Gallio; he was the brother of the philosopher Seneca, and perished with him under Nero. An inscription found at Delphi (see top illustration on p. 183) reproduces a letter of the emperor Claudius in which Gallio is referred to; as it was written late in A.D. 51 or in the first half of A.D. 52, it helps to establish the chronology of St. Paul's travels. The case against Paul was brought before the proconsul in the agora of Corinth (see the view above) where archaeologists have found a structure which could be a remnant of a proconsular *bema* or tribunal (see p. 74); it is also possible, however, that one of the basilicas adjoining the market place was used for this purpose.

Disputing daily in the school of one Tyrannus.

(Acts 19 : 9)

From Corinth St. Paul left Europe and proceeded to Ephesus, the capital of the Roman province of Asia (although the proconsul still resided at Pergamon). After the usual beginnings in the synagogue, came the inevitable eviction, and St. Paul transferred his place of instruction to the "school" (*scholê*, lecture hall) of one Tyrannus, where he continued for two years. It would be entirely in accordance with Greek usage if such a place of disputation were attached to a place of exercise, a stadium or a gymnasium; for the word *scholê* originally meant "leisure", and was then transferred to a place where one passed one's leisure — according to the Greek conception either in bodily or in mental exercises. We have evidence that the Greek gymnasia were combined with lecture halls; e.g. the inscription (see illustration below) found scratched in a scholarly script on the walls of a room adjoining the stadium at Sebaste and probably of the third century A.D. It reads "May the learned master Martialis and his friends be remembered by the Kore" and shows that the room was used by a teacher and his circle. The "school" of Tyrannus was probably of the same character. The fact that St. Paul could teach there in peace for two whole years lends special importance to his sojourn there.

MANY of them also which used curious arts brought their books together, and burned them before all men . . .   (Acts 19 : 19)

One of the powerful effects of St. Paul's preaching at Ephesus was the conversion of a large number of people who had dabbled in magic arts, a common phenomenon in times of religious decline. With the loss of belief in the gods of the Greeks came an increased faith in mystery religions and magic. Collections of magic formulae, several of which have been preserved, were made and written down. The illustration above shows one page of the so-called "Great Magic Papyrus of Paris" written on papyrus leaves (not rolls, as would have been the case with earlier books of this kind in Egypt), c. A.D. 300. It consists of a mixture of pagan and Jewish spells. Belief in the occult powers of the Jewish exorcists was widespread in antiquity (cf. the sorcerer Elymas, in Cyprus, whom St. Paul confounded at Paphos, Acts 13 : 8-11), and contributed not a little to the creation of the class of the "God-fearing" semi-proselytes. This class, which had lost its ancestral beliefs but had not yet absorbed Jewish teaching, or only a little of it, was easily attracted to Christianity.

AND when they heard these sayings, they were full of wrath, and cried out, saying, Great is Diana of the Ephesians! And the whole city was filled with confusion: and having caught Gaius and Aristarchus, men of Macedonia, Paul's companions in travel, they rushed with one accord into the theatre. (Acts 19 : 28-29)

St. Paul's stay at Ephesus continued unmolested until he came into conflict with the powerful guild of silversmiths who were preparing votive images of the great goddess of the city, the Diana of Ephesus, for the many pilgrims who came to see her famous temple. Diana, or Artemis, of Ephesus was an Asiatic fertility goddess who, though identified with the Artemis of the Greeks, was actually quite different in character. The centre of her worship in the temple was originally a stone supposed to have fallen from heaven. In later times the image of the goddess, which has been found in many places (see illustration on the left), represents her standing with her arm outstretched. She is clad in a closely clinging dress, upon which are represented in relief the images of many gods. In front of her are pendants, which some scholars hold to represent many breasts symbolizing the fecundity of nature, while others regard them as ornaments. The outraged multitude of worshippers of the goddess collected in the theatre, which in Greek cities was the usual place of assembly for the masses. The remains of the theatre of Ephesus have been excavated (see illustration on the right). Visible in the foreground of the photograph are the remains of the stage and orchestra, with some of the seats rising tier upon tier behind them. Thanks to the intervention of some friendly men among the authorities, the people were calmed and St. Paul left Ephesus alive.

AND there sat in a window a certain young man named Eutychus, being fallen into a deep sleep: and as Paul was long preaching, he sunk down with sleep, and fell down from the third loft, and was taken up dead. (Acts 20 : 9)

From Ephesus St. Paul returned for a short time to Macedonia, and revisited Philippi; thence he returned to Asia and preached at Troas. The meeting was held in an upper room on the third storey; one of those present fell down from a window, and was taken up for dead; St. Paul revived him. To understand this incident we must remember that the Greco-Roman house of the period was of two different types. Usually it was a low building, with a central courtyard to which there was access from the various rooms. Such houses, of the predominant Mediterranean type, were built in the country-side and small towns, where space was no consideration. In the bigger towns, on the other hand, and above all in Rome and other great cities, only the very rich could allow themselves such spacious luxury. The normal house in the cities (called *insula,* "block" in contrast to the former type of *domus* or "house") was a high and narrow structure, with as many as six storeys or more. Houses of several storeys are still standing near the Forum of Trajan in Rome (see illustration above). A fall from a third-storey window of such a high house on to the paved street could easily be fatal.

ND when we had finished our course from Tyre, we came to Ptolemais, and saluted
the brethren . . .   (Acts 21 : 7)

From Troas St. Paul proceeded along the coast of Asia Minor to Miletus, where he met the elders of Ephesus, and
thence to Rhodes, Patara in Lycia, and on by a Phoenician ship (see p. 197) to Tyre. From Tyre he and his
companions continued overland to Ptolemais (see view below). The biblical city of Accho, originally a Phoenician town, was given the name Ptolemais in the time of Ptolemy II of Egypt (c. 262 B.C.) and was known by
this name for the rest of antiquity; only after the Arab conquest did the old name (Akka in Arabic) revive.
In the time of St. Paul the city was about to receive a settlement of Roman veterans of various legions and with it
the titular rights of a Roman colony. It had a considerable Jewish population, although from the time of the
Maccabean revolt it had pursued a policy hostile to the Jews. It was the headquarters of Herod in his campaign
to conquer Judaea, and later on fulfilled the same function in the campaign of Vespasian against Galilee in A.D. 67
For commercial and geographical reasons, it remained at all times the port of Galilee. The city of Ptolemais-Accho
was originally built on a rocky promontory jutting out into the sea at the northern end of Haifa bay (see photograph below); in Hellenistic and Roman times it spread over a wide expanse of the adjacent plain. Politically
Ptolemais was, in Roman times, part of Phoenicia.

CRYING out, Men of Israel, help: This is the man that teacheth all men every where against the people, and the law, and this place; and further brought Greeks also into the temple, and hath polluted this holy place.

(Acts 21 : 28)

Upon his return to Jerusalem, St. Paul was recognised in the Temple by some men of Asia and accused of profaning its sanctity. Like most of the sanctuaries in antiquity, the Temple of Jerusalem consisted of various parts, with different regulations governing admission to each of them. The Holy of Holies could be entered only by the High Priest, and even by him only once a year, on the Day of Atonement. The Temple proper and the court in front of it (see p. 139) — except the altar — could be approached only by priests. Male Israelites could enter the Inner Court; women could only go as far as the Women's Court, the outer of the two courts of the Inner Temple. Gentiles were free to enter the Temple esplanade up to the low barrier encircling the Inner Temple, but might not pass beyond. Any infringement of these regulations was punished by death by the Roman authorities and the mere suspicion of such illicit entry would arouse the wrath of the populace. In order to prevent incidents, inscriptions were set up beside the barrier of the Inner Temple warning non-Jews against trespassing. One such inscription was found intact in 1870 and is reproduced here. It reads: "Let no one of the Gentiles enter inside the barrier around the sanctuary and the porch; and if he transgresses he shall himself bear the blame for his ensuing DEATH". For another fragment of these warning inscriptions see page 232.

B<small>UT</small> Paul said, I am a man which am a Jew of Tarsus, a city
in Cilicia, a citizen of no mean city . . .   (Acts 21 : 39)

In his speech of defence, as on several other occasions, St. Paul proudly mentions the fact that he was a native of the city of Tarsus, the chief city of Cilicia, a border province between Syria and Asia Minor. This city is already referred to in ninth century Assyrian inscriptions. In the Persian period it was the seat of a Persian governor, and its god, the Baal of Tarsus (*Ba'al Tarz*), was widely worshipped. At that time it was a Semitic city; but in the Hellenistic period it became Greek in character. When Cilicia became a Roman province in 64 B.C., Tarsus was made its capital; it was favoured by Julius Caesar and Mark Antony. The city was situated on the banks of the river Cydnus, about 12 miles from the sea. Among its population there was a Jewish community, which was well represented among the Jews in Palestine in later periods as well. The linen-workers of the city were famous for their skill and turbulence; the craft of tent-making, which was practised by St. Paul (Acts 18 : 3), was closely linked with the weaving of linen. Among the principal remains of the ancient city is the Roman gate (see view above), now called St. Paul's Gate.

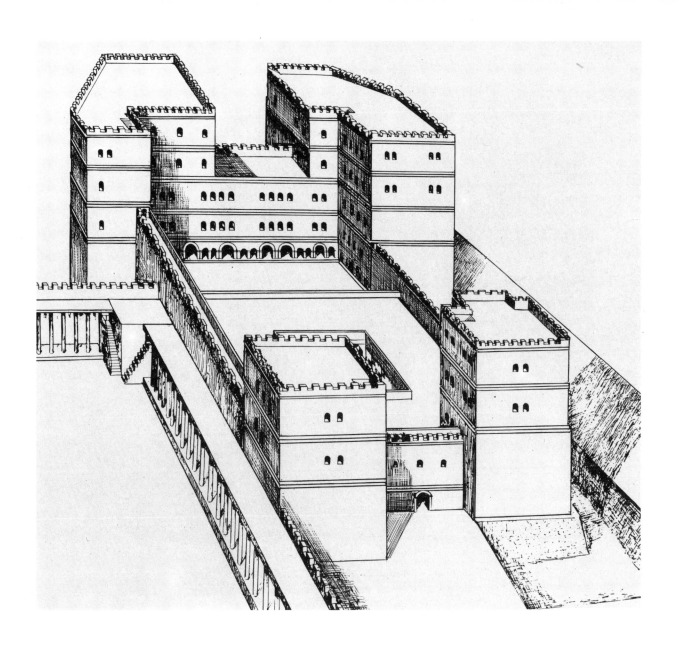

THE chief captain commanded him to be brought into the castle . . . (Acts 22 : 24)

The castle into which St. Paul was taken, and from the stair of which he spoke to the multitude assembled in the Temple court (Acts 21 : 35), was the fortress of Antonia adjoining the Temple at its north-western corner. In the time of the Judaean Monarchy, the saddle connecting the Temple Mount with the hills north of it was fortified by the towers of Meah and of Hananiah (see Vol. II, p. 220). In Nehemiah's day a fortress bearing the Persian name *Baris* (*Birah* in Hebrew) stood here. It was strengthened by the Hasmonaeans and for a time served as a royal residence. When Herod transferred his palace to the north-west corner of the Upper City, he fortified the *Baris* again and named it Antonia, in honour of the triumvir Mark Antony (82-30 B.C.) who was at that time the ruler of the Orient. The fortress consisted of four high towers, not symmetrical in shape, with an interior court; the latter is sometimes supposed to be the *lithostrotos* mentioned in the Gospel of St. John (see p. 152). Since the Antonia, with its high position and great strength, dominated the Temple, it was garrisoned with Roman troops, who kept the vestments of the high priest there. From it they could intervene quickly in case of any tumult in the Temple court, as the fortress communicated by stairs both with the court itself and with the roofs of the porches surrounding it (see reconstruction above).

191

Aɴᴅ he called unto him two centurions, saying, Make ready two hundred soldiers to go to Caesarea, and horsemen threescore and ten, and spearmen two hundred . . .

(Acts 23 : 23)

From Jerusalem St. Paul was sent to Caesarea, the official seat of the governor, to be tried. In view of the dangers threatening his life, the Roman commander at Jerusalem provided St. Paul with a very strong escort: two hundred soldiers, seventy horsemen, and two hundred "spearmen". The two hundred soldiers were probably part of a cohort stationed at Jerusalem and drawn from the Roman citizens living in the oriental cities of Caesarea, Sebaste or Ascalon. These troops were trained in the Roman manner and had Roman officers and centurions (see p. 167). On this occasion they were accompanied by a troop of auxiliary cavalry. After the Punic Wars, the Romans gave up the training of a cavalry of their own, and substituted for it cavalry troops levied from various peoples famed as especially good horsemen, such as the Celts or Mauretanians. The third group of soldiers, here translated "spearmen", is in the Greek original *dexiolaboi,* "holding (the spear) with the right", or, in some Mss. *dexioboloi,* "throwing with the right". They seem to have been some kind of light troops, perhaps native levies, armed only with a spear and no shield, and as such different from the heavily armed Roman cohorts. In the illustrations we see, on the right, a Roman soldier in full panoply (from the tomb of one C. Valerius Crispus, a soldier of the 8th Augustan Legion, who died at the age of 40 after 21 years of service; it was found in Germany), and, on the left, another tombstone, found at Neapolis (Nablus) in Palestine, showing a Mauretanian cavalryman named Augindai, who died on active service at the age of thirty.

THEN the soldiers, as it was commanded them, took Paul, and brought him by night to Antipatris.

(Acts 23 : 31)

The problem of swift communication between the city of Jerusalem, with its masses of potential trouble-makers, and Caesarea, the seat of the governor of the province, was solved only after the destruction of Jerusalem in A.D. 70, and the establishment of the camp of the Tenth Legion on the ruins of the city. A road was then made running north-west from Jerusalem, across the mountains, and coming out into the coastal plain at Antipatris, now Rosh ha-ʿAyin, from where it proceeded northwards to Caesarea. In the case of St. Paul, however, it is more likely that he and his escort went down by the usual route via Beth-Horon (called by Josephus the "public road"), and thence by way of Lydda to Antipatris. This city, the biblical Aphek, was in Hellenistic times called *Pegai* (the "Springs"), and possibly also Arethusa. There Herod built a city, which he called Antipatris in honour of his father; the name remained till the end of the ancient period, although the city had by then lost its importance. It was a convenient stopping-place on the coastal road, and survived as such. The tell of Rosh ha-ʿAyin contains remains of all the periods from the Middle Bronze Age onwards; it is at present crowned by the ruins of a Mameluke castle (see view above).

AND the next day sitting on the judgment seat . . .　　(Acts 25 : 6)

In Caesarea St. Paul was brought before the Roman procurator of the province, Felix, who kept him in custody for two years. In A.D. 55 (or according to some authorities 60) Felix was succeeded by Porcius Festus, who re-examined Paul's case. As we have already seen, a Roman magistrate was supposed to try cases seated on an elevated tribunal (judgment seat) and surrounded by his council (see v.12). A grotesque version of a hearing before a Roman magistrate is given in a painting found at Pompeii; the painting seems to represent the Judgment of Solomon or a similar tale. A woman is seen on her knees pleading before a raised podium, on which sit three judges. They are surrounded by soldiers, and other soldiers stand below the tribunal. In spite of its being a caricature, the painting gives a good idea of the appearance of the judgment seat of a provincial governor.

AND after certain days, king Agrippa and Bernice came unto Caesarea to salute Festus . . . (Acts 25 : 13)

In Caesarea St. Paul was not kept in close confinement and was able to continue his missionary activity, sometimes even before highly-placed personages. The king Agrippa mentioned here is Marcus Julius Herodes Agrippas II, the last Herodian ruler (A.D. 50 to c. 95). He was the son of king Agrippa I (see p. 170) but on the death of his father was considered too young to rule. In A.D. 50 he was at last nominated ruler of Chalcis and the Hauran (the tetrarchy of Philip), and in 54 parts of Galilee and of Jewish Trans-Jordan were added to his domain; he was also entrusted with the supervision of the Temple in Jerusalem, including the right to appoint the High Priest. At the beginning of his reign Agrippa II showed some independence, and even struck coins with his portrait (see illustration above). On the outbreak of the war with the Romans he tried to pacify the people. Failing in that, he sided with the Romans and succeeded in keeping his realms; but he had to witness the destruction of the Temple and of the Holy City. Agrippa II was, on the whole, a much feebler character than his father, as is also evident in his attitude to Christianity. Berenice, his sister, was famous for her beauty; she captivated Titus the son and successor of Vespasian, who for some time thought of making her his empress, but gave up the plan under the pressure of public opinion at Rome. She was married to her uncle Herod of Chalcis, and later on to king Polemon II of Cilicia. Her moral character was not above reproach.

THEN Paul stretched forth the hand, and answered for himself.   (Acts 26 : 1)

The peoples of the Mediterranean, with their volatile temperament, have at all times accompanied their speech with appropriate gestures. This tradition has been preserved till this day in Southern Italy and in the Orient; indeed, the gestures made by persons represented as speaking on the Pompeian wall-paintings have been much better understood by comparison with the gestures of the Neapolitans of to-day. Gestures were, above all, an important part of the studied rhetoric of speakers in popular assemblies and of preachers, whether philosophical or religious. St. Paul, who during his arrest and confinement at Caesarea had had long experience in addressing assemblies or important personages (having spoken before at least two provincial governors, various city rulers, the Sanhedrin, etc.), would naturally have known how to suit his gestures to his discourse. In the many ancient works of art representing orators, they usually appear with one arm raised. Reproduced above is a statue of an Etruscan speaker, one Avle Metle, of about 100 B.C.; he is addressing a meeting with hand uplifted. The sculptor was probably a Hellenistic Greek who knew how to combine the refinements of classic art with the stern realism favoured in Italy.

AND when it was determined that we should sail into Italy, they delivered Paul and certain other prisoners unto one named Julius, a centurion of Augustus' band. And entering into a ship of Adramyttium . . .

(Acts 27 : 1-2)

When St. Paul, as a Roman citizen, appealed to Caesar, the governor Festus had no choice but to send him to Rome. The right of appeal to the people against a judicial sentence was one of the most cherished privileges of the Romans in the time of the Republic; and when the Republic was abolished (in fact, although not in theory) the hearing of appeals devolved from the people on the emperor, who personified popular sovereignty. As St. Paul was, however, still a prisoner, he had to be accompanied by a guard; besides he was not the only prisoner being sent to Rome, as we learn from this verse. The officer in charge of the group was a centurion of one of the cohorts stationed in Judaea, which had the honour to bear the appellation "Augustan", probably with some addition indicating its place of recruitment, as in the case of other such bodies, e.g. "the Augustan cohort of the Sebastenes" etc. The centurions (see p. 167) were dependable men to whom such delicate missions could be entrusted; moreover, they were usually Italians, and Julius might have been well pleased at the chance of visiting his home town, after safely delivering his prisoners (see p. 203). The embarkment took place at Caesarea, but the ship was from the city of Adramyttium, a harbour in Mysia (Asia Minor, near Troas). Probably there was no ship sailing direct to Italy from Caesarea at the time, which, from the subsequent story, we learn was probably late in the autumn of A.D. 60. As Judaea was not among the provinces sending regular supplies to Rome, ships calling there must have been somewhat rare, especially so close to the period when shipping stopped altogether owing to the approach of winter. The map below shows the course of this eventful voyage, as described in the following pages.

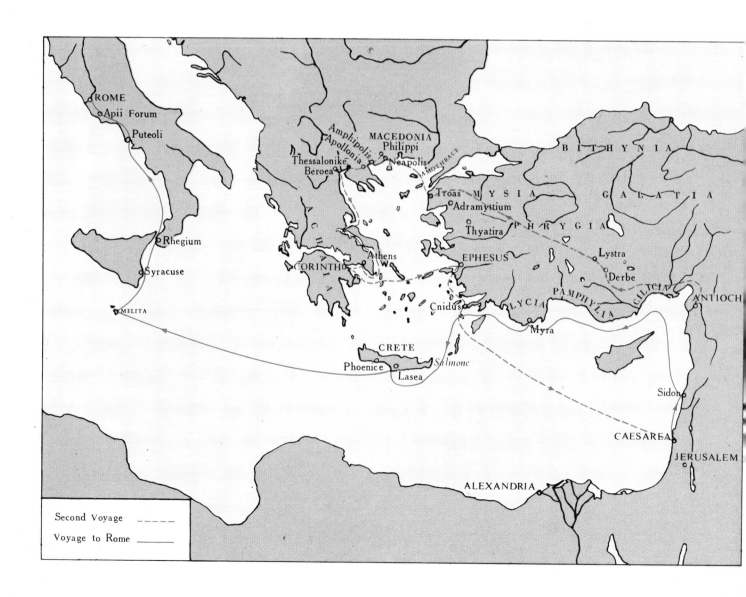

AND there the centurion found a ship of Alexandria sailing into
Italy; and he put us therein.   (Acts 27 : 6)

Proceeding along the coasts of Phoenicia, Syria and Cilicia, the ship from Adramyttium finally reached the port of
Myra; from there it probably returned to its home town. At Myra, the centurion commanding the convoy transferred his charges to a bigger ship, which was en route from Alexandria to Italy. This was one of the principal
trade routes of the Mediterranean in St. Paul's time; for the populace of Rome depended, for the free distributions
of wheat to which it was accustomed, on the two great grain-producing countries of the Empire, Africa and Egypt.
No wonder therefore that, in spite of the late season, ships still were sailing from Alexandria, the great harbour of
Egypt, to Italy; but, unwilling to risk the open sea, the captain of this ship took it along the coast and so came to
Myra, where his new passengers awaited him. The illustrations above shows a big merchant ship of antiquity as
represented on a sarcophagus from Sidon. In contrast to the naval vessels, such merchant ships used only sail-power.
They were massively built, with big storage capacity. The passengers were accommodated, as far as possible, in a
cabin on the poop or on the forecastle. The illustration below shows the loading of an Egyptian grain-ship, called
the Isis Geminiana, as represented in a painting found at Ostia, dating to the third cent. A.D. The owner, one
Abascantus, is standing on the deck, with the captain, Farnaces, behind him on the deck of the cabin. Porters carry
the sacks up to the decks, where they pour the grain into a receptacle, supervised by a counting clerk.

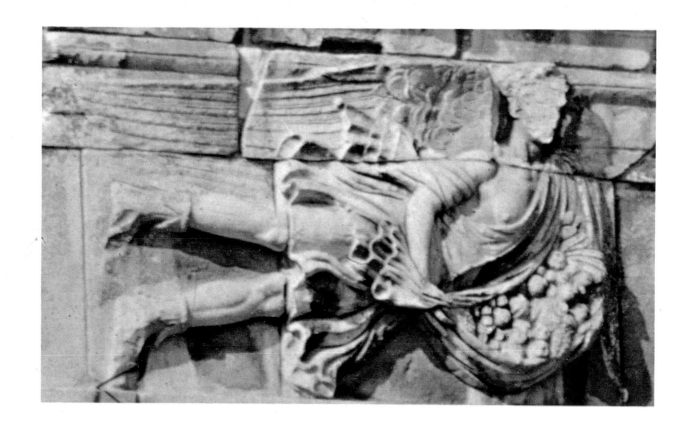

B<small>UT</small> not long after there arose against it a tempestuous wind, called Euroclydon. (Acts 27 : 14)

With the exception of the banked oars of fighting vessels, which could be used only for relatively short spurts, the ancients depended on wind to supply the motive power of their ships. Moreover, it was the winds which brought the rain clouds or kept them away and thus directly influenced agricultural yields. The winds were therefore regarded — in accordance with the general tendency of ancient religions to personify all forces of nature — as a group of semi-divine beings kept in the Cave of the Winds by Aeolus, to whom Zeus had entrusted this charge. Aeolus released them one by one, according to the season or at the special request of a deity. Amongst the winds, Boreas, the North Wind, was especially feared (he is represented on the fourth century B.C. Tower of Winds at Athens — see illustration — as a bearded personage, with high boots, blowing a shell and carrying the rain in his mantle). Euroclydon is a composite Greek name, made up of the word for the South-East Wind *(Euros)* and *klydon,* "wave". The tempestuous wind blowing from the south-east was especially dangerous to ships sailing along the south coast of Europe, as it threatened to wreck them on the coastal rocks. Another version of this name, found in some Mss., is Euraquila, the North-East Wind. One of the kinder winds *(Zephyros)* is represented in the enlargement above.

AND we being exceedingly tossed with a tempest . . . (Acts 27 : 18)

The frail craft of antiquity were an easy prey to the storms which swept across the Mediterranean from time to time. If we consider that the largest ship of which we hear in ancient times was about 1500 tons — an Alexandrian wheat-ship driven into port by rough weather — (as compared to the 30–40,000 ton vessels of our day), and that a boat of 30 tons is already called a "ship" in the Mishna (*Zabim* 3 : 3), we can understand the nature of ancient navigation. Ships hugged the coastline as far as possible and did not venture upon the open seas at all in winter. In addition, one should remember that navigation was entirely by the stars or the sun, without any of the appliances which were known even in the Middle Ages, such as the compass; this meant that there was no possibility of ascertaining the position of the ship on cloudy nights. The saying of the Roman poet Horace that "he who dares to cross the sea must have a heart bound in brass" sums up the whole ancient attitude towards navigation. The illustration, from a Roman relief of the third century, shows a series of ships being tossed by a storm, a predicament which the ancient mariner tried to avoid as far as possible. The ship on which St. Paul travelled must have been fairly large, as it had 276 passengers and crew, but it was wrecked nevertheless.

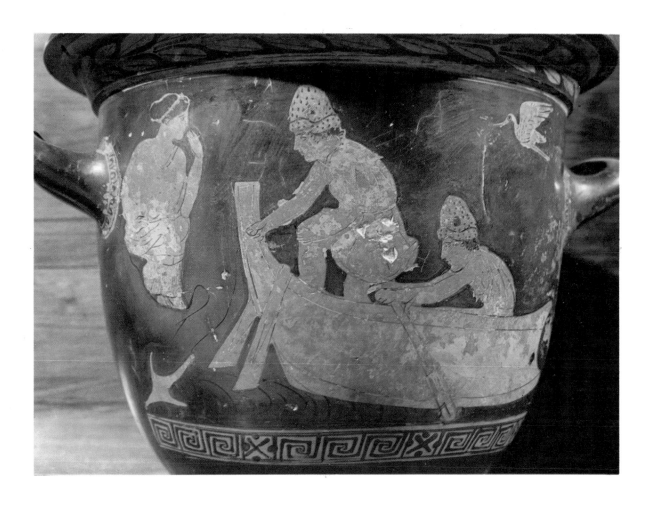

THEN fearing lest they should have fallen upon rocks, they cast four anchors out of the
stern, and wished for the day.   (Acts 27 : 29)

Since ancient ships were at the mercy of wind and waves, some means had to be devised to keep them steady when
not moving; this was the task of the anchor. Originally any heavy object, in particular a heavy stone, served
for this purpose; it was attached to a rope and flung into the sea. Soon, however, it was found that the most
effective form of anchor was an iron bar, with a curved cross-piece at the end. The curved ends caught on to the
sea-bottom, but still allowed the whole anchor to be drawn up when necessary. The illustration (taken from a
Greek vase of the fourth cent. B.C.) shows a mariner casting out an anchor while standing on the stern of a
ship, between the two big rudders by which it was steered. The anchor already has a modern shape; the addition
of a hooked end to the curved part was a later invention, dating from the first cent. B.C. In Roman times the
anchors, made of cast-iron, did not differ in shape from the modern ones. After a long period of cloudy weather
had prevented any taking of bearings (v. 20) and St. Paul's ship had been tossed for fourteen days on the Adriatic
sea, land was seen near it. In order to avoid being dashed on the rocks, soundings were made with a plumb line,
the first cast showing twenty *orgyas* (a Greek measure of depth, equivalent to the outstretched arms, and estimated
at 24 palms or 6 feet, the length of an English fathom). The next sounding was only fifteen fathoms. As the bottom
of the sea was apparently rising rapidly, it was more prudent to cast anchor and try to ride out the storm than
risk being dashed upon the rocky shore.

A ND when they were escaped, then they knew that the island was called Melita. And the barbarous people shewed us no little kindness . . .

(Acts 28 : 1-2)

After a long period of drifting before a south-easterly tempest (see p. 198), St. Paul's ship was finally wrecked on the island of Melita (now Malta). Everyone on board was saved, although the ship itself was a total loss (vv. 41-44). The traditional place where the passengers came ashore is the so-called St. Paul's creek (see view above). Malta is the largest of five islands at the eastern end of the strait between Sicily and Tunis. It has been inhabited since prehistoric times, but the first settlers of whom we have historical information were the Phoenicians of Carthage. Their Semitic language, a dialect of Phoenician, is still spoken on the island and was also written in ancient times. Evidence of the mixed culture of ancient Melita, which became part of the Roman empire after the Punic Wars, is provided by the bilingual inscription on the base of a dedicatory obelisk found there (see illustration). The upper part is in the Phoenician script; the lower three lines are in Greek and contain a dedication by two Tyrians to Heracles (Melkarth), the national god of Tyre. The "barbaric" character of the people of Melita refers to their language and culture, which were non-Hellenic and therefore barbaric in the eyes of civilized people of St. Paul's time, but by no means to their manners, which are attested here to have been surprisingly kind.

AND after three months we departed in a ship of Alexandria, which had wintered in the isle, whose sign was Castor and Pollux.

(Acts 28 : 11)

In Melita the travellers found another wheat-ship, also from Alexandria, which was luckier than their own vessel — or perhaps had a more prudent captain —and which had remained in harbour there, awaiting the passing of the winter season. Its captain no doubt judged it better to deliver his cargo at a later date than to risk its total loss at sea. After three months, he ventured to sail out and completed his voyage successfully. Like most of the vessels of ancient times, this one was dedicated to some god (cf. the "Isis Geminiana" of p. 197), in this case to Castor and Pollux, the two "Children of Zeus" (Dioskuroi) by Leda, and the brothers of Helen of Troy. The two youths, whose emblem was a high cap with a star above it (see the reproduction, right of a relief found at Sebaste-Samaria) were popular among the Romans, as they were supposed to have saved the state at a time of grave national danger. They were also the protectors of mariners; hence the naming of the ship after them was peculiarly appropriate. No doubt the images of the Twins were engraved on its poop, as was usual with ancient ships. We can see such images on the ship on a relief (above) found at Rome. It represents the unloading of one ship and the arrival of another at Ostia, the harbour of Rome. The second ship is sailing into the port past a light-house. Images of the gods (Isis at the upper left, Good Fortune in the centre, Dionysius at the upper right, Neptune the ruler of the seas in the lower centre) show the close connection between ancient maritime activities and religion.

ᴀɴᴅ we came the next day to Puteoli . . . they came to meet us as far as Appii forum, and The three taverns . . . And when we came to Rome, the centurion delivered the prisoners to the captain of the guard . . .

(Acts 28 : 13, 15, 16)

The travels of St. Paul ended safely at Puteoli (modern Pozzuoli), the harbour of Rome, north of modern Naples. The mouth of the Tiber, the river of Rome, was hardly navigable in the early days of the empire, and only after long labours in the reigns of Claudius and Trajan was it made ready to receive ships; at the time of St. Paul's voyage the harbour of Ostia was still under construction. The landscape reproduced above (from a Pompeian painting) is presumed to show the port of Puteoli, with its moles and shipping. From Puteoli the party travelled to Rome by the Appian way (see view in the middle), the "Queen of the Roman Roads". The first part of this highway, from Rome to Capua, was built as early as the fourth cent. B.C. by the censor Appius Claudius the Blind; later on it was prolonged to Brindisium. It also served the Romans as a cemetery, both its sides being lined with funerary monuments. The hamlet of Apii Forum was 40 miles from Rome, about one third of the whole distance from Puteoli. In Rome, St. Paul was delivered to the "captain of the guard", probably some officer of the Praetorian Guard (see relief at right) which had, since Augustus, been entrusted with the protection of Rome and the emperor. Originally scattered all over Italy, they were concentrated in Rome by Tiberius and thus became a political power which could soon make and unmake emperors. The praetorian soldiers were distinguished from the ordinary legionary of the line by better pay and a splendid uniform.

EPISTLES

PAUL, a servant of JESUS CHRIST, called to be an apostle, separated unto the gospel of God. (Rom. 1 : 1)

The Gospels, giving an account of the life, teaching and death of Jesus, are followed by the Acts of the Apostles, which continue the story of the early days of Christianity till the arrival of St. Paul at Rome. The Acts are followed by the Epistles, twenty-one in number, ten or perhaps thirteen of which were written by St. Paul. The series opens with the epistle to the Romans, setting out the doctrine of God's wrath against unrighteousness, the wrongs done by both Jews and Gentiles, the Christian doctrine of salvation, and an exhortation to a life of righteousness, the performance of civil and social duties, charity and unity. Though placed first in the list of St. Paul's letters, Romans is by no means the first chronologically; the New Testament arrangement of them is roughly in descending order of length. Romans is unique in the Pauline canon in that it was written to a church neither founded nor yet visited by the Apostle, probably from Corinth in about A.D. 56. The illustration is taken from a codex of the Pauline epistles of the third century A.D., fragments of which were found in 1930; it shows Romans 8 : 15-25.

I AM debtor both to the Greeks, and to the Barbarians ...   (Rom. 1 : 14)

The apostle includes here within the scope of his teaching the two groups then constituting the civilized world. The term "Greeks" as used in this context is not confined to the Greek or Hellenic nation, which evolved the Greek culture and then spread it across the world in the Hellenistic period, till it was adopted by Rome. One of the factors which aided this spread of Hellenism was the absence of any racial or religious discrimination in the Hellenistic world; a man was measured only by the degree of his adoption of Hellenic culture (see p. 89). St. Paul himself was to a great extent an inheritor of the Greek tradition, as were most of the Jews living in the Diaspora. The growth of Christianity was already helped by the uniform culture, including language and literature, thus created by the Hellenistic world. At the same time, many peoples of antiquity — and above all the Jews — became increasingly conscious of their own traditions as opposed to those of Hellenism; although classed as "barbarians" (originally meaning "people of uncouth tongue", as opposed to the mellifluous Greek), they were no less important for the spread of Christianity. As a Hellenized Jew, St. Paul declares himself a debtor to both types of culture then prevalent.

Reproduced, on the left, is a typical Greek from the Mausoleum of Halicarnassos, 4th cent. B.C.; and, on the right, the bronze head of a Cyrenian barbarian, fashioned by a Greek artist in the first century A.D.

AN instructor of the foolish,
a teacher of babes . . .
(Rom. 2 : 20)

In the complex world of Hellenistic culture, a man's education counted more than any other factor in his social standing. It was therefore extremely important to go to the right teachers from the beginning. The rich could engage a special slave, called a pedagogue (lit. "leader of children") to take care of the education of their offspring. Such a teacher is portrayed on the Greek vase of the fifth century B.C., reproduced above. He is an oldish, balding man, with a thick beard; the laurel wreath on his brow indicates his dedication to Apollo, the god of poetry. His stick is leant against his chair. He is holding his left hand behind his back, while instructing his (invisible) pupils with his right, in which he is holding a stylus (writing stick). It is quite likely that St. Paul is here referring to a Jewish teacher of "babes" or small children; for in the days of the Hasmonaeans, Rabbi Simon ben Shetah had decreed universal instruction in reading and writing, and illiteracy thereafter became rare among the Jews. After completing their elementary education, more advanced pupils were entrusted to the schooling of a teacher of rhetoric (which then included literature and the art of expressing oneself in writing and speech). The illustration below, taken from a tomb relief of the third cent. A.D. found in Germany, shows a teacher (bearded, seated on the cathedra — see p. 63) in the centre, with a seated student holding a roll on either side of him. A third student is just seen arriving on the right.

BEING justified freely by his grace through the redemption that is in CHRIST JESUS. (Rom. 3 : 24)

The original meaning of the Greek word translated "redemption" in this verse (*apolytrosis*) is the emancipation of a slave. Although the institution of slavery is recognised both in the Old and New Testaments, as it was in the whole of the ancient world, yet all ancient religions as well as systems of law conceded that, just as a free man could become enslaved, so a slave could regain his freedom. Jewish law did not allow the enslavement of a Hebrew to continue beyond the sabbatical year (Ex. 21 : 2-6). In Greek religion the setting free of a slave was a pious act, as is shown by the many inscriptions at Delphi commemorating such emancipations. Roman law too admitted the freeing of a slave, either by payment of a sum of money or by the last will and testament of his master. Certain ceremonies had to be performed to make the freeing of a slave valid; they are portrayed on the relief shown in the illustration from the first century A.D., in which two slaves are being freed. One of them, already a free man, shakes the hand of his former owner; the other is kneeling to be touched by the magistrate's rod (*vindicta*) as a sign of his manumission. Both are wearing the high cap called *pileus*, the cap worn by freemen.

FOR the scripture saith unto Pharaoh, Even for this same purpose have I raised thee up, that I might show my power in thee ... (Rom. 9 : 17)

The great miracle at the beginning of the history of Israel, the Exodus, and in particular the passage of the Red Sea and the destruction of Pharaoh and his host, has left an indelible impression on the consciousness of the Jewish people down the ages. It is referred to again and again in the prophetic and poetical literature of the Old Testament (Neh. 9 : 11; Ps. 135 : 9; Ps. 136 : 15 etc.) and occupies a prominent position in the frescoes of the synagogue of Dura Europus. As an outstanding example of the salvation effected by God's grace it figures in the prayers, both Jewish and Christian, which list this kind of miracle. As such it is also represented in early Christian art. The example shown here is a mosaic panel in the church of Santa Maria Maggiore in Rome, now attributed to the time of Pope Sixtus III (432-440), but based on earlier Jewish representations originating in Judaeo-Greek circles at Alexandria. The scene depicts, on the right, the "City of Egypt", with Pharaoh's forces issuing from it and precipitating themselves into the Red Sea. On the left Moses, with his miraculous rod, is parting the waters, with the Israelites behind him. Pharaoh, represented as an old man with white beard and hair, is drowning in the sea, still clad in the purple of royalty and with his shield held high, as if to protect himself from the wrath of Heaven.

HATH not the potter power over the clay, of the same lump to make one vessel unto honour and another unto dishonour?   (Rom. 9 : 21)

The craft of pottery is one of the oldest of the manual occupations of mankind; it reaches back at least to the Neolithic period. The ancients regarded the making of a vessel as an act of creation not unlike that by which God created the world, and regarded the helplessness and absolute dependence of the clay in the hand of the potter as a figure of the relation between the Almighty and His creatures. We find this type of simile in the utterances of the prophet Isaiah (Isa. 29 : 16) and the prophet of the deliverance (Isa. 45 : 9; 64 : 8), as well as in the sayings of Jeremiah (18 : 6 — see Vol. III, p. 114 for ancient representations of the potter). Here St. Paul employs the same simile to illustrate his teaching of the election of some to Divine grace and the rejection of others, just as the potter determines the various uses to which his vessels shall be put. The illustration, from an ancient relief of the Roman period, shows a potter working on his wheel and attaching a handle to a vessel. The wheel used then was of the same shape and construction as those of the earlier period; but the clay was usually much better prepared and the ovens heated to a higher temperature, thus ensuring the production of finer vessels.

AND if some of the branches be broken off, and thou, being a wild olive tree, wert graffed in among them, and with them partakest of the root and fatness of the olive tree.   (Rom. 11 : 17)

The simile here employed by St. Paul is somewhat remarkable in being contrary to the usual practice of tree-grafting. The general rule is that a branch of a cultivated variety of tree is grafted on to a robust, wild variety, thus improving the latter's fruit. The city-born and city-bred St. Paul was not, it is true, as conversant as Jesus had been with the ways of the cultivator of the soil; but even so, he would hardly have made such a mistake as that attributed to him here, and have presumed that a wild olive was grafted on to a cultivated one. We must, on the contrary, assume that he used this exceptional case deliberately, in order to stress the uniqueness of the event he was discussing, namely the mystery of the rejection of the new religion by the people of God, the elected nation of Israel. The illustration shows some of the olive trees recently transplanted in Jerusalem, with grafts beginning to put forth small and as yet insignificant leaves.

F<small>OR</small> it has pleased them of Macedonia and Achaia to make a certain contribution for the poor saints which are at Jerusalem.
(Rom. 15 : 26)

Both the early Christian and the Jewish faiths centered on a group of people living in the Holy Land, but too poor to support themselves. It was therefore regarded as the duty of their co-religionists living in the Dispersion (Diaspora) to supply their needs, as befitted those believers who lived in comparative affluence, but in alien lands on a lower spiritual level than the focal area of their faith. With the rejection of the Jewish Law, Christianity in fact detached itself from the belief in the exclusive holiness of the country where it had originated. Yet enough of the old sentiment still remained for St. Paul to arrange for the needs of the Jerusalem Christian community, which in his time was small and living in hostile surroundings. Collections for the "saints" in Jerusalem, are referred to here and in 1 Cor. 16 : 1, where they are called *logia*. Exactly the same term is used in the ostracon shown below and dated to the 4th August, A.D. 63. In it a certain Psenamunis, the son of Pekysis, acknowledges the receipt of 4 drachmae, 1 obolus, as a contribution *(logia)* to the worship of Isis, the Egyptian goddess. It will be seen from this example that the type of collection mentioned in this verse was a common practice in antiquity.

PAUL, called to be an apostle of JESUS CHRIST through the will of God, and Sosthenes our brother, Unto the church of God which is at Corinth . . .　　　(1 Cor. 1 : 1-2)

The prominence of Corinth as a commercial centre and capital of the province of Achaia, and the comparatively long time that St. Paul laboured in the city (see p. 181), gave the Christian community established there a special importance. In the course of his missionary activity, St. Paul wrote no less than four letters to the Corinthians, two of which have been included in the canon of the New Testament; when difficulties arose in this community he addressed to it some of his most important pronouncements. The first letter to the Corinthians was apparently written in A.D. 54 from Ephesus, where St. Paul stayed for several years (see p. 183). This letter deals, first, with the divisions in the church at Corinth, leading to rivalry among the various parties and to an attempt to undermine his own prestige; with problems of sex, morality and marriage (especially pertinent in a city of light morals, as was Corinth in antiquity); with matters of contact with heathen society; and especially with the Apostle's well known views as "to the more excellent way" and the resurrection from the dead.

The photograph above shows the site of modern Corinth, with the Gulf of Corinth in the background and the mountains of Central Greece rising beyond it.

215

The main doctrine of Christianity, that the Son of God appeared in history as the man Jesus Christ, suffered death on the cross and thereby became the means of the salvation of mankind, was unacceptable to the two great groups with which it came into conflict. To the Jews such claims were indeed "a stumbling-block" (St. Paul's term). The Gentiles, it is true, were more used to the concept of incarnation, through contact with mystery religions, and the idea of gods appearing on earth. But their deities were triumphant gods; the idea of God suffering the ignominious death of a convicted felon must have seemed utter nonsense to the pagan mind. Statements to that effect are not lacking in the pagan polemics against Christianity, as far as they have been preserved in the writing of the Church Fathers. A graphic illustration of the hatred and contempt sometimes evoked by the Christian faith was found in 1856 in one of the guardrooms of the Palatine in Rome, the site of the imperial palace. It is a crude graffitto scratched on the wall in the first half of the third century A.D. and shows a man kneeling to a crucified figure with an ass's head; the inscription states that there is "Alexamenos worshipping his god". The allusion to Christianity is evident; similar calumnies regarding the worship of an ass had already been uttered by the enemies of the Jews in the Hellenistic period.

Y ET not the wisdom of this world, nor of the princes of this world, that come to nought.

(1 Cor. 2 : 6)

In the time of St. Paul, humanity was quite clearly divided into the governing and the governed. With the subjugation of the whole Mediterranean world by the Romans, most of the peoples of this area lost control of their destinies. Even in Rome itself, the common people had, after the establishment of the empire, no more say in the ruling of the world nominally ruled by them; politics were now a matter for the Roman aristocracy which governed in the name of an all-powerful emperor. The "princes" (lit. *archontes* — "rulers") of the world were the governors and commanders appointed by him. Although the Epistles here advocate the acceptance of their authority (see p. 245), St. Paul was nevertheless well aware of the transient nature of their power as compared with the eternity envisaged in his religious teaching. The illustration above shows what was probably the central group of those ruling the world at this time — a procession of senators and members of the imperial family on their way to do sacrifice. It was found on the frieze of the *Ara Pacis* ("Altar of Peace") erected by Augustus in Rome on his triumphal return after the pacification of Gaul and Spain, in 13 B.C. It gives a clear idea of the haughty, yet public-spirited, character of this ruling aristocracy of St. Paul's time.

ACCORDING to the grace of God which is given unto me, as a wise master-builder, I have laid the foundation, and another buildeth thereon . . .   (1 Cor. 3 : 10)

As a citizen of "no mean city" (see p. 189) and a great traveller all over the eastern part of the Roman Empire, St. Paul was familiar with the immense building activity which was going on throughout the Roman world in the first decades of the empire. As soon as the civil wars which had troubled Rome in the first century B.C. ended with the establishment of the rule of Augustus (see p. 104), increasing prosperity in Rome and the provinces led to a wave of constructional works. Augustus himself boasted that he had found Rome a city of brick and had left it a city of marble; and building on a similar scale went on everywhere in his time. In his simile St. Paul compares himself to a wise master-builder who laid the foundations of an edifice, while others completed the walls. With the increase of building activity the actual work of construction naturally became specialized and was divided among various contractors and workmen, one laying the foundations, another erecting the wall, a third adding the ornament. The illustration shows the building of the walls of Rome; it was found on a relief in the Roman forum, dating to the first century A.D.

W HAT will ye? shall I come unto you with a rod . . .   (1 Cor. 4 : 21)

The use of the rod to enforce judgments, and in general to uphold the authority of magistrates and courts, was common in antiquity. The Mosaic Law had on several occasions (e.g. Deut. 25 : 3) prescribed the use of stripes; and St. Paul himself (2 Cor. 11 : 24) had undergone the punishment thus prescribed. The Roman magistrates also relied on the use of the rod to punish anyone who opposed their authority; indeed the rods carried by the lictors were the symbol of their power (see the illustration, a relief from the time of the Early Empire, found at Portogruaro near Venice). The lictors, who were usually freedmen, carried bundles of rods, called *fasces*. In Rome, where the magistrate's power of sentencing to death was limited by the right of appeal to the people, they carried the rods only (as on the relief shown here); but in the provinces where the governors wielded absolute power of life and death, they had axes attached to the fasces. The number of lictors varied in accordance with the rank of the magistrate: praetors had six, consuls twelve and the emperor twenty-four. They walked in solemn procession in front of the magistrate, whenever he went about his official duties. In this verse St. Paul offers the Corinthians the alternative of being treated by him as an apostle or as a Roman magistrate.

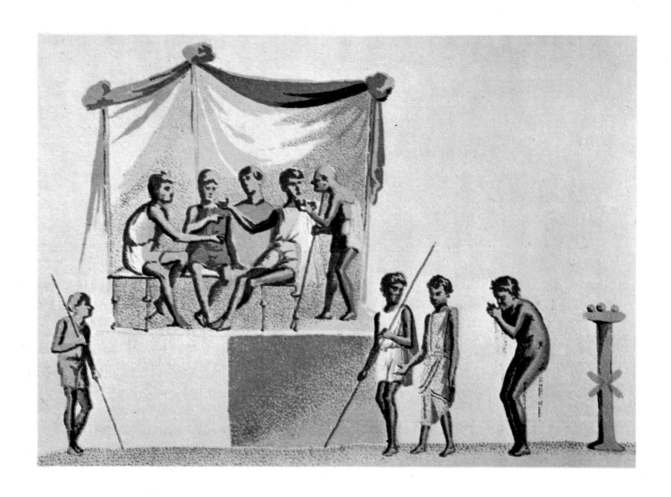

DARE any of you, having a matter against another, go to
law before the unjust, and not before the saints?

(1 Cor. 6 : 1)

Although the standard of justice in the Roman courts had improved under the empire in comparison with the
unsettled times of the late republic, the various religious communities, such as the Jews, nevertheless preferred
to settle disputes between their own members before their own tribunals, instead of having recourse to the
Roman authorities. Only in the case of outsiders or outcasts, such as St. Paul appeared to be in the eyes of the
leaders of the organized Jewish communities in the Diaspora, did their opponents appeal to the Romans or the
city rulers (see pp. 176 and 182). How a Roman tribunal functioned we can see from the illustration above
which is a detail from a fresco found in the dyers' quarter (the *Fullonica*) in Pompeii. The whole fresco depicts
a festivity of the dyers' guild, followed by disputes which end in a fight. Those accused of disturbing the public
peace are brought before the magistrate who is represented sitting on his tribunal in informal dress (he is wearing
a tunic and not a toga) and flanked by his assessors (see p. 253). Witnesses are brought before him, while the
court-usher hands in two more of the disputants, one of whom is bleeding freely.

M EATS for the belly, and the belly for meats . . .   (1 Cor. 6 : 13)

The fundamental materialism of the Roman mind found its most grotesque expression in the prosperous times of the Early Empire in a spread of gluttony unparalleled in history before or since. Latin literature abounds in descriptions of the gargantuan and ingeniously devised repasts eaten by wealthy Romans, from Lucullus, whose name became proverbial, to the emperor Vitellius, whose bloated countenance and many chins betray the nature of his favourite vice. A typical Roman meal, and a relatively simple one at that, is represented on the border of a mosaic found at Antioch and reproduced here. It dates to the third century A.D. The meal begins with eggs (hence the Roman saying "*ab ovo*" — lit. "from the egg", meaning from the beginning) and continues from right to left by way of a course of fish, ham and poultry, to its conclusion in the shape of a rich cake. Multiplied tenfold this would serve to give an idea of the récherché gastronomical titillations indulged in by many of the highest circles of the Gentile world, from which St. Paul draws his warning simile.

L ET every man have his own wife, and let every woman have her own husband.

(1 Cor. 7 : 2)

In this verse St. Paul is proclaiming the Christian doctrine of marriage as opposed to the laxer morality of the pagan world, a subject on which the Roman satirical poets furnish us with only too much information. Yet there is as much contrary evidence to show that among the Greeks and Romans, especially in the middle and lower classes, conjugal ties were much respected and the standard of morality was high. The main proof of this is supplied by gravestones, with their inscriptions in which husbands or wives praise the virtues of the departed spouse. One such example is reproduced above; it is the tombstone, found at Rome, of one Aurelius Hermia, a butcher from the Viminal hill, and his wife Aurelia Philemation. The husband and wife are represented in the centre clasping hands affectionately. The accompanying inscription serves to emphasize the union of their spirits; in it the husband praises the virtues of his wife "the chaste, modest, faithful to her husband", while the wife speaks highly of her "loving husband and fellow-freedman, who was more than a father to her". Such examples could be multiplied to show that all was not rotten in the Roman world in the first century A.D.

F<small>OR</small> though there be that are called gods, whether in heaven or in earth, (as there be gods many and lords many)... (1 Cor. 8 : 5)

In ancient religions the boundaries between gods and men were not drawn as strictly as in the monotheistic faiths which superseded them. Gods descended from Olympus and mixed with men; great heroes were taken up to heaven and worshipped after their deaths as gods. If Heracles, who was a benefactor of humanity, became a god, why not Alexander the Great, whose deeds were at least as magnificent? The Hellenistic kings profited from this belief and established cults of themselves as "gods manifest" (*epiphanoi*); the cases of Antiochus IV of Syria and of the Ptolemies, kings of Egypt, are especially well documented. Such deification of a living Greek ruler was supposed to have a great effect on his Oriental subjects who were used to regarding their dynasts as gods. The Roman emperors were usually deified only after their deaths, following the example of Julius Caesar; and Augustus discouraged worship of himself, if unaccompanied by that of the goddess Roma (see p. 292). Gaius Caligula, on the other hand, firmly believed himself a god and acted accordingly; and even his more reasonable successor, Claudius, was worshipped in his lifetime in the provinces. St. Paul was therefore alluding to a well-known practice of the Gentile world when he mentioned the gods in heaven and on earth. The illustrations show, for comparison, a representation of Jupiter, the principal deity of the Roman pantheon, on a Pompeian painting, with his sceptre and the eagle at his feet, and a statue of the emperor Claudius as a god, with the same attributes.

223

Wнo goeth a warfare any time at his own charges? who planteth a vineyard, and eateth not of the fruit thereof? or who feedeth a flock, and eateth not of the milk of the flock?

(1 Cor. 9 : 7)

Although the examples quoted in this verse refer to the limitations imposed on the Hebrew rulers in calling up the people for military service (Deut. 20 : 5-8), the underlying realities are those of the period in which St. Paul lived. Those familiar with Roman military and economic activities could easily supply the background of these similes for themselves. There was continuous warfare of some sort on one or another of the imperial frontiers; while agriculture (or rather viticulture, in the example chosen) and the rearing of flocks were common pursuits within those borders. The illustrations show two of the three occupations mentioned in the verse. In the relief above, the emperor Trajan (98-117) is seen starting for the Second Dacian War. The relief is part of the decoration of the column dedicated to this emperor at Rome. It shows the emperor standing in his ship and setting sail from a harbour, with a lantern shining in front of him and citizens holding lighted torches on the left above. The other relief, also found at Rome, shows the peaceful life of farmers and shepherds; a shepherd is milking the flock, while another above is cutting down a tree to make a hut. These idyllic scenes form a sharp contrast with the martial scene above them.

KNOW ye not that they which run in a race run all, but one receiveth the prize? . . .
Now they do it to obtain a corruptible crown; but we an incorruptible. I therefore so run,
not as uncertainly; so fight I, not as one that beateth the air.   (1 Cor. 9 : 24–26)

St. Paul, although of Jewish origin and learned in the Law, was nevertheless a Roman citizen and a member
of a wealthy family living in a Hellenistic city. He was therefore thoroughly familiar with the Greek way of life
in which athletics played a most important part. Contests of skill in chariot-riding, racing on foot (see lower
picture) or on a horse, hurling the spear and the discus, wrestling and boxing, were held in all Greek cities and in
those cities of the Orient which had adopted Greek culture. Naturally, therefore, the apostle uses metaphors
drawn from the world of athletics to illustrate his case when addressing the Corinthians. He here refers to the
foot race and to the crowns obtained by those victorious in the contests. The illustration on the left illustrates part
of the tombstone, found at Athens, of one Nikokles the son of Aristokles, a Greek of the Roman period. No less
than sixteen crowns are represented on the whole monument, standing for as many victories in athletic contests,
including the Great Panathenaic, the Games at Delphi, the Isthmian Games at Corinth, besides many others.
"Beating the air" refers to the sport of boxing, which is illustrated above from another vase of the fifth century
B.C. Two men are seen boxing in the centre, with onlookers standing by to assist the boxers and to judge the
contest (upper picture on right).

AND did all drink the same spiritual drink . . .   (1 Cor. 10 : 4)

The miracle at Rephidim (as related in Exodus 17 : 1-7 and again in Numbers 20 : 7-13), when Moses smote the rock and water came out of it, made a profound impression on succeeding generations; it is referred to again in Deut. 8 : 15 as "water brought out of the flinty rock" (cf. Vol. I, p. 263) and in the poetic and prophetic literature of the Old Testament. The symbolic interpretation of the event here adopted by St. Paul has remained one of the basic tenets of the Christian church. Hence we find Moses' smiting of the rock represented in the catacomb paintings more than any other scene from the Old Testament. In the example chosen for illustration above, we see Moses as a bearded figure striking the rock in front of him with his staff. Water is gushing from the rock and an Israelite is bending down to drink from the spring which appears in such a miraculous way in the desert. This scene is combined with another to the left: there we see Moses loosing his sandals, as ordered by God who is represented by a hand issuing from a cloud above. The painting was discovered in the Catacomb of St. Callixtus at Rome and is now assigned to the fourth century A.D.

As some of them also tempted, and were destroyed of serpents.

(1 Cor. 10 : 9)

In alluding to the people who tempted God and were destroyed by serpents, St. Paul is of course referring to the plague of serpents which punished the Israelites in the desert, as told in Numbers 21 : 5-9 (cf. Vol. I, p. 221). There was also a similar event in Greco-Roman mythology, represented in the famous work of art illustrated above. Laocoon, a Trojan priest, incurred the wrath of Apollo who sent serpents to destroy the sinner and his two sons. This story was the subject of a Late Hellenistic sculptured group (ca. 50 B.C.) which was later set up in Nero's palace on the Esquiline where it was discovered in 1506, profoundly influencing the art of the Renaissance. The artist represented the father in the centre of the group struggling with the two serpents; the younger son on the left has already perished, while the elder on the right tries to free himself from the reptiles' coils. The choice of the psychological moment of agony and despair, and the technical excellence of the execution render this sculpture one of the most striking and characteristic examples of the emotional art of the period. The disaster which befell Laocoon was also interpreted symbolically as an evil augury of the coming fall of Troy. As St. Paul was in Rome when this sculpture was about to be set up in Nero's Palace, he might well have seen it.

EVERY man praying or prophesying, having his head covered, dishonoureth his head. But every woman that prayeth or prophesieth with her head uncovered dishonoureth her head; for that is even all one as if she were shaven.

(1 Cor. 11 : 4-5)

The apostle intends to make the ritual practices of the Christians as different as possible from those of both the Jews and the Gentiles. Thus, it was a common Jewish custom, and one shared with many of the oriental nations, to keep one's head covered as a sign of respect and reverence. As, of course, the greatest reverence was due to God, He had to be worshipped with the head covered. In the same way the Romans, who normally went about bare-headed, used to draw a fold of their voluminous mantle, the toga, over their head when praying or sacrificing. The statuette reproduced on the left, which dates to the early empire, shows a Roman performing a libation; he has lifted his right hand towards heaven and has his head covered (cf. also the procession of senators on the *Ara Pacis*, p. 217, where the principal personages have their heads covered). Women in the Greek world, on the contrary, sacrificed with their heads uncovered (see on the right the drawing of a fresco found on the Aventine hill at Rome). In demanding that women keep their heads covered while praying, St. Paul conforms with Jewish usage, in which the uncovering of the head of a married woman was regarded as improper in the highest degree; but for men to pray bare-headed was an innovation.

WHEN I was a child, I spoke as a child, I understood as a child, I thought as a child; but when I became a man, I put away childish things. For now we see through a glass, darkly . . .

(1 Cor. 13 : 11-12)

Classical Greek art followed an idealizing tendency which did not regard the immature as a fit subject for artistic representation; hence, if we wish to learn about the games played by Greek children, we have to turn to the material provided by the craftsmen who painted the Attic vases, or to the Hellenistic period in which interest in children awoke. The example chosen here to illustrate the words of the apostle is taken from a Late Roman sarcophagus (see above) which was certainly the coffin of some child. As usual, the deceased is represented in his happiness in the other world, following his avocations during life. In this relief, a group of boys and girls is shown playing various children's games. The next verse contains an allusion to the mirrors used by the ancients. The word translated "glass" *(eisoptron)* refers to the common bronze mirrors, which could be polished till they imperfectly reflected the features of those looking into them (see, left, the reproduction of such a bronze mirror in its unpolished state); no clear image could be obtained in mirrors till as late as the 14th century A.D. when glass backed with tinfoil began to be used.

AND even things without life, giving sound, whether pipe or harp, except they give a distinction in the sounds, how shall it be known what is piped or harped? For if the trumpet give an uncertain sound, who shall prepare himself to the battle?

(1 Cor. 14 : 7-8)

The two verses above (together with 1 Cor. 13 : 1) list the most common musical instruments known in antiquity (cf. also Vol. IV, pp. 62-63). They are here illustrated from three monuments. Above is a Pompeian mosaic, probably the copy of an Alexandrian painting. It depicts a street scene with strolling players. On the left a woman is playing the double pipe; in the centre an actor is dancing, accompanying himself with cymbals held in his hands (for a reference to the "tinkling cymbal" see 1 Cor. 13 : 1). The third actor is beating a hand-drum. All three figures are masked. The illustration on p. 231 (left), reproducing a wall painting from a Roman villa of the first century A.D., shows a woman harpist holding her instrument and conversing with another woman holding a drum. In contrast to these instruments, which were much played in civilian life, the use of the trumpet was reserved for fighting. The Roman army employed several kinds of trumpet, some straight and some curved, and similar instruments were used in the gladiatorial contests. In the relief reproduced, right, we see fighting gladiators, and opposite them a group of trumpeters blowing their long, straight trumpets, the *salpinx* mentioned in the Greek original of our verse.

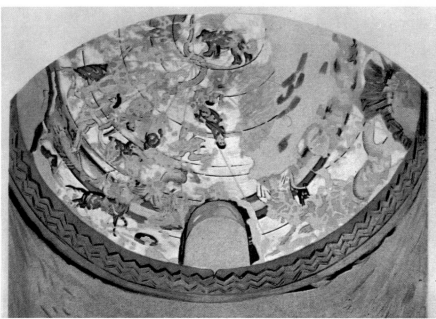

THERE are also celestial bodies and bodies terrestrial: but the glory of the celestial is one and the glory of the terrestrial is another.   (1 Cor. 15 : 40)

Although both the Jewish and Christian religions rejected the astrological conception of the universe which was most common in the later centuries of antiquity (and which was officially adopted by the then prevailing Stoic philosophy), the conception of "celestial" and "terrestrial" bodies originating in it was nevertheless used in common parlance. The belief that the movement of the stars in heaven influenced the fate of men on earth has also left some traces in the Bible, as in the Song of Deborah (Judg. 5 : 20 — "the stars in their courses fought against Sisera"). It did not end with the end of the ancient world; horoscopes are found in later periods too, both in the Christian and in the Islamic world. The example shown here is a fresco from the Umaiyyad desert castle of Quseir ʿAmra, in the wilderness beyond the Jordan, dating to the eighth century A.D. It shows the various constellations seen in the heavens at a certain date, and is painted on a dome in the palace which served as a hunting-lodge for the caliphs and was equipped with dining-rooms, a bath and other amenities.

W RITTEN not with ink,
but with the Spirit of the living
God; not in tables of stone, but
in fleshy tables of the heart.

(2 Cor. 3 : 3)

St. Paul contrasts the witness of the spirit with the various kinds of material record common in his time. Any kind of record for temporary use was made with a sharp pointed instrument on a tablet covered with wax; but this method of writing is not mentioned here. Writing of a more permanent character was done on papyrus or parchment with reed or bronze pens which had split nibs rather like their modern counterparts. The ink was kept in metal or faience ink-pots, with narrow openings or with covers to prevent the ink from spilling (see illustration on the right). Still more permanent in character was monumental writing on stone or bronze tablets. The ancients used to chisel out the dedications of both religious and civil buildings, as well as treaties, laws, and funerary inscriptions on monuments, on stone or metal tablets; as the metal tablets have mostly perished the writing on stone supplies the bulk of epigraphical information preserved. The specimen given here is a fragment of the Temple inscription (see p. 188 for the whole text) found at Jerusalem, which forbade Gentiles to pass beyond a certain point in the Temple Court. It is a fairly good example of this kind of writing, with the guiding lines and the paint inside the letters still visible. When in Jerusalem, the apostle must have glanced at this inscription or at one of its copies.

As the serpent beguiled Eve . . .   (2 Cor. 11 : 3)

One of the fundamental tenets of the Christian religion is the belief that the Original Sin caused by Adam and Eve's fall in Paradise was redeemed by the sacrificial death of Jesus on the cross. We therefore find references to the Fall both in apostolic literature (as here and in Rom. 5 : 12-21; 1 Cor. 15 : 22, 45) and in early Christian art. These artistic representations of Adam, Eve and the serpent are probably derived from a cycle of pictures illustrating the biblical story which was evolved in the Hellenized Jewish circles at Alexandria, and has been preserved to some extent in the frescoes of the synagogue at Dura-Europus, the catacomb paintings, and illuminated Bible manuscripts. Adam and Eve are usually shown on either side of the tree, with the serpent winding round the trunk. The whole composition recalls the scenes illustrating the myth of the Argonauts, with Jason and Medea and the dragon serving as counterparts of Adam and Eve and the serpent. Another motif influencing this representation is the serpent guarding the golden apples of the Hesperides. Reproduced here is a fresco from the catacomb at Naples.

IN Damascus the governor under Aretas the king kept
the city of the Damascenes with a garrison, desirous to
apprehend me.   (2 Cor. 11 : 32)

St. Paul here gives a rather different version of the circumstances of his escape from Damascus from that in Acts
9 : 23-25 (see pp. 165-6). Instead of attributing his danger to the Jews, as stated by the author of the Acts, the
apostle mentions that it was the governor of Damascus under king Aretas who tried to have him arrested. The
Aretas referred to can, chronologically, only have been Harithath the Fourth, king of the Nabataeans, called
Aretas in Greek; he ruled from 9 B.C. to A.D. 40. The Nabataeans were a people of Arab origin, who in the
Persian period occupied Edom and the Negeb, developed the trade routes and agriculture around Petra, their capital,
and in the arid areas under their control, as well as an art of no mean quality (see Vol. III, pp. 246-7). They main-
tained themselves as vassals of Rome till A.D. 106, when they were subjected by Trajan and their country turned
into a province named Arabia. While the dynasty lasted, it extended its sway over the desert east of the Jordan,
and occasionally also ruled Damascus (once from 85-66 B.C. and again in the days of Caligula). It is to this
latter period of their rule that St. Paul refers here. The interruption in the series of coins of the city of Damascus
during this time (ca. A.D. 37-40) attests that the city was then not autonomous. The illustrations show a coin
of Aretas with his portrait, on the left; and, on the right, an inscription in Nabataean found at Eboda ('Avdat) in
the Negeb, bearing the names of Harithath and other Nabataean princes.

WHEREFORE take unto you the whole armour of God, that ye may be able to withstand in the evil day, and having done all, to stand. Stand therefore, having your loins girt about with truth, and having on the breastplate of righteousness; And your feet shod with the preparation of the gospel of peace. Above all, taking the shield of faith, wherewith ye shall be able to quench all the fiery darts of the wicked. And take the helmet of salvation, and the sword of the Spirit, which is the word of God.   (Eph. 6 : 13-17)

The whole passage in verses 13-17 is based on reminiscences of Isaiah 59 : 17; but, naturally, in describing the "armour of God" St. Paul had before his eyes the type of defensive and offensive weapons which were common in the Greco-Roman world. The defensive part of the armour consisted of a helmet to protect the head, a breastplate to protect the chest (with a belt to keep it in place and to hold the sword), greaves to protect the legs, and a shield to ward off the blows of the enemy's sword and spear, and the darts from his bow (v. 16). The low penetrating power of ancient offensive weapons, which — except for the dreaded bow — depended on muscular power alone, made the use of armour worth while, even though it slowed down the movement of the soldier. In the period of the Roman empire the weight of the armour was gradually reduced till the revival of the armoured cavalry in the third century. In the illustration, taken from a vase painting by the Attic artist Duris (ca. 490 B.C.), we see Odysseus handing over to Neoptolemos the arms of his father Achilles. Although the vase is much earlier than St. Paul's epistle, the essential aspect of armour had not changed and we can see the various parts referred to in the above verses: the helmet, breastplate — made of metal scales — the shield, and the spear. (For a sword see p. 278).

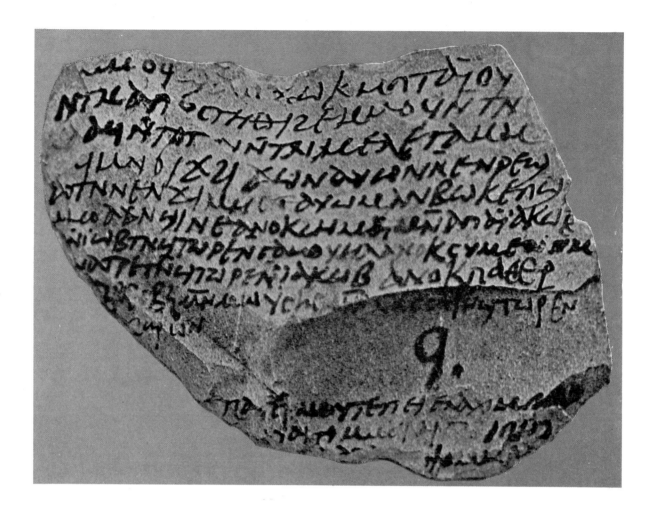

PAUL and Timotheus, the servants of JESUS CHRIST, to all the saints in CHRIST JESUS which are at Philippi, with the bishops and deacons. (Phil. 1 : 1)

The early Christian Church, like all similar organizations, required the appointment of officials who could take charge of the common property of its members and administer it for the benefit of those entitled to help (Acts 6 : 1-6). These administrators were called *diakonoi* "servants"; their spiritual and moral qualifications are laid down in 1 Tim. 3 : 8. The "bishops" (Greek *episkopoi*, lit. "overseers") were appointed in the larger communities (Acts 20 : 17, 28) and were entrusted with the care of the faithful, like shepherds watching over their flocks. In the early days of Christianity the number of such overseers in one community was not limited to one, as in later times; at Philippi and at Ephesus there were several of them. An organization, however, was not contemplated at the outset, but developed gradually as the need for supervision of gatherings, regulation of conduct and a system of charitable relief required it. Women were not disqualified by their sex. All were expected to qualify for office by blamelessness of conduct and holiness of character. Office clearly meant service, and further implied prior discipline. The ostracon shown above, written in Egypt, ca. 600 A.D., sets forth the relations between bishops and deacons many centuries after St. Paul addressed the two groups in his letter to the Philippians. By then, it shows, candidates for the office of deacon pledged themselves to the organizational disciplines of the period.

ALL the saints salute you, chiefly they that are of Caesar's household.
(Phil. 4 : 22)

SALVIVS CAESAR
SER
SVPRA ARGENT

Roman aristocratic households comprised hundreds of slaves, some of whom laboured in the personal service of their master and others on his estates. In several cases slaves were even allowed to set up in a trade or craft, paying part of their profits to their owner. The imperial household was, from the time of Augustus to that of Trajan, organized on the aristocratic Roman model, but on a vastly larger scale. It contained thousands of slaves, some of whom, especially those who succeeded in obtaining their freedom, rose to the summit of political power. They in fact constituted the civil service of the early empire and, as such, wielded almost absolute powers in the emperor's name. In such a numerous community, many of whom came from Greece and the Orient, Christianity early found a foothold, especially because of its appeal to those of lowly social status (see also the next page). The Alexamenos whose devotion to Jesus was ridiculed in a caricature (p. 216) was also a member of the imperial household. Reproduced here is the bust of Salvius, a servant of the emperor Tiberius, who was in charge of the silver plate *(Salvius Caesari servus supra argentum)*; it was found in the Second Columbarium (cemetery) of the Vigna Codini on the Appian Way, near Rome.

WHERE there is neither Greek nor Jew, circumcision nor uncircumcision, Barbarian, Scythian, bond nor free ...

(Col. 3 : 11)

The human appeal of Christianity, as taught by St. Paul, lay in its complete disregard of the social hierarchy of the early Roman empire. To the various communities of national or religious origin, each regarding the others with suspicion and occasionally with contempt, the apostle stresses their unity in the new faith. Greeks, who regarded the rest of the world as barbarians (see also pp. 201, 208), Jews, who drew a difference between those who had entered the covenant of Abraham and all others, barbarians who suffered from inferiority of status because of their lack of Greek culture, and even the uncouth Scythians, the most savage of barbarians — all could equally hope for redemption. So could even the slaves, who had lost their freedom in this world, but would participate in the salvation of Paradise. The manual tasks performed by slave labour are illustrated by a Roman relief, showing the placing of blocks on a sumptuous funeral monument in the shape of a temple (on the right); the work is carried out with the aid of a machine consisting of a high mast, with ropes attached to it by pulleys, the motive force being supplied by a treadmill (lower left) worked by the exertions of slaves. The relief comes from the tomb of the Haterii at Rome, from the first cent. A.D.

FOR I bear him record, that he hath a great zeal for you, and them that are in Laodicea, and them in Hierapolis. Luke, the beloved physician, and Demas, greet you.   (Col. 4 : 13-14)

At the end of his epistle to the Colossians, the inhabitants of a city in the upper part of the Lycus Valley in the province of Asia, St. Paul conveys the greetings of one of his disciples, Epaphras, a native of the city, and adds an appreciation of his zeal for the Christian communities at Colossae and the neighbouring cities of Laodicea and Hierapolis. The former was situated about twelve miles west of Colossae, and was probably founded by Antiochus II Theos (261-246 B.C.) and named in honour of his wife Laodice. It had a famous temple of the Phrygian god Men, with a medical school attached. It was also a centre of the wool trade and of banking. Hierapolis, now called Tambuk Kalessi, was situated north-west of Laodicea, between the Lycus and the Meander; it was famous for its hot springs which were used for baths, and for its temple of the goddess Kybele. It had a long main street (see view above) with colonnades on either side, and a gymnasium, temples and theatres. It is first mentioned c. 190 B.C. and was a flourishing city till an earthquake in A.D. 60. Luke the physician, mentioned here, is generally identified with the Evangelist and the companion of St. Paul on his voyages. The profession of physician was highly esteemed in the Greek and Roman world; some of its practitioners, especially the physicians of the emperor, were able to do great services to their native towns and were honoured by them (p. 130). The illustration below is a reproduction of a Roman relief, the tombstone of a physician named Jason, who is seen auscultating a patient.

P AUL, and Silvanus, and Timotheus, unto the church
of the Thessalonians . . .   (1 Thess. 1 : 1)

Two of St. Paul's epistles are addressed to the community of Thessalonica (modern Saloniki), the great city on
the coast of Macedonia. Originally called Thermae, after the hot springs in its vicinity, it was renamed in 315 B.C.
by Cassander after his wife Thessalonike, the sister of Alexander the Great. The city prospered owing to its
position at the junction of the Egnatian way, the principal line of communications across the Balkans, and the
northwards route to the Danube, and also because of its magnificent harbour. Under the Romans it was the
capital of the Second province of Macedonia, and a free city from 42 B.C. onwards. In the time of St. Paul there
was a Jewish community there with its own synagogue (Acts 17 : 1-13). The church at Thessalonica was founded
by St. Paul on his second missionary journey. On being forced to leave the city, the apostle wrote from Athens,
after having received a report from Timothy as to the state of the community. The main doctrinal points of the
letter treat of the imminent return of Christ; the second epistle is presumably a later reiteration. The illustration is a
view of the city and its harbour on the Thermaic Gulf as it was called in antiquity, now the Gulf of Saloniki.
The view is taken from the heights surrounding the city and forming its principal line of defence.

T HEREFORE let us not sleep, as
do others; but let us watch and be
sober.   (1 Thess. 5 : 6)

Among the exhortations with which St. Paul concludes his epistle to the Thessalonians is one to the
faithful to watch vigilantly for the second coming of
Jesus, the time of which was uncertain though the
event itself was sure and would probably occur with
dramatic suddenness. In the following verse (8) the
faithful are adjured to put on "the breastplate of faith
and for an helmet the hope of salvation". These military metaphors (for which compare p. 235 and Ephesians
6 : 14), as well as the exhortation to "keep watch and
be sober", make it probable that the apostle here
intended a comparison with the splendid discipline
of the Roman army, with which he must have
become familiar on his travels and in the course of
his perils. It was owing to this unquestioning obed-
ience to orders that the Romans were able to make
good their defeats and to take full advantage of their
victories. The vigilant alertness referred to is illustrated by the bronze statuette, about 9 in. high (on
the right) of a Roman soldier in full armour. It shows
the legionary with a crested helmet on his head, and a
cuirass made of overlapping bands of metal which
are fastened down in front, with a kilt of leather or
metal strips underneath. He is also wearing trousers
and shoes. The spear, sword and shield which completed the Roman soldier's equipment are missing
here.

F OR we hear that there are some which walk among you disorderly,
working not at all, but are busybodies.   (2 Thess. 3 : 11)

In referring to the "busybodies" who shun all work, the apostle most likely had in mind the parasite, a common
figure in ancient Greek and especially Roman society. The term originally meant anyone "feeding with" *(para-
sitos)* someone else, such as the assistants of an official who helped him to collect taxes in kind; then those dining
at the public expense; and, finally, anyone who succeeded in worming himself into the good graces of the rich
and feeding at their tables. Such types were the standing butts of ancient satire. Their eternal hunger and their
readiness to undergo any humiliation for the sake of food are in particular an inexhaustible source of jokes in
Greek and Roman comedy. As the ancient actors appeared in masks, which indicated the type of person they
were supposed to represent, the audience could at once distinguish the parasite. One such representation, from
a Pompeian fresco, is shown here. We see, on the left, the paunchy and ever hungry parasite conversing with a
courtesan and her servant and making a sign to avert the evil eye. All of the three are common characters in the
comedy of manners, which was the standard type of entertainment in Hellenistic and early Roman times in the
Greek world and thus quite familiar to an educated person like St. Paul.

THE salutation of Paul with mine own hand, which is the token in every epistle . . .   (2 Thess. 3 : 17)

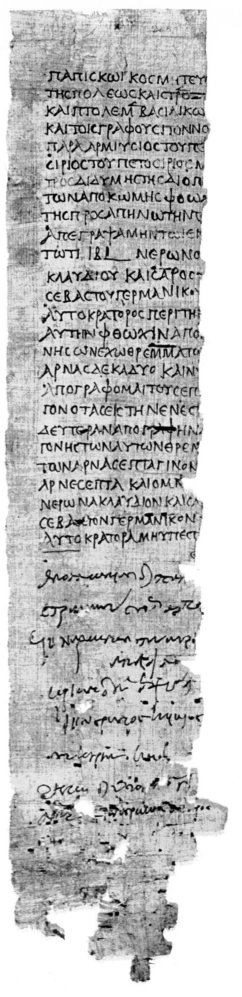

The art of writing, and especially of writing legibly, was much rarer in antiquity than to-day; therefore, anyone who could do so employed trained scribes to whom he dictated his letters. This was also the practice of St. Paul who, in another letter (Gal. 6 : 11), refers to the large letters written in his own hand. In order to assure the recipient that the letter was authentic, the sender usually added a note in his own hand, such as the word "Greeting", the date and the like. St. Paul authenticates his letters by adding a "salutation in his own hand", as did most of the letter writers whose letters have been preserved on papyrus. As an example of a letter indited in two hands we reproduce here a letter written on the 24th of August A.D. 66, on behalf of the peasant Harmyisis, to Papiscus, governor of Oxyrhynchos. It is written in a clerkly hand, with additions in another cursive script.

NEITHER give heed to fables and endless genealogies . . .
(1 Tim. 1 : 4)

In his warning against false doctrine the writer refers to the "fables and endless genealogies" of the pagans. After a period in which Greek myths evolved spontaneously and freely, they were systematized by scholars and linked together by a genealogy of the gods, in which they were arranged in generations and related to each other by supposed family ties. Another prolific source of fables and genealogies was the desire of every Hellenized city — and for this purpose Rome could also be counted as one — to be connected in one way or another with a Greek god or hero as its founder. In Rome especially an elaborate line of descent was fabricated, and apparently also believed in. The founders of Rome, Romulus and Remus, were described as the sons of the god Mars and the Vestal Rhea Silvia; exposed in the Tiber, they were given suck by a she-wolf, till they were discovered by shepherds and brought up among them. The illustration shows this legend as represented on an altar found at Ostia: the she-wolf and the twins are seen below, protected by an eagle; the shepherds with their characteristic crooks are visible above them, while the god of the River Tiber watches over the twins in the lower right corner of the relief. The altar is dated by an inscription to 124 A.D.

PRAYERS... be made for
all men ... for kings and for
all that are in authority ...
(1 Tim. 2 : 1-2)

The request made here to pray "for kings and all that are in authority" is the more astonishing if we remember that, at the time of the composition of this letter, A.D. 63-67, the Roman world was governed by Lucius Domitius Ahenobarbus, the son of Agrippina (the daughter of Germanicus and later on the second wife of Claudius the emperor) and C. Domitius Ahenobarbus, a Roman noble. After his adoption by the emperor Claudius, the young man was named Nero Claudius Drusus Germanicus Caesar; he ascended the throne in A.D. 54. After a period of five years during which his ministers governed well for him, Nero began a career of tyranny and debauch which rendered his name a byword. He removed the members of his family one by one and terrorized the aristocracy. His artistic aspirations to shine as poet and singer rendered him odious in the eyes of the serious-minded Romans. After the great fire in Rome, in 64 A.D., during which he appeared as a vocal artist commemorating the Fall of Troy, he directed popular suspicion away from himself as the arsonist and persecuted the Christians; St. Paul seems to have lost his life in this persecution. Finally, the armies in the provinces rose against the deranged emperor, and he perished in 68 by his own hand. Nevertheless, it was this worst emperor of the great apostle's lifetime that is singled out as one to be prayed for. Reproduced above is one of the many portraits of Nero, made at Rome.

245

I WILL therefore that men pray every where, lifting up holy hands, without wrath and doubting. In like manner also, that women adorn themselves in modest apparel, with shame-facedness and sobriety . . .

(1 Tim. 2 : 8-9)

The raising up of the hands to heaven was the common attitude of prayer in the East, as contrasted with the covering of the head and folding of the arms in the Roman form of supplication (see p. 228). In the paintings of the catacombs we find many representations of the early Christians praying with lifted hands. The reproduction above is a painting in the catacomb of St. Callixtus at Rome. In this scene we see a woman, dressed in long robes, with her head veiled, and without jewels or other ornaments such as are roundly condemned by the apostle in other epistles (see p. 259). The woman, on the left, is wearing the long tunic or *stola,* which was the principal female garment among the Romans; the tunic has long sleeves and is adorned solely by two broad stripes of colour. Over it she has in addition a mantle, the *palla,* of a darker colour. Her head is modestly veiled. On the right is a youth clad in a tunic, also lifting up his hands in prayer. Many similar representations have been found in other catacombs, indicating that the teaching of the apostle bore fruit among the Christians of Rome. It should, of course, be remembered that the early adherents of Christianity were of the lower and middle classes, always more sober in their apparel than the aristocracy.

THE husbandman that laboureth must be first partaker of the fruits.   (2 Tim. 2 : 6)

Agriculture was the basic occupation of man in antiquity, even more than in modern times; for, without scientific methods of production and in the absence of any source of power beyond that supplied by man and beast, the amount of food produced was usually barely sufficient to keep the population alive. Another factor which made cultivation of the soil imperative in every suitable spot was the difficulty experienced in transporting large quantities of produce from one country to another; the wheat trade of Egypt with Italy was an exception (see pp. 197, 202). The feeding of the large cities, and above all of the capital, Rome, with its huge and unproductive population, presented an especially serious problem. For, since the Punic wars with their attendant ruin of the independent peasantry, the great Roman nobles had bought up the small cultivators and created huge estates *(latifundia)* which served mainly for the luxuries and pleasures of their owners. In his simile here, the apostle stresses the importance of the farmers and their right to their produce, a right endangered by the taxes and dues exacted by the landlord. The illustration shows a farmer of Italy, Titus Paconius Caledus, the son of Titus, supervising the bringing in of the harvest. He is standing on the right with a book of accounts in his hand, watching his servants bring in the produce of his farm.

BUT in a great house there are not only vessels of gold and of silver, but also of wood and of earth . . .   (2 Tim. 2 : 20)

In listing the materials of which the vessels found in the great houses of antiquity were made, the apostle states facts amply confirmed by modern archaeological discoveries. The finest vessels were of gold and silver; not many of these have survived, because the precious metals were naturally the first objects to be stolen and melted down. But, even so, there has been a series of finds of treasures of gold and silver ware. The illustration shows a vase from the famous find made at Hildesheim in Northern Germany. It consisted of the complete table service of a Roman noble — 74 pieces in all. The treasure was probably booty taken by the Germans from the Romans in the first century A.D. and buried in the earth. The costliness and variety of the objects (one of which, a mixing krater, ornamented in relief with plants and animals, is reproduced on the right) vividly illustrates the verse above. Pottery vessels were, of course, much more common; they formed the staple household ware and their sherds are found in great quantities on every ancient site. The example shown right, is a spindle-shaped bottle, typical of the Herodian period, the time of Jesus and St. Paul. Wooden vessels have only rarely been preserved in the Holy Land; they are much more numerous in Egypt with its drier climate. The example shown here on the left is a small wooden box, found in one of the caves near the Dead Sea which served in the second cent. A.D. as places of refuge for Jews hiding from the Romans.

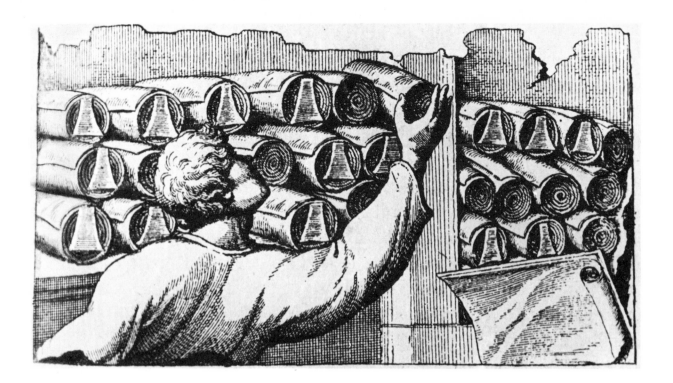

THE cloke that I left at Troas with Carpus, when thou comest, bring with thee, and the books, but especially the parchments.

(2 Tim. 4 : 13)

Even if St. Paul could be demonstrated not to be the author of 1 and 2 Timothy as they have come down to us the passage 2 Tim. 4 : 9-21 is regarded as a genuine Pauline fragment. The cloak left by him at Troas is called *phelone,* a rare word which is generally assumed to be a corruption of *phainole,* corresponding to the Latin *paenula.* This was a mantle made of coarse wool, usually with a hood attached, which was the normal dress of the common people in the Roman empire, and especially of travellers (see the illustration below taken from a Pompeian design, showing a traveller settling his accounts with an inn-keeper). An apostle, whose life was spent in journeying from one place to another, was especially in need of such a warm and comfortable garment to protect him from the vicissitudes of the road. Of still greater importance to St. Paul, however, were the books, and especially the parchments, that he had left behind. The books *(biblia)* were rolls of papyrus, the usual material for ancient books; they were kept rolled together, each with an identifying tag, as we can see in the illustration above, which is a reproduction of a relief showing a librarian looking for a roll. The parchments (in Greek *membrana*) were thin skins of animals (mostly sheep or goats) prepared for writing. As they were more durable than papyrus, they were used for more important writings, and were usually bound together in the form of a book (not a roll), the so-called *codex.* The parchments which St. Paul was so anxious to receive were perhaps sacred texts, most useful in missionary work.

E XHORT servants to be obedient unto
their own masters . . .   (Titus 2 : 9)

As we have already seen, the social message of early Christianity was not revolutionary; it stressed the relative unimportance of social divisions between Greeks and barbarians, slaves and free men (see p. 208), as compared to the importance of eternal salvation through faith. Kings and those in authority are to be prayed for (p. 245), although they are but lords and masters of this world. In the same way the institution of slavery is not condemned, but a mitigation of its initial harshness is sought. Slaves are to obey their master. This was not always an easy command to follow, and sometimes the slave took matters into his own hands and became a fugitive. Formerly the runaway slave, when caught, had been cruelly punished by being branded. In Christian times this brutal branding was replaced by a badge, like the one illustrated here on the left. It reads "I have escaped, hold me, if you return me to my master (follows a name) you shall receive a *solidus* (gold coin)". The badge is a round piece of metal, 2¾ in. in diameter, provided with a hole for a string by which it was attached to the neck of the runaway.

NOX(II
ΛΜΙΙΙ ΟΛΤΕΓΙΙΛΙΙΛΤΟΛ
ΤΠΙΛ· ΙΙΕΓ' ΙΛΥΙΙ
ΠCΟ
ΓΙΥΙ
IT IS
ΓΟΛΙS
ΛΙΧΙΛΖΙS

To speak evil of no man, to be no
brawlers . . . (Titus 3 : 2)

The lower classes of Roman society, with their lack of any intellectual interests, naturally tended to various types of gross enjoyment and pastimes requiring no mental effort. Such inclinations were easily satisfied by frequenting the numerous taverns with their facilities for drinking and gambling. The writer on many occasions warns the members of the communities he has founded to abstain from this type of life, with its attendant moral dangers. A vivid illustration of the brawling which was the almost inevitable accompaniment of visits to such low haunts is provided by the illustration on p. 250, left, and above, reproduced from a Pompeian painting. It shows two scenes of gambling and its consequences. In the first picture on the left the two gamblers begin to quarrel about the results of a throw; in the second they start fighting and insulting each other in the grossest terms, while the terrified landlord begs them to "Go, quarrel outside". The artist has not given us a third picture showing the end of the quarrel, but it can easily be imagined (see p. 220). The second scene is now defaced, but a design, made while it was entire, gives an idea of how it looked originally.

The emerging Christian communities, small in numbers, despised by the masses, occasionally persecuted by the Roman authorities, and in constant conflict with the local Jewish synagogue, were naturally not over-anxious to advertise their existence. Their places of worship were therefore mostly located in the interior of private houses which, if built in the prevailing Mediterranean style, with the rooms grouped round a courtyard and enclosed on all sides, could not easily be looked into by an unfriendly eye. There was such a church in the house of Philemon of Colossae, a man of standing and the owner of a slave Onesimus; the latter is here returned to his master with a message from St. Paul. We can form an idea of the external aspect of such a domestic church from another of the same kind uncovered in the excavations of Dura-Europus on the River Euphrates, and dating to the third cent. A.D. (see plan above). This church was indistinguishable from a private house; it was entered from the street by way of a colonnaded court and consisted of a chapel, with walls covered by wall-paintings (reproduced above), a big room for the love-meal *(agape)* of the community, and an assembly hall, made by joining together two separate rooms, with a seat for the head of the community, probably a bishop. In the first centuries of the Christian era most Christian worship, even in times of relative quiet, must have taken place in such domestic churches.

SAT down on the right
hand of the Majesty . . .
(Heb. 1 : 3)

In placing Jesus "on the right hand of majesty" the author of the Epistle to the Hebrews evidently had before his
eyes the public appearance of the Roman emperor or a high magistrate. It was the general Roman usage for all
officials of the republic, not excepting the emperor, to have assessors who sat with them during the judicial
proceedings and advised them on the verdict to be pronounced, although legally only the magistrate himself
was responsible for the decision, his advisers being there merely in a consultative capacity. Nevertheless, the
advice of learned jurists given to an emperor unlearned in the law must have been fairly decisive; in the later
empire the right to be consulted was granted to eminent lawyers even when not in attendance on the emperor.
Reproduced here is a representation of the emperor in council from the Arch of Constantine ar Rome. (As we
know, the head of the emperor was changed when the reliefs were taken down from their original setting and
placed in their present position). The original reliefs seem to have depicted Marcus Aurelius seated on the magistrate's curule chair and surrounded by his assessors; he is shown distributing some sort of favours to the populace
assembled at the foot of his tribunal.

THOU art a priest for ever after the order of Melchisedec. (Heb. 5 : 6)

Melchisedec is mentioned in Genesis 14 : 18 as "king of Salem and priest of God most high" (See Vol. I, p. 50).
He received Abraham with bread and wine after the victory over the allied kings, Chedorlaomer and others,
and received a tithe of the booty. The Canaanite king-priest, whose dynasty continued to reign in Jerusalem at
least till the time of the Israelite conquest (cf. Josh. 10 : 1, 26) was transformed later on into the prototype of
a priestly ruler of superior order; the kings of the Davidic dynasty were assured in Psalm 110 : 4: "The Lord
has sworn and will not repent: Thou art a priest for ever after the order of Melchisedec".
In the epistle to the Hebrews (chapters 5-7) the argument is taken further. In attempting to show that Jesus
had superseded the Jewish high priest, the author first argues that there was a priesthood in the order of Melchisedec parallel with, but superior to, that descended from Aaron. For as Abraham paid tithe to Melchisedec, he
admitted his superiority; and as Levi and his descendants the priests were as yet unborn, they were represented
by their ancestor Abraham in admitting this superiority. The name and title of Melchisedec, interpreted as "king
of righteousness" and "King of Salem, which is king of peace", were in the eyes of the author attributable to
Jesus.
The meeting of Abraham and Melchisedec is represented in a sixth-century illuminated manuscript of Genesis
(the so-called "Genesis of Vienna"). Abraham approaches on the left, his hands covered,to accept the wine and
bread; Melchisedec comes towards him from the right. He is dressed in the raiment of the Byzantine emperor,
with diadem, purple mantle and red shoes; he carries a loaf and a jug. Behind Melchisedec is a symbolic representation of the Temple.

A MINISTER of the sanctuary, and of the true tabernacle, which the LORD pitched, and not man.

(Heb. 8 : 2)

Following his general line of reasoning, the author of the Epistle to the Hebrews describes Jesus as the minister of the true tabernacle, set up by the Lord, as opposed to the Tabernacle which accompanied the Israelites on their wandering through the desert and was the work of man, although prepared by divine command (see Vol. I, p. 160). The Tabernacle, which was later transferred to Shiloh and superseded by the Temple of Solomon, was throughout the ages revered by the Jews as the visible symbol of the pristine purity of their faith in the desert wanderings. One of the earliest representations of the Tabernacle in its wanderings is to be found on the frieze of the Capernaum synagogue (see p. 112), probably from the late second cent. A.D. This object was for a long time misunderstood; some scholars considered it to represent a wagon, or the carriage which was a prerogative of the Jewish Patriarch in Roman times. However, since the discovery of the synagogue frescoes of Dura Europus it has become clear that the relief represents the Tabernacle during its wanderings in the desert. It has here, as at Dura, the shape of a temple mounted on wheels, and corresponds to the carriages shaped like sanctuaries in which the Romans transported the images of their gods from one place to another.

T<small>HEY</small> were stoned, they were sawn asunder, were tempted, were slain with the sword . . . (Heb. 11 : 37)

The author of the Epistle to the Hebrews seems to refer here to the legendary death of the Prophet Isaiah. According to this legend, which has been preserved both in Jewish midrashic literature and in a Greek apocryphal work called "The Ascension of Isaiah", the prophet was put to death on the orders of the idolatrous king Manasseh of Judah, the unworthy successor of the pious Hezekiah whom Isaiah served as counsellor. Isaiah is said to have been put between two halves of a tree trunk and sawn asunder. A Coptic painting (reproduced above) found in the necropolis of Bagawat, in the oasis of el-Khargeh (Egypt), shows the prophet in a sitting position with two executioners, one on either side, sawing at him. A Greek inscription "Isaiah" over his head identifies the subject. The painting dates to the fifth century A.D.

BEHOLD, we put bits in the horses' mouths, that they may obey us; and we turn about their whole body. Behold also the ships, which though they be so great, and are driven of fierce winds, yet are they turned about with a very small helm, whithersoever the governor listeth.

(Jas. 3 : 3-4)

In order to illustrate his thesis of the dangers inherent in the wrong use of such a small organ of the human body as the tongue, the author has recourse to two comparisons. The first is with the bit put in the horse's mouth, a small piece of metal which nevertheless governs the movement of the large animal. Bits have been found in excavations from the time of the Hyksos invasion of Palestine and Egypt; the invaders, whose strength lay in their chariots, had learnt to tame the horse and control it by the use of bits. The example reproduced below shows a bit found at Pompeii. Similar to the bit is the ship's helm (see illustration above). In antiquity ships were generally small (see p. 197) and, instead of the elaborate rudder-mechanism used in modern vessels, they were steered by oars of larger than usual size; two such oars were passed through the stern, and the desired direction was given to the vessel by moving them to the right or left. Reproduced above is a ship on a Late Roman sarcophagus with the steering oars clearly visible.

Yᴇ have heard of the patience of Job . . .   (Jas. 5 : 11)

The book of Job, one of the most profound as well as one of the most poetical books of the Bible, must have recommended itself to the early Christians as an example of sufferings meekly and patiently borne. In their tribulations they found encouragement in the example of Job's patience and his ultimate reward by God, along with that of the husbandman who patiently awaits his crops; all the greater will be the reward at the coming of the Lord. This reference to Job in the Letter of St. James has undoubtedly led to the inclusion of Job among the representations of the just in the stock themes of early Christian art. The illustration shows the sufferer sitting on the ash-heap (Job 2 : 8) with his wife and a friend standing by to console him. The relief is part of the decoration of the sarcophagus of Junius Bassus, prefect of the city of Rome, who died on the 25th August 359. The coffin can thus be dated exactly. Its façade is divided into two storeys, with columns separating the various scenes, each of which is surmounted by a gable or an arch. The scenes shown include, besides Job, Adam and Eve, the Sacrifice of Isaac, Daniel in the lions' den, and several scenes from the lives of Jesus, St. Peter and St. Paul.

WHOSE adorning let it not be that outward adorning of plaiting the hair, and of wearing of gold, or of putting on of apparel.

(1 Pet. 3 : 3)

Female fashions in Roman society in the first century A.D. entered on a phase of fanciful adornment, in contrast with the simpler fashion of the preceding Augustan era and of the Antonine period which followed. Already in the time of Nero fashionable ladies began to pile up their hair in monstrously high curled coiffures; and in the succeeding Flavian period this fashion reached a pitch of absurdity equalled perhaps only in eighteenth century Europe. Reproduced on the right is a portrait bust, supposed to represent Julia the daughter of the emperor Titus. Her hair is dressed as a veritable tower of locks piled high up over her forehead; such a construction could hardly have been held in position without some inside support, probably furnished by false hair. In view of such a style of hairdressing we can understand how Roman ladies passed hours in the hands of the slaves who prepared their coiffures, a frivolous waste of time strongly condemned by the apostles. The wearing of costly jewelry and of gorgeous raiment, on the other hand, is not bound up with any special fashion; in the Orient it has existed since time immemorial, witness the strictures of the prophets, especially Isaiah (see Vol. III, pp. 22-23) and Amos (Ibid. p. 236). The lady Bithnaia represented in a fresco from Dura-Europus, with her high tiara, abundance of ornaments and purple garment, is but one example of the many that could be given in this connection.

WE have also a more sure word of prophecy; whereunto ye do well that ye take heed, as unto a light that shineth in a dark place, until the day dawn . . .　　　(2 Pet. 1 : 19)

As we have seen in another connection (cf. pp. 31 and 69), the only form of artificial light in ancient times was that provided either by wicks burning in oil, or by candles or torches; in any case the quantity of illumination, even when a large number of lamps were placed together, was very small. The same applies also to the streets; apart from nights on which the moon shone, there was no street-lighting at all. Anyone who ventured out into the night had to carry a lantern, and such a light was highly welcome in a dark place. The example reproduced here was found at Pompeii. The bronze body of the lantern is suspended by chains from a handle; inset into the bronze at the bottom there is a wick which is fed by oil supplied, drop by drop, from a receptacle. The frame of the lamp contained some transparent material which allowed the light of the wick to shine through. The lantern is marked with the name of the maker or owner.

FOR the time past of our life may suffice us to have wrought the will of the Gentiles, when we walked in lasciviousness, lusts, excess of wine, revellings, banquetings, and abominable idolatries.

(1 Pet. 4 : 3)

The pagan religions of antiquity regarded man and nature as fundamentally one; the gods, men, animals, trees, sea and earth were blended in a way which endowed anything in nature with divine approval. The Hellenes, who were the leading devotees of this pantheistic creed, were thus able to rise to the highest peaks of a lofty idealism, but at the same time, especially when influenced by the ancient Oriental mystery religions, they could sink into natural brutishness. Certain religious festivals in particular, combined with banquets, could end in orgies which released man's worst instincts. In marked constrast to this pantheism, both Judaism and Chrisianity adopted a dualistic attitude, sharply distinguishing God from the world or devil, and regarded all forms of sensual indulgence as abominable idolatries to be shunned by all true believers. Two examples of such orgiastic worship are given here: one — on the right — is the sacrifice to the Egyptian goddess Isis as depicted in a Pompeian painting. This Egyptian goddess was enormously popular with the Romans of the first century A.D., and was worshipped in particular by the women. We see, in the middle, an altar with horns, on which incense is smoking; worshippers approach the steps of the temple, while priests with shaven heads play the sistrum and pray on their knees. The second example (on the left) is from the design on an Attic vase of the second half of the fifth century B.C., showing the orgiastic dance of nymphs in honour of the god Dionysus.

L<small>ITTLE</small> children, keep yourselves from idols . . .   (1 John 5 : 21)

St. John concludes his First Epistle, in which he has discussed the relations of God to light, justice and love successively, with a final warning against idolatry, addressing the faithful as "little children". The dangers of idol-worship were naturally greater with children used to following the teaching of their fathers than with adults who could reason for themselves. Quite possibly St. John had in mind the common artistic representations of children worshipping Greek gods, like the one in the procession reproduced above from a fresco found at Rome. One of the favourite subjects of ancient art was the portrayal of children (usually indentified with Cupid or Amor, the child-god of love and son of Venus) practising the various professions or in general behaving like grown-ups; the contrast between the childish figures and the seriousness of their acts was found especially attractive. The painting here in which children are seen worshipping Diana and forming a procession, might well have been executed in the same spirit.

TREES whose fruit withereth, without fruit, twice dead, plucked up by the roots.
(Jude 12)

In its polemics against the teachings and practice of those who had perverted the doctirne of God's forgiveness of sins into an excuse for immoral living, the pseudonymous letter of St. Jude cites Cain (godlessness), Balaam (cupidity) and Korah (disobedience) as prototypes from whose punishment Christians may deduce the certainty of the awesome judgment these present sinners are bringing down upon their heads. They are likened to clouds without water, carried about by winds; trees whose fruit withereth, twice dead; waves of the ocean, full of sound, casting up the foam of shame; wandering stars, fated to burn out into nothingness. A barren tree as a figure of wretchedness was used in Isa. 56 : 3, Jer. 8 : 13, Matt. 3 : 10. In the dry districts of Judaea, especially, a barren tree was a common sight (see illustration above).

REVELATION

I AM Alpha and Omega . . .   (Rev. 1 : 8)

The last book of the New Testament is the Revelation of St. John the Divine; its subject is the Second coming of Christ, the Day of Judgment and the End of the World, to be followed by the New Heaven and New Earth; but before this consummation the wicked are to perish and humanity — save the elect — be decimated by the messengers of divine wrath. The book of Revelation contains a number of symbolical allusions to contemporary politics, the reality of Roman power, the wicked emperor and his predecessors, the danger of invasion from the East, and similar subjects. In the first chapter of the Book, God is symbolically described as the Alpha and Omega, the first and last letters of the Greek alphabet, and hence by implication the first and last of things, as all the secrets of the universe can be expressed by these letters and what comes between them. On account of this verse, the letters Alpha and Omega are usually added to the cross in many works of early Christian art. The example chosen above is taken from the sixth century mosaic in the church of Saint Apollinare in Classe in Ravenna. Drawn on a background of stars in heaven is a golden cross studded with jewels, with the head of Christ in its centre. The letters Alpha and Omega appear to the left and right respectively of the horizontal arms of the cross.

AND being turned, I saw seven golden candlesticks.

(Rev. 1 : 12)

The Revelation begins with a vision connected with the seven principal churches of Asia, symbolized here by seven golden candlesticks. In the period following the destruction of Jerusalem in A.D. 70 the golden candlestick of the Temple (see Vol. I, p. 163) became the recognized symbol of Judaism; here, however, it is still treated as the heavenly symbol of divine light (cf. Zechariah 4). Ancient representations of the candlestick, beginning with that on the Arch of Titus, are very numerous and the type seems to change with the ages. It appears sculptured in relief in Galilean synagogues (but without the predominant position it achieves later on), on Jewish lamps both from Palestine and the Diaspora, on gold glasses (see the illustration above of a gold glass found at Rome), on bone and ivory carvings and on the mosaic pavements of later synagogues, on Jewish coffins, and painted on the walls of Jewish catacombs. On the gold glass above the seven branched candlesticks are accompanied by the full array of Jewish ritual objects: the Ark of the Torah flanked by two lions, and below them the candlesticks accompanied by ram's horns *(shofar),* citrons *(ethrog),* a palm branch *(lulab)* and an oil jar.

THE seven stars are the angels of the seven churches: and the seven candlesticks which thou sawest, are the seven churches.

(Rev. 1 : 20)

The seven churches symbolized by the seven stars, seven angels and seven candlesticks, are listed in detail in the rest of the chapter. They are (see map) those of Ephesus, Smyrna, Pergamos, Thyatira, Sardis, Philadelphia and Laodicea. Some of these cities had been connected with the missionary activity of St. Paul. He himself had been active for a long time in Ephesus, the capital of Asia (see p. 183); his disciple Epaphras had laboured in Laodicea (Col. 4 : 12, 13); and his convert Lydia was a native of Thyatira (Acts 16 : 14). The other churches, mentioned here for the first time, are those of Pergamos (see p. 271), the great trading city of Smyrna, Sardis, the ancient capital of the Lydian kingdom, and Philadelphia, one of the main road-junctions in the Hermus valley. All these were among the most important cities of the Roman province of Asia and, as we learn from this chapter, had Christian communities established in them at an early date; we may also presume that there were Jewish communities in all of them (see also next page).

Roman Roads _____

And unto the angel of the church in Smyrna write . . . (Rev. 2 : 8)

The Smyrna which is mentioned as the second of the seven churches of Asia was the city refounded (near the ruins of an earlier Ionian colony) in the fourth cent. B.C. Its geographical position at the head of a deep bay ensured its commercial prosperity; loyal to Rome, it flourished under imperial rule and vied with Ephesus and Pergamon for the primacy of the province. It was allowed first to erect a Temple to Tiberius, Livia and the Senate and thus obtained the title of "Warden of the Temple". The Jewish community in Smyrna seems to have existed since Hellenistic times; numerous inscriptions attest its importance and wealth into the third century. It seems to have given special trouble to the Christians living in the town, and was singled out for blame at the end of the message here. The photograph shows the present harbour and city of Smyrna, looking north.

AND to the angel of the church in Pergamos write ... I know thy works, and where thou dwellest, even where Satan's seat is ...

(Rev. 2 : 12-13)

Pergamon ("Pergamos" here) rose to greatness as the capital of the royal dynasty of the Attalids (283-133 B.C.) who founded a powerful kingdom in the north-western corner of Asia Minor. The last ruler of the dynasty, Attalus III, bequeathed his kingdom to the Romans, and under them it became the nucleus of the province of Asia; Pergamon remained the capital of the province till the end of the first century B.C., when it was transferred to Ephesus. The Attalids had embellished their capital with splendid palaces, temples and other public buildings. The most famous of their works was the Great Altar of Zeus and Athene, erected by king Eumenes II (197-159 B.C.) in commemoration of Attalid victories over the Gauls. This building (see reconstruction above) stood on a large terrace overlooking the agora of the city. It measured 120 by 112 feet and consisted of a colonnaded court surrounded by walls on three sides, with an altar in its centre (see the reconstruction). Around the outer wall of the court ran the great frieze, 400 feet long and 7 ft. high, depicting the battle of the gods against the giants who attempted to storm Olympus. (The lower illustration shows the three-headed Hekate fighting a serpent-legged giant with a torch). The frieze is one of the most magnificent works of Hellenistic sculpture, and the deep impression it made on even a hostile beholder is still evident from the appellation "Satan's seat" given it here.

A ND will give him a white stone . . .   (Rev. 2 : 17)

The mystic "white stone" enumerated among the other objects passed on to the church of Pergamon is a sign of acquittal. A stone (*psephos* in Greek, also used for mosaic stones) was used for voting by the judges of the Athenian courts (occasionally beans were used instead of stones). To vote with a white stone meant acquittal, while a black stone stood for condemnation. The legendary origin of this custom goes back to the trial of Orestes, the son of Agamemnon king of Mycenae, in the Areopagos (see p. 179), the ancient supreme court of Athens. Orestes had avenged his father by killing Clytemnestra, his mother, and her paramour, Aegistheus. Pursued because of his matricide by the Erinnyes, the goddesses of vengeance, he stood his trial before the Athenian judges. As the votes were evenly divided, Pallas-Athene, who favoured him, threw in a white stone (the *calculus Minervae*) and thus got him acquitted. The illustration above (taken from a Greek vase of the painter Duris, c. 490 B.C.) shows the Greek heroes voting as to who should receive the arms of the dead Achilles; Athena, standing behind the altar on which the stones are placed, decides in favour of Odysseus.

HE that overcometh,
the same shall be clothed
in white raiment ...
                    (Rev. 3 : 5)

White raiment was the hallowed garb of purity among the pagans, as well as among the Christians and Jews.
Thus, the Israelite priests were dressed in white linen (Ex. 28 : 40-42); and white is the colour symbolic of
purification from sins in Isa. 1 : 18. In the Gospels an angel who came to sit by Jesus' tomb (Mark 16 : 5)
is dressed in a long white garment; and elsewhere in Revelation the armies of heaven appear in spotless white
linen, riding on white horses (Rev. 19 : 11, 14). Representations of saints and martyrs in white raiment abound
in early Christian art. The illustration chosen is earlier than most of these: it depicts the priests at Dura Europus
(third cent. A.D.). On this fresco the chief priest and his assistant are both dressed in long white robes and are
wearing a high conical cap of the same colour. In the religious philosophy of Philo personages enveloped in white
light appear endowed with mystic-symbolic significance.

HIM that overcometh will I make a pillar in the temple of my God, and he shall go no more out: and I will write upon him the name of my God, and the name of the city of my God, which is New Jerusalem . . . (Rev. 3 : 12)

In the vision here recorded reference is made to writing upon the pillars of a temple. This custom is borne out by archaeological evidence from many ancient sites. Sometimes statues of prominent persons were placed against the upper part of a column and their names and titles written on the column underneath. At Palmyra, a whole street had been thus decorated; the statues have perished, but the inscriptions have remained. In other places, the name of the person dedicating the column was written on it. This was especially the custom in the Galilean synagogues of the third-fourth centuries A.D. Since the Jewish communities in Galilee had no members rich enough to donate a whole building, every benefactor gave part of the edifice, and his name was written on the part donated by him (see the inscription in memory of a donator on the "cathedra of Moses", p. 63). The illustration chosen here shows a column in the synagogue at Capernaum (see p. 112); it bears a dedication in Greek by Herod, the son of Mokimos, and his descendants. A second column is dedicated in Aramaic. Both prove that the custom of writing on pillars was a wide-spread one.

A<small>ND</small> anoint thine eyes with eyesalve, that thou mayest see.
(Rev. 3 : 18)

Medicine in the Roman empire was not a regulated profession; anyone could practise it, and the better physicians succeeded mainly because of the higher class of client they were able to treat. Usually the physicians prepared their medicines themselves, but for certain special diseases they were provided by pharmacists who had compounded the specific or who had inherited the prescription. Such remedies were peddled throughout the length and breadth of the empire by itinerant vendors and marked with specially prepared stamps. Such stamps have been found in large quantities. They usually bear the name of the manufacturer or inventor, and the name of the malady against which the ointment was supposed to be effective. Oculists' salves occupy a prominent place among them. Reproduced here is one such stamp which marked, amongst other remedies, an eyesalve — obviously of the kind referred to above. Occasionally such remedies actually helped: Galen mentions among his prescriptions one entitled "Eyesalve applied by Florus to Antonia the mother of Drusus, when she was in danger of losing her eyesight through applications of other physicians".

AND I saw in the right hand of him that sat on the throne a book written within and on the backside, sealed with seven seals.

(Rev. 5 : 1)

The sealing of written documents was intended to protect their contents from unauthorized eyes and, at the same time, to authenticate them. Prominent personages, such as emperors, had their own seals executed by engravers skilled enough to make the counterfeiting of the seal most difficult. We know, for example, that the emperor Augustus used to seal his letters with the image of Alexander the Great, specially cut for him by the famous engraver Dioscorides. Multiple sealings were used to safeguard signatures. As an example, one may mention the receipt books of the Pompeian banker, Lucius Caecilius Jucundus (see illustration below). These books consist of six pages, the outer ones (1 and 6) being blank, while 2 and 3 contain the text of the receipt which is sealed on page 4 by a series of seals, with the name of the witness recorded beside each. The figure of the book with the seven seals, which were broken one by one, must have been modelled on some such document, the implication being that the divine judgment against the world written on its pages was to remain a secret, till the time came to break the seals open.

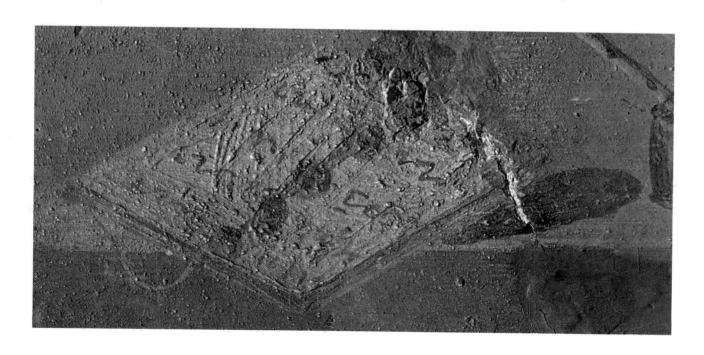

A<small>ND</small> I saw, and behold a white horse: and he that sat on him had a bow; and a crown was given unto him: and he went forth conquering, and to conquer. (Rev. 6 : 2)

The world in which the Book of Revelation was written was that of the Roman empire at the peak of its tremendous and apparently unshakeable power under the early emperors. The vision therefore dwells on the destruction of the nerve-centres of the existing order by the various enemies whom divine omnipotence could raise up against Rome. The first of these are the Parthians, those inveterate enemies first of the Hellenistic kingdoms, and then of the Romans who succeeded Hellenism and managed to save it at least as far as the River Euphrates. The Parthians were the successors of the ancient Persians in their struggles with the Seleucids, whom they gradually drove back from the highlands of Iran and, late in the second century, from Babylonia. In 54 B.C. they defeated a Roman army under the triumvir Crassus at Carrhae in Upper Mesopotamia, and thus saved themselves from Roman domination. Wars between the Romans and the Parthians continued throughout the centuries, with now one power gaining the upper hand, now the other. The peoples subject to Rome and restive under its yoke hoped for the Parthians to put an end to Roman rule. Thus, one of the Jewish sages who was opposed to Rome expressed the opinion that the days of the Messiah would come, if a Persian (Parthian) horse was seen tethered to the monuments of the Holy Land. The paintings at Dura Europus contain many representations of mounted Parthian horsemen (see above); their kings are usually portrayed as conquerors holding a bow, which was the Parthian weapon par excellence. The Parthians excelled especially in shooting from horseback, and could even shoot backwards when galloping in full retreat.

AND there went out
another horse that was red :
and power was given to
him that sat thereon to take
peace from the earth, and
that they should kill one
another : and there was given
unto him a great sword.

(Rev. 6 : 4)

The second rider on a red horse seems to symbolize civil war. If the assumption is correct that the Revelation was written in the time of the emperor Domitian, the author would vividly remember the convulsion which shook the Roman empire when the emperor Nero (see p. 245), by his madness, finally provoked a general uprising against his rule. Within the short span of one year no fewer than four emperors were proclaimed and three of them, Galba, Otho and Vitellius, perished by assassination, suicide or execution. The various provincial armies vied with each other in raising their commanders to the status of emperor, in the hope that their candidate would prevail and that they would enjoy his largesse. In the end Vespasian, the contender chosen by the armies of the East, was victorious and established the Flavian dynasty; but in the civil war of the years 68/69 the insta-bility of the imperial government had been fully exposed and all the enemies of Rome could hope for a repetition of similar events. The rider of the red horse was to cause the Romans "to kill one another"; his great sword was a typical Roman cavalry weapon, the *spatha* (as distinguished from the short Spanish sword of the Roman infantry). Reproduced in the illustration is the tombstone of Titus Flavius Bassus, son of Dansala, a cavalryman of the Norican troop, who died at the age of 46 after 26 years of service. He is seen mounted on his horse and trampling down a fallen enemy. His spear is in his right hand and his long sword hangs at his side.

AㅤND I beheld, and lo, a black horse; and he that sat on him had a pair of balances in his hand. And I heard a voice in the midst of the four beasts say, A measure of wheat for a penny, and three measures of barley for a penny; and see thou hurt not the oil and the wine.

(Rev. 6 : 5-6)

The third rider, on a black horse, stands for a natural disaster — that of famine (cf. Acts 11 : 28) — which is to overwhelm existing society. In the primitive conditions of production, and especially transport, prevailing in antiquity, a drought and failure of crops in one place could only with difficulty be remedied by shipping the produce of another place to the areas affected. The rider is enjoined not to touch the wine and oil, as these are not essential to human life. He is given a balance (called in Greek "a pair", from the pair of scales which, together with the bar and tongue, constituted the normal balance — see the illustration above, one of the balances found at Pompeii). The balance was used for weighing; here, however, it is largely symbolical, because dearth is expressed not in terms of weight, but of measure. The Greeks and Romans employed standard measures, inscribed with the quantity they contained. The example reproduced here was found at Carvoran (England) and belongs to the reign of Domitian, the time when the Revelation was written. It is marked with the date and a line showing a capacity of 16 sextarii — equalling one modius, or "measure". The measure mentioned here is the *choinix*, calculated at 1.08 litres or .98 quarts. One choinix of wheat was sufficient for one day; but as the pay for a day's work was only one denarius (see Matt. 20 : 9) — here translated "penny" — it was outrageous to have to pay a whole day's wage for one measure only. Barley, of course, which was consumed only in time of need and was — except in poor districts — normally reserved for horses or donkeys, was three times as cheap as wheat even in times of famine.

CLOTHED with white robes, and palms in their hands.   (Rev. 7 : 9)

The vision of the blessed stresses the purity of the elect, symbolized by their white robes (see p. 273) and their ultimate victory, symbolized by the palm branches (see also p. 148). Palm branches were, from early times, presented to the victors in Greek athletic contests, together with the crown (see p. 225). They served as a symbol of triumph on the occasion of the Maccabaean conquests, as well as at the triumphal entry of Jesus into Jerusalem. There are many illustrations showing victorious athletes holding palm branches, or judges in a contest standing by with a palm branch to be handed to the victor. In the statue reproduced here a charioteer, the winner of a circus race, is seen holding a palm branch. In the symbolical significance given to the term *agon* (contest) by St. Paul, the struggle of the believer with the world around him was likened to the contest in the palaestra. The victor, i.e. the steadfast martyr, who sealed his faith with his life, received a crown and a palm branch in the other world. Such scenes are frequently represented on catacomb paintings and in church mosaics.

AND another angel came and stood at the altar, having a golden censer... (Rev. 8 : 3)

The burning of incense, i.e. spices which gave off a cloud of fragrant smoke, before the altars of the gods was common to most nations of antiquity. The importance attached to this rite can be gauged from the fact that the raw materials required were quite often imported from remote lands (in particular Southern Arabia), regardless of cost. The Books of Exodus and Leviticus contain long and detailed descriptions of the elements from which incense was to be compounded (see Vol. I, p. 176). The incense placed on the altar — see the reproduction above, from a third century painting found at Dura Europus, representing a sacrifice made by a Roman tribune and his soldiers — was burnt in special containers called censers. These were of two kinds: the closed type which was swung at the end of a chain and has been adopted by the Church; and the open type, apparently the more ancient, which is illustrated here. It consisted of a flat shovel on which glowing coals were heaped (see below). To prevent the heat of the metal burning the hand of the sacrificer, the handle was coated with some heat-resistant material. The incense itself was either held in the hand (see Vol. I, p. 19), or kept piled up in two flat receptacles attached to the two upper corners of the incense-shovel from where it was taken between pinched fingers and thrown upon the coals. Representations of such shovels are common in mosaic synagogue pavements, accompanying the seven-branched candlestick.

AND there was given me a reed like unto a rod: and the angel stood, saying, Rise and measure the temple of God, and the altar, and them that worship therein.　　(Rev. 11 : 1)

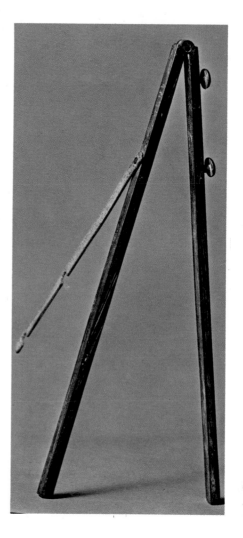

In several prophetic visions in the Old Testament an angel or messenger of God appears with a measuring rod, to mark out the ground-plan of the future Temple (Ezek. 40 : 3; Zech. 2 : 1). The instruments referred to in these books were, in all probability, similar to those which we find represented on Egyptian or Babylonian monuments. However, the measuring rod seen by the author of Revelation in his vision was more probably of the type employed by the Romans, which is illustrated on the right. This rod is made of metal, with a hinge in the middle; its full length is one Roman foot. Of the four faces of the rod, the broad outer one is divided into 16 digits; the large inner face has 8 palms marked on it, four on each side of the hinge; and one of the two narrower faces is divided into 12 unciae. In this way the Roman measuring rod enabled its user to subdivide the foot by 8, 12 and 16, as required. Other similar instruments, made of bone and marked with dots, have also been found.

AND their dead bodies shall lie in the street of the great city . . .   (Rev. 11 : 8)

The dead bodies lying in the "streets" of the great city obviously refer to a disaster which is to overtake the city of Rome. Instead of the usual word for street, the Greek original here reads *plateia,* meaning "broad street". At the time when Revelation was written, the imperial city had begun to be transformed by the building activities of successive emperors. In particular, the area north of the old Roman Forum had been developed by a series of new fora, beginning with that of Julius Caesar in which stood the temple of Venus Genetrix, the legendary ancestress of the Julian family. Then Augustus built another forum with the Temple of Mars the Avenger (of the assassination of Julius Caesar); Vespasian built a third with the temple of Peace; and Nerva added a fourth, small forum. But all these were surpassed by the forum of Trajan, with its large semi-circular wings (see illustration above). The building and town-planning activities which changed the face of imperial Rome justified the title of "the Great City" given it in this verse.

AND I stood upon the sand of the sea, and saw a beast rise up out of the sea, having seven heads and ten horns, and upon his horns ten crowns . . .

(Rev. 13 : 1)

The vision of the beast with many heads and horns, as described here, is clearly related to the similar vision of Daniel (Chap. 7); only here we have to understand the reference to the Roman empire and its vassal states, instead of to the Hellenistic kingdoms. The seven heads are apparently the seven emperors who appear also in chap. 17 (see pp. 290-1); the ten heads wearing ten crowns are most probably the vassal kings of Rome. In general, the Romans tried as far as possible to avoid direct rule, especially in the case of the East with its long-established political institutions. A few dynasties which were too big and powerful to acquiesce in Roman overlordship (such as those of the Antigonids in Macedonia, the Seleucids in Syria and the Ptolemies in Egypt) were deposed; but minor rulers, if sufficiently pliant and in control of peoples inclined to revolt, were left in the possession of their thrones. Only gradually, in the course of the first century A.D., were these vassal kingdoms absorbed one by one. In the time of Augustus, a fringe of such vassal states protected the eastern borders of the Empire. They included the Bosphoran kingdom in the Crimea, Colchis in the Caucasus, the kingdoms of Armenia, Pontus, Cappadocia and Commagene in Asia Minor, Judaea under Herod, Chalcis and the Nabataean kingdom in Syria and Arabia, and Mauretania in Africa. One of the kings of Commagene, Antiochus I (69-34 B.C.), erected a magnificent monument in Nimrud Dagh, with statues and reliefs representing himself and his ancestors. One of these reliefs (reproduced above) portrays this Antiochus, with the god Mithras.

T o receive a mark in their right hand, or in their foreheads. (Rev. 13 : 16)

The seal (Greek *charagma*) is applied to the elect to mark them on their right hand or forhead. The writer alludes to the well known custom of applying such seals — with the name and year of the reigning emperor — to letters of purchase and similar documents. One such seal, dated to the thirty-fifth year of Augustus (A.D. 5-6) and inscribed "In the year 35 of Caesar. The Secretariat", is reproduced here. It is made from soft limestone and is in mirror-writing, so as to reproduce the wording on the documents stamped in the right way. The dating made it necessary to prepare a new seal every year; hence the soft and provisional character of the stone which was used for this kind of seal.

THRUST in thy sharp sickle, and gather the clusters of the vine of the earth; for her grapes are fully ripe.   (Rev. 14 : 18)

The necessity of cutting the grape-clusters from the vine neatly and quickly, without injuring the delicate fruit led to the introduction of a specially sharp curved sickle for the use of vintagers (see illustration, above right). We see this sickle in use in a vintage scene reproduced on a sixth century mosaic pavement, found in the ruins of the monastery of Lady Mary at Beth-Shean. Depicted in the mosaic, within a framework of winding trellises which form circular medallions, are villagers cutting the grapes and carrying them to the wine-press in baskets. The man in the middle right medallion is holding a sharp sickle in his right hand and a big bunch of grapes in his left. The proportions are not exact, as in most Byzantine pavements; the artist was more interested in making his meaning clear than in giving each object its proper relative size. It is to such an operation that St. John compares the gathering of the vine of the earth — "for her grapes are fully ripe".

AND the sixth angel poured out his vial upon the great river Euphrates; and the water thereof was dried up, that the way of the kings of the east might be prepared.

(Rev. 16 : 12)

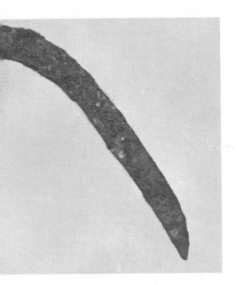

As in a previous verse, the author of Revelation here voices the aspirations of the oppressed Orientals and their desire to see the hated Roman power humbled before the Parthian kings of the East (see also p. 277). The River Euphrates, which formed the boundary between the two empires (for a view of the river see Vol. I, p. 226) will suddenly dry up, thus in an instant removing the security of the Roman frontier behind it and giving the Parthians an unobstructed passage into the Roman province of Syria and beyond. This vision took some time to realize; it was only in the third century A.D. that the re-invigorated Persian empire, under its new Sassanian dynasty, came to serious grips with the Romans. The greatest moment in Sassanian history was the surrender of the emperor Valerian in A.D. 260 to the Persian king Sapor I, after a defeat in battle. Even before that the Persians had successfully invaded Syria and taken its capital Antioch in 255. This moment of triumph is represented on a rock relief at Naqsh-i Rustam showing Sapor I on his horse, with the Roman emperor kneeling at his feet.

AND he gathered them together into a place called in the Hebrew tongue Armageddon.   (Rev. 16 : 16)

The place of the last battle of the kings of this earth is described as Armageddon, which is a corruption of Har Mageddon or the "Mountain of Megiddo". This site, now identified with Tell el-Mutesellim at the point where the Valley of 'Iron and the Via Maris (Sea Road) debouch into the Valley of Esdraelon, was not inhabited at the time when the Revelation was written. Its strategic position, however, was still important; the Roman camp of the Sixth Legion was placed by Hadrian at near-by Legio (Lajjun), later on the city of Maximianupolis (see Vol. III, p. 292). The broad expanse of the Valley of Esdraelon at the foot of the mountain (see view above), and the vital importance of the great trade-routes crossing it, seem to have influenced the choice of this place as the locality of the last battle. Possibly also memories of the great conflict between Josiah king of Judah and Pharaoh Necho may have contributed to this localization; for it is hardly likely that the still older battle at Megiddo in the time of Thotmes III of Egypt could have still been remembered in the first century A.D.

ᴀɴᴅ I saw a woman sit upon a scarlet coloured beast, full of names of blasphemy, having seven heads and ten horns. And the woman was arrayed in purple and scarlet colour, and decked with gold and precious stones and pearls . . .   (Rev. 17 : 3-4)

After the opening of the book with the seven seals, followed by the revelation of the great wonders of heaven and the coming of the seven angels with the seven last plagues, there appears the great enemy of god, Rome — thinly disguised under the appellation of "Babylon the Great". The imperial city is represented as a woman arrayed in purple and scarlet, and riding upon a scarlet beast. The components of this vision are obviously taken from the female statues personifying the great cities, or rather their tutelary goddesses or Tyches. From the time that the sculptor Eutychides created the prototype of such a goddess in his famous work representing the Tyche of Antioch, the personification of cities as dignified females wearing mural crowns became a generally accepted convention. There were local variations: thus Alexandria, the great port of Egypt, is represented wearing a crown formed by ships; and Rome, the warrior city, appears with helmet and breastplate, like a second Minerva (see also the next page). The illustration below, which is a reproduction of a painting found on the premises of one Verecundus, a cloth-maker in the "Street of Abundance" at Pompeii, shows another such symbolical image. It is the Venus of Pompeii, majestically draped in blue and crowned with gold, riding on a chariot drawn by elephants, with Cupid in attendance on her and winged genii hovering to their right and left. This hieratic figure, which recalls those of the Oriental gods, is of a type not unlike the vision of "Babylon the Great" in the Revelation.

THE seven heads are seven mountains, on which the woman sitteth. And there are seven kings: five are fallen, and one is, and the other is not yet come; and when he cometh, he must continue a short space. And the beast that was, and is not, even he is the eighth . . .

(Rev. 17 : 9-11)

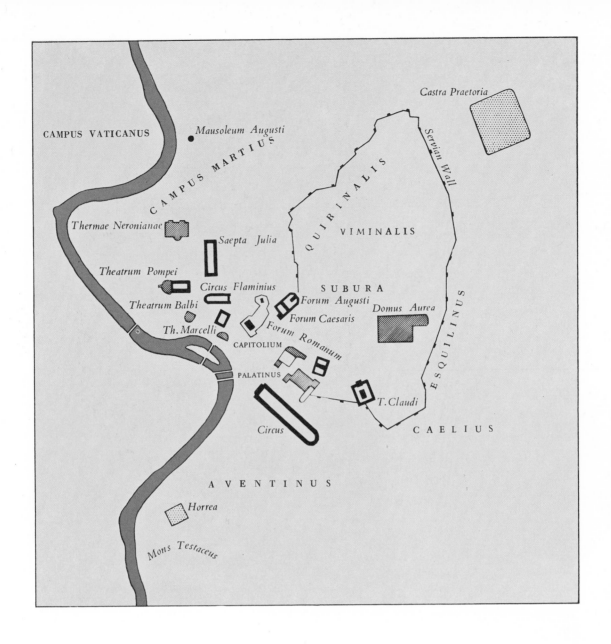

The city of Rome was founded beside the ford of the River Tiber nearest to the sea. The first settlement was built on a hill called the Palatine (see map on p. 291). Then the steep hill of the Capitol was crowned with a castle. In the time of the Republic five other hills (Aventine, Caelius, Esquiline, Viminal and Quirinal) were included within the city walls; they were all situated in the plain adjoining the ford across the Tiber (where later on the oldest bridge over the river was erected). Although imperial Rome extended far beyond these original seven hills, including parts of those on the left bank of the Tiber and various others still more distant, it retained its traditional designation as the "City of the Seven Hills"; and the same number of hills was later on assigned to its successor, Constantinople.

The interpretation of the mystic number of the seven kings (emperors) of Rome referred to here depends on the date assigned to the composition of the Book of Revelation. If we assume that the "beast that was and is not" is Domitian, then the five fallen kings would be the five emperors of the Julio-Claudian dynasty (see their coins above): Augustus (31 B.C. - 14 A.D. — upper left); Tiberius (14-37 — upper centre); Caligula (37-41 — upper right); Claudius (41-54 — lower left) and Nero (54-68 — lower centre). The "one that is" would be Vespasian (69-79 — lower right) — (omitting the three short-lived emperors of the civil war year 68-69, viz.: Galba, Otho and Vitellius). The one who "is to come and rule for a short time" would be Titus (79-81), to be followed by the "beast", Domitian (81-96).

ᴀɴᴅ the woman which thou sawest is that great city,
which reigneth over the kings of the earth.

(Rev. 17 : 18)

The goddess Roma, the incarnation of the city which became an empire, is here revealed as the true identity
of the "Babylon" in the text. As long as Rome was a republic, the guardian spirit of the state appeared on its
coins in the shape of a woman adorned with jewels and wearing a winged helmet surmounted by a griffin.
This symbol was transformed in the Orient into a goddess and worshipped together with the emperor. The representations of this patron deity were of two types: one that of the warrior goddess, modelled on Minerva or
Pallas Athene, or sometimes even appearing as an Amazon with helmet, high boots, spear and shield; and the
other, that of a city Tyche, with a mural crown (see p. 291). The illustration above, which is a reproduction of
the interior of a gilt silver bowl, found with the Hildesheim treasure (see p. 248), shows a compromise between
the two. Roma is here represented in the dress of a matron, with *stola* (robe) and *palla* (mantle), but wearing
the helmet of Minerva surmounted by a griffon flanked by two sphinxes, and leaning on a shield.

AND every shipmaster, and all the company in ships, and sailors, and as many as trade by sea, stood afar off.

(Rev. 18 : 17)

One of the results of the fall of Babylon-Rome will be the cessation of its maritime trade. To understand why this is singled out as the sure sign of disaster one has to appreciate the basic facts of the imperial city's existence. Its population was swollen by an enormous number of aliens, many of them slaves or freedmen, all of whom relied for their maintenance on the imperial bounty. Any failure of this bounty was, therefore, fraught with danger for the emperor and his court. Only by supplies of wheat from Egypt and Africa could the population of Rome be kept quiet. The importance of the wheat-ships can be seen from the references to them in the Acts; St. Paul continued and completed his voyage on Alexandrian ships carrying this cargo to Italy. One of the plans of the Jews who revolted against Rome in the time of Nero was to interfere with this trade and thus rouse the Roman proletariat against the imperial government. The importance of these cargoes is also evident from the fact that the emperors most mindful of their duty to the capital improved its harbour facilities by developing the port of Ostia at the mouth of the Tiber. Reproduced here is a mosaic of the third century found at Ostia; it shows two ships being unloaded in the port. It is the stopping of such supplies that is envisaged in the verse above.

AND he treadeth the winepress of the fierceness and
wrath of Almighty God.   (Rev. 19 : 15)

The treading of the winepress as an image of the wrath of God occurs
in the prophecy of Isaiah (see Vol. III, p. 89) ; the red of the grape-juice
calls to mind the colour of blood, and the pulping of the grapes
symbolizes the fate of those who oppose the will of the Deity. To the
representations of the winepress from Egypt, reproduced in the
previous volumes, we can here add another from a relief found near
Venice. It shows two labourers holding hands and leaning on sticks;
they are rhythmically jumping in a vat filled with grapes. A third
man on the left is bringing more grapes for the winepress. In the
Roman period more and more use was made of mechanical presses,
but these were in appearance far less picturesque than the primitive
method shown here.

AND I saw an angel come down from heaven, having the key of the bottomless pit and a great chain in his hand.

(Rev. 20 : 1)

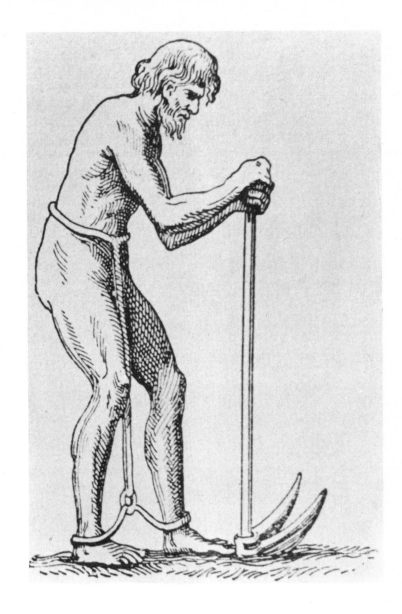

After the destruction of the wicked and the overthrow of Rome, the great temporal adversary of God, the time shall come to inaugurate the thousand years of the second reign of Christ on earth by chaining and locking up the power of evil, the great dragon which is the Devil and Satan. The locking up is done with a key, the key of the bottomless pit. Roman keys have been recovered in large numbers; the example shown on the right above was found in one of the caves near the Dead Sea, among the booty carried there by the last remnants of the armies of Bar Kokhba (see p. 75). The way in which such a key worked can be seen in Vol. II, p. 78. The protruding studs of the key fitted into corresponding holes in the bolt and lifted the pins which kept the bolt in the locked position; the bolt could then be withdrawn and the door opened. The locking operation, as here, reversed the process. The chain which was brought by the angel for the binding of the dragon corresponded to the ordinary Roman chains found in large numbers wherever there were slaves to be kept bound, as in the illustration on the left. The chaining of the dragon and the locking of the pit indicate the necessity of taking double precautions to prevent the forces of evil from breaking out and wrecking the millennium.

Aɴᴅ had a wall great and high, and had twelve gates ... (Rev. 21 : 12)

With the final elimination of Evil, the time has come for a complete regeneration of the universe; a new heaven and a new earth appear, and the Holy City of Jerusalem, which has waited in heaven for this time, comes down on earth to take the place of the sinful city which had been punished by the abomination of desolation (see p. 67). This concept of a Heavenly Jerusalem as opposed to the earth-bound city is common to both the rabbinical sources and to early Christianity. We find a pictorial representation of Heavenly Jerusalem in the frescoes of the synagogue of Dura Europus (see the illustration). The artist actually intended to depict the Temple of Solomon standing in the middle of the earthly city; but he has encircled the latter with the seven walls of the celestial Jerusalem, each in a different colour. The Temple, in the form of a Hellenistic sanctuary, stands in the middle of the city. The three gates of Jerusalem are adorned with various images of pagan character, such as could be seen on the gates and temples of the cities of the period. Such details, so far from seeming incongruous with the general conception of the Heavenly City, served only to augment its splendour.

HE which testifieth these saith, Surely I come quickly; Amen. Even so, come, LORD JESUS. The grace of our LORD JESUS CHRIST be with you all. Amen. (Rev. 22 : 20-21)

The Book of Revelation ends with the solemn assurance that the things described therein would quickly and surely come to pass, and with a blessing to all the faithful. Although the expectation of the return of Christ in the near future and the imminent end of the world was a powerful factor in winning converts for the new faith, it was disparaged by the Church authorities, and above all by St. Paul in his epistles to the Thessalonians. The concluding illustration is taken from the last page of one of the earliest manuscripts of the Greek Bible, the Codex Sinaiticus (fourth cent. A.D.).

INDEXES

SITES, MONUMENTS AND OBJECTS

129. Coin — Hebrew University, Jerusalem
     Relief above — Louvre Museum, Paris
     Below — National Museum delle Terme, Rome
130. Alexandria Museum, Egypt

ST. JOHN

137. John Rylands Library, Manchester
149. National Museum, Naples
150. National Museum, Naples
155. British Museum, London

ACTS

159. Biblioteca Medicea — Laurenziana, Florence
161. Shrine of the Book, Jerusalem
162. Inscription — Palestine Archaeological Museum
     Dipinto — Beth She'arim, Catacomb 14
163. National Museum, Damascus
164. Relief — Museo civico, Verona
167. Relief — Museo della Civiltà romana, Rome
169. National Museum, Damascus
170. Coin — Hebrew University, Jerusalem
174. Statue — Vatican Museum, Rome
     Relief — Lateran Museum, Rome
175. Relief — Vatican Museum, Rome
     Statue — National Museum delle Terme, Rome
177. Fresco — National Museum, Damascus
     Shells — Department of Antiquities, Israel
179. Areopagus, Athens
     Acropolis, Athens
183. Inscription — Ecole francaise d'archéologie, Athens
     Graffito — Palestine Archaeological Museum, Jerusalem
184. Bibliothèque nationale, Paris
185. Statue — National Museum, Naples
186. Market of Trajan, Rome
188. Museum of Antiquities, Istanbul
191. Cavalryman — Palestine Archaeological Museum, Jerusalem
     Legionary — Museum, Wiesbaden
193. National Museum, Naples
194. Münzkabinett, Munich
195. Archaeological Museum, Florence
197. Relief — National Museum, Beirut
     Fresco — Vatican Library, Rome
198. Tower of the Winds, Athens
199. Ny Carlsberg Glyptothek, Copenhagen
200. National Museum, Naples
201. Above — St. Paul's Bay, Malta
     Below — Malta Museum, La Valetta
202. Above — Villa Torlonia, Rome
     Below — Palestine Archaeological Museum, Jerusalem
203. Painting — National Museum, Naples
     Landscape — Via Appia antica, Rome
     Relief — Louvre Museum, Paris

EPISTLES

207. Chester-Beatty Collection of Papyri
208. British Museum, London
209. Vase — Staatliche Museen, Berlin
     Relief — Landesmuseum, Trier
210. Musée de Mariemont, Belgium
211. Sta. Maria Maggiore, Rome
212. Museum of Fine Arts, Boston
214. Staatliche Museen, Berlin
217. Ara Pacis, Rome
218. Antiquarium of the Forum, Rome
219. Museo Concordiese, Portogruaro, Italy
221. Museum, Antioch, Hatay (Turkey)
222. British Museum, London
223. Statue — Vatican Museum, Rome
224. Above — Column of Trajan, Rome
     Below — National Museum delle Terme, Rome

225. Above — National Museum of the Villa Giulia, Rome
     Below — Metropolitan Museum of Arts, New-York
226. Catacomb of St. Callixtus, Rome
227. Vatican Museum, Rome
228. Statue — British Museum, London
229. Relief — Vatican Museum Rome
     Mirror — Hebrew Museum, Rome
     Mirror — Hebrew University, Jerusalem
230. Mosaic — National Museum, Naples
     Relief — Glyptothek, Munich
231. Harpist — National Museum delle Terme, Rome
232. Inscription — Palestine Archaeological Museum
     Pen and inkstand — British Museum, London
233. Catacomb of S. Gennaro, Naples
234. Coin — Hebrew University, Jerusalem
     Inscription — 'Avdat Expedition, Israel
235. Vase — Kunsthistorisches Museum, Vienna
236. Egypt Exploration Fund, London
237. Catacomb, Vigna Codini, Rome
238. Lateran Museum, Rome
239. Relief — British Museum, London
241. British Museum, London
242. National Museum, Naples
243. University Library, Cambridge
244. National Museum delle Terme, Rome
245. Municipal Museum of Antiquities, Haifa
246. Catacomb of St. Callixtus, Rome
247. Vatican Museum, Rome
248. Box — Hebrew University, Jerusalem
     Vase — Staatliche Museen, Berlin
     Jar — Hebrew University, Jerusalem
250. Disk — National Museum delle Terme, Rome
     Painting — National Museum, Naples
253. Arch of Constantine, Rome
257. Relief — National Museum delle Terme, Rome
     Horse bit — National Museum, Naples
258. Crypt of St. Peter's, Rome
259. Bust — Capitol Museum, Rome
     Painting — National Museum, Damascus
260. Lamp — National Museum, Naples
260-1 Vase — Louvre Museum, Paris
262. Vatican Library, Rome

REVELATION

267. San Apollinaire in Classe, Ravenna
268. Vatican Library, Rome
271. Relief — Pergamon Museum, Berlin
272. Kunsthistorisches Museum, Vienna
273. National Museum, Damascus
275. British Museum, London
276. National Museum, Naples
277. National Museum, Damascus
278. Museo della Civiltà romana, Rome
279. Corn-Measure — Chesters Museum, Northumberland
     Scales — National Museum, Naples
280. Vatican Museum, Rome
281. Shovel — Hebrew University Jerusalem
     Fresco — National Museum, Damascus
282. Rod — British Museum, London
283. Forum of Trajan, Rome
284. Nimrud Dagh, Turkey
286. Mosaic — Beth-Shean, Israel
     Siekle — British Museum, London
287. Relief — Naqsh-i Rustam, Persia
289. Fresco — Pompeii
290. Coins — Hebrew University, Jerusalem
292. Staatliche Museen, Berlin
293. Mosaic — Ostia
294. Archaeological Museum, Venice
295. Key — Hebrew University, Jerusalem
296. National Museum, Damascus
297. British Museum, London

300

PHOTOGRAPHS

ST. MATTHEW

The Orient Press Photo Company: 21, 23, 25, 27, 28, 29, 30, 35, 36 left, 37 right, 41, 43, 47, 51 below, 52, 59, 61, 66, 78
A. Allon: 34, 44, 61, 68
Placed at the disposal of the editor: 22, 24, 26 below, 53, 58, 72

ST. MARK

The Orient Press Photo Company: 84, 91 (mill)
Placed at the disposal of the Editor: 94-95, 96
A. Allon: 85 (wheat)

ST. LUKE

The Orient Press Photo Company: 105, 109, 110-111, 112, 113, 124, 125, 126, 128, 132
A. Allon: 119
Placed at the disposal of the Editor: 133

ST. JOHN

The Orient Press Photo Company: 138, 143, 144-145, 147, 151
Placed at the disposal of the Editor: 141, 142, 152
A. Allon: 148
B. Rotenberg: 140

ACTS

The Orient Press Photo Company: 167 (view), 170, 187, 192
Placed at the disposal of the Editor: 165, 166, 168, 172-3, 176, 178, 181, 182, 185 (view), 189

EPISTLES

The Orient Press Photo Company: 213, 255, 263
E. Nash, Rome: 216

Placed at the disposal of the Editor: 215, 239, 240

REVELATION

The Orient Press Photo Company: 274, 288
Placed at the disposal of the Editor: 270

RECONSTRUCTIONS

by Eva Avi-Yonah: 118, 139, 153, 190, 256

MAPS

by Eng. P. Yoeli: 76, 131, 160, 171, 196, 269, 291

302